The Decline of Agrarian Democracy

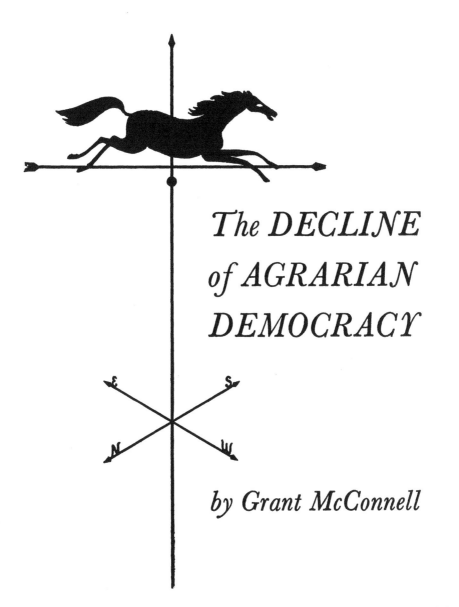

The DECLINE

of AGRARIAN

DEMOCRACY

by Grant McConnell

UNIVERSITY OF CALIFORNIA PRESS
Berkeley & Los Angeles : : 1953

UNIVERSITY OF CALIFORNIA PRESS
Berkeley & Los Angeles, California

CAMBRIDGE UNIVERSITY PRESS
London, England

Designed by Adrian Wilson

CONTENTS

ACKNOWLEDGMENTS

A large debt of gratitude has been accumulated in the preparation of this book. Advice, criticism, and help have come from many people. I wish particularly to thank the following: Lloyd H. Fisher, Varden Fuller, Robert A. Gordon, Peter H. Odegard, and Paul S. Taylor. My task would have been more difficult without the intelligent and cheerful help of numerous librarians, especially of Miss Orpha E. Cummings and Mrs. Aileen R. Jaffa. It would have been impossible without the help and toleration of my wife, Jane McConnell,

I wish also to thank the following for permission to use quotations from their publications: Cornell University Press, E. P. Dutton and Company, Harper and Brothers, Houghton Mifflin Company, O. M. Kile, The Macmillan Company, *The Nation's Agriculture,* University of North Carolina Press, Charles Scribner's Sons, and *Wallaces' Farmer and Iowa Homestead.*

G. M.

INTRODUCTION

More than half a century has elapsed since the death of the last great mass movement of farmers in America. When Populism vanished as an effective force, something much more important than its organizations or its movement passed irrevocably from the scene. Before the turning point of the century, agrarianism in America was democratic in character. In part this was the result of a simple fact: until recently farmers had been in the majority. But there was more to it than this. The great farmer movements of the nineteenth century were upwellings of protest against the system of power growing out of the raw and turbulent capitalism of the era. The protest was made not merely against injustice to farmers but against injustice to all common men. Agrarianism spoke in the name of all. The enemy which it challenged was power.

In the first five decades of the twentieth century, the quality of agrarianism has been transformed. The monumental fact of the period is the rise of a structure of political power based on farm organization that extends from thousands of localities through every level of government to the highest councils of the nation. This structure not only represents a repudiation of the traditional agrarian distrust of power, but in its development has been the direct cause of some of the most disturbing passages in American politics.

How did agriculture become the site of this power structure? Why should agrarian organization assume such a character? The tendency of the day is perhaps to say, with urban cynics, that no

1

more was ever to be expected from the tillers of the soil. An alternative view is that this structure of power actually is not a farmers' structure but one of business and other interests so sinister as to be hardly discoverable.

The answers are at once less simple and more concrete. They lie in the nature of the organizations out of which power in rural life has emerged. No single body comprehends the whole of the structure. One of the essential parts is the system of agricultural education that has been growing since the latter part of the nineteenth century. Another is the United States Department of Agriculture. Most important of all, however, is the great farm organization of modern times, the American Farm Bureau Federation. Each organization has had an influence upon the development of the others, and each has been dependent upon all the others.

The pattern of their interrelationship has emerged gradually over a period of many years. Insensibly, the sheer needs of power itself have determined this development. Organization, to survive, must not be passive, but must secure its outposts. If the objectives which at first were ends in themselves have been forgotten, if ends have become means and means ends, this is but the dynamic of a salient characteristic of our time, organization.

The principles of organization are matters of the first importance. The manner in which organization develops and gathers power or stagnates and fails must be examined. The organizational structure seen here is not a failure; it is one of the most conspicuous successes in all America. It will not be comprehended by the singling out of selfish men. The conditions of power can be explained not so much by social structure as, perhaps, social structure by the conditions of power.

The transformation of agricultural politics has been accompanied by a kind of success that measures itself against that of other parts of the community. Even more significant is the fact that the success is not that of "agriculture" as an entity but of one segment of those who speak in its name. And here the measure, indeed the means, of this success is failure and defeat for those who have been excluded.

I

The OLD
TRADITION

In 1892 three major parties presented candidates for the office of president to the people of the United States. The old established parties, Republican and Democratic, were abruptly forced to adjust their strategies to meet the attack of a new political organization, the People's party. Out of the West and out of the South it rose, like one of the great storms that sweep the plains, unpredictable, incalculable, and elemental. Its onslaught shook to their foundations the structures of organizations and political alignment which had been long in building. Even more, it seemed to threaten the destruction of all the economic winnings of a capitalism so far everywhere victorious. For here was the fury of common men; if all manner of things were lifted up and flung before the wind, this was no less than the uncertain yet inevitable concomitant of the release of a force of nature.

Retrospectively, as perhaps with most storms, the scope of the disturbance was less than it seemed, and the destruction was trifling in comparison with what had been expected. It was also less sudden, less abnormal, and less unreasoning than it appeared to those who were compelled to bend before its transitory wrath. The Populists, as those of the People's party came to be known, made a mark in the elections of the year, but their success did not suggest that either of the old parties had been supplanted. General Weaver, the Populist candidate for president, won more than a million popular votes, an impressive total, certainly, and one that justified a claim to major party status, but it was scarcely enough to call for dissolution of the

3

Republican or Democratic parties.[1] Elsewhere on the ballots, the new party won eight congressional seats, three governorships, and innumerable county offices.

Yet this success was not the measure of the event. At best, it gave no indication of the intensity of the turbulence. The florid but vivid recollection of one who saw the movement's unfolding is a better gauge: "It was a religious revival, a crusade, a pentecost of politics in which a tongue of flame sat upon every man, and each spake as the spirit gave him utterance."[2] This was the atmosphere of Populism. It combined a deep sense of outrage with a righteousness that could come only from long-standing religious certainty. Bitterness and hate were there too, and all the frustrations of undeserved and unexpected failure, which had descended, many felt, because of the greed of a few and the disastrous course of the business cycle. To some among the Populists, it was evident that the rapacity of corporations was the sole and adequate cause for the ills that beset men. Money and monopoly had usurped power throughout the land, and the common people were becoming slaves.

Jerry Simpson, "Sockless Jerry" as his opponents dubbed him, wrote down the questions:

> How could it be possible under such a system that the rich should fail to grow richer and the men of moderate means should rapidly fall into the ranks of the extremely poor? Then is it any wonder that the men who followed "old John Brown" into Kansas, on the principle that it was wrong to rob the black man of the fruits of his toil should rebel when their own welfare is at stake?[3]

When such language was printed in pamphlets and cried from platforms, can it be doubted that builders of corporate empires and men of money generally looked with apprehension upon this rise of a new political power? The apprehension was one that would not rapidly fade or be forgotten.

Populism was a movement before it became a political party. It was a popular movement and, more importantly, an agrarian movement. It came near the end of the period in which the belief could still prevail, with some justification, that the common man was typically a farmer. According to the census of 1790 the nation's population was 95 per cent rural; by the census of 1890 it was 64 per cent rural.' During the hundred years that intervened, the assumption held that Everyman tilled the soil. The cause of the majority in nearly every instance was an agrarian cause. If the nation was a democracy, it was an agrarian democracy.

From the nation's beginning to the end of the nineteenth century the character of the farmer's active participation in political affairs was on the pattern of Populism, sporadic and explosive. For long periods of time he was quiescent, almost passive. The industrial advance and the steady commercialization of all phases of life went on relentlessly in these periods. Then, at irregular intervals, when the industrial machine faltered and economic disaster came, the farmer rose and asserted his right to political consideration. His movements were always touched with passion and seemed temporarily to sweep all before them. To some, these interludes of agrarian fury were no more than febrile attempts to bilk the nation's industrial destiny. Henry Adams, surveying the election of 1892, so dismissed it:

> A capitalistic system had been adopted, and if it were to run at all, it must be run by capital and by capitalistic methods, for nothing could surpass the nonsensity of trying to run so complex and so concentrated a machine by Southern and Western farmers in grotesque alliance with city day-laborers, as had been tried in 1800 and 1828 and had failed even under simple conditions.[5]

Yet, in 1892, as in 1800 and 1828, the farmer's movement was something more than a challenge to industrialism. There were economic demands, the class demands of agrarianism, to be sure. A lower tariff, restrictions on alien landholding, removal of fences on public lands, expansion of the supply of money—these were characteristic. But, equally, farmers demanded a graduated income tax, restraints on monopoly, education, the direct election of senators, the Australian ballot, the initiative, and the referendum.[6] These were not narrow class demands. They were honest and genuine attempts to ensure the operations of democracy, to make certain that *no* group was excluded from sharing in the political process.

These demands derived partly from a confidence that farmers were in the majority. But the nineteenth-century agrarian movement was more than sheer faith in majority rule. It meshed repeatedly with the other great commoners' movement, that of organized labor, though the latter was far the weaker and even seemed at times to represent opposing interests. More important than this, however, was the steady and consistent attempt to open and to maintain political channels for the expression of dissent, and to guarantee that the least among the nation's people should have protection. The Declaration of Purpose of the National Grange, for example, was not mere rhetoric:

> We acknowledge the broad principle that difference of opinion is no crime, and hold that "progress toward truth is made by difference of opinion," while "the fault lies in bitterness of controversy."
> We desire a proper equality, equity and fairness; protection for the weak, restraint upon the strong; in short, justly distributed burdens and justly distributed power. These are American ideas, the very essence of American independence and to advocate the contrary is unworthy of the sons and daughters of an American republic.[7]

The association between democracy and agrarianism in nineteenth-century America was real. In practice, agrarian democracy had peculiarities that were alarming to those who were building the great institutions of capitalism—intemperance of language, a near-fanaticism, and a tendency to single out for attack just those focal points of capitalism that were most sensitive: banks, grain exchanges, and trusts. It was also a notably inconstant force.

As a body of doctrine, agrarian democracy is elusive. The name with which it is most readily associated is that of Thomas Jefferson, himself a gentleman farmer. He founded his political strategy upon an appeal to farmers and frontiersmen. He laid extravagant praise upon their solid excellences. In an almost lyrical passage he declaimed, "Those who labor in the earth are the chosen people of God if ever He had a chosen people, whose breasts He has made his peculiar deposit for substantial and genuine virtue."[8] Jefferson's emphasis on agriculture, however, is easily exaggerated. His interests and sympathies were far wider than such passages might suggest.[9]

The best exponent of agrarian democracy in our history was Jefferson's friend and political associate, John Taylor of Caroline. Taylor, like Jefferson a prosperous Virginia planter, was convinced of some inner moral light shining forth from the farmer's way of life.[10] Unlike Jefferson, however, he never experienced doubt that farmers were the chosen people for whom the nation was founded. He was thus far more clearly an agrarian. Agrarianism, indeed, is commonly rooted in such a faith. Agrarians who find it impossible to accept the old physiocratic belief that only agriculture is productive tend to take refuge in the conviction that agriculture is more fundamental and basic than other occupations, and therefore that its practitioners are better than others. This conviction is widely held even in our contemporary industrial society.[11]

Taylor, however, represented a great deal more than his own simple class interests.[12] His great concern was rather with the "publick interest," which he saw threatened by a small group of "aristocracies of interest." The latter consisted of capitalists (a word used by Taylor) who were exploiting the rest of the nation through inflated public paper, bank stocks, and a protective tariff. By conquest and use of governmental power, the capitalists had fastened a new tyranny upon the common people, that is, upon farmers. The interests of a rising and powerful faction of a few rich men thus stood in direct opposition to the common interest; it was a class struggle between capitalists and agrarians.

The central problem was the power exercised by the newly risen class of exploiters. Its source was economic. No one has ever laid stronger emphasis on the economic bases of political power in America than Taylor. His conception has remained basic in agrarian thought. This power, as Taylor saw it building in his own time, was rooted in the inequality that resulted from the capitalists' rapid accumulation of wealth.

Taylor's solution lay in restoring the nation to an agrarian course. With its apparently limitless expanses of unoccupied land, America could look forward to a unity of interest, and that an agricultural interest. With a nation of free and equal farmers, there need be no clash of factions, for there would be no diversity of economic interests. Such a society would have no great agglomeration of power, either public or private, to threaten tyranny. There would be no gross inequality. To ensure such a pattern, Taylor demanded expropriation of the exploiters and a thorough division of power, both aspects of the same thing.

At some point in the nineteenth century, perhaps in Taylor's own time, the pattern became chimerical. The banishment of power, either economic or governmental, and the unification of society in farming were not to be achieved. Yet this remained the substance of agrarian thought throughout the century. It never again received the full rationalization given it by Taylor, but all its variants—the Jacksonian attacks on the Bank of the United States, the assaults of the Granger period on the railroads and grain exchanges, the Populist attacks upon monopoly—had the same conviction, that the power which capitalists continued to fashion from economic inequality was the enemy of democracy.

And in this sense agrarian democracy differed little from other currents of democratic thought in America. The two ideas around which all its programs centered were equality and freedom. The latter was conceived almost wholly as the condition in which power had been fragmentized. The former was the essential condition to such fragmentation. This conception of democracy had its limitations, but it was shared by other than agrarians, and was perhaps the most characteristic of the nineteenth century.

In all the agrarian movements flowed an undercurrent of something approaching intolerance—an unshakable air of superiority about men of the soil, the belief that farmers were the chosen people of God. It was implied that there was a necessary and inherent connection between agrarianism and democracy. The only justification for this implication was that farmers had been in the majority throughout much of our history. For the rest, the connection was mystical. The still surviving attitude has provoked the sardonic remark that farmers have been called the backbone of nearly every form of government that has ever existed.[13]

The association between agriculture and democracy, though real, was not to be taken for granted. It was the nation's good fortune that it existed, but there was, in truth, little more than the force of tradition to ensure its continuance. The most hopeful sign was the form of organization toward which the farmers' movement had been evolving since the Civil War. Neither the Grange nor the Farmers' Alliance ever had the characteristics of exclusive organizations. Both were broad in their appeals and solidly based in the great mass of the farming population. Even more important, the Alliance gave birth to a genuine political party. This implied that the agrarians were prepared to accept the responsibility of building a majority, even if that majority included other than farmers. It implied a willingness to seek political solutions of a general character. This was the ultimate promise of agrarian democracy, just when its old basis in a farming majority was passing.

In the 1890's the tradition of agrarian democracy was at its peak. It had never appeared more steadfast or more vigorous. The Populists returned to the elections of 1896. Something had begun to go wrong, however. The party found itself coalesced with the Democrats and driven off in the byway of free silver. The movement faltered and its explosive force was suddenly spent. The quiet of lethargy returned to the farms.

2

The ECONOMIC SETTING

The stillness which fell on agrarian politics at the end of the nineteenth century demonstrated one thing: whatever political form the mass movements of farmers had taken in the period just ended, much of the driving force behind them had been economic. The factor which more than any other accounted for the failure of Populism to recover from its disaster of 1896 was the rise in prices which came thereafter. And this factor, once seen, provided the key to much of what had gone before.

Perhaps the most obvious feature of the era ended with the century was the long decline of prices. With some large fluctuations, prices of agricultural products dropped seriously and continually during this period. There were furious moments of speculation in Western lands, moments when the delusion prevailed that the rain belt had moved west and when land was taken up not merely for inappropriate cultivation but even for never-to-be-built cities of the plain. Yet the period as a whole was not one of optimism and the trend of farm prices was downward. And, whatever the obscurity of the large event, the price a farmer got for his crop was the plainest and simplest fact he had. In wheat the farm price per bushel was more than two dollars at the end of 1866; it fell below one dollar in 1874. For a few years it was above one dollar, but then it dropped to forty-nine cents in 1894. In corn the average farm price went from sixty-six cents a bushel in 1866 down to twenty-one cents in 1896. And these were great historic crops of America.[1]

This decline in prices, especially in view of the large indebtedness incurred by many farmers in the period of enthusiastic expansion, is probably sufficient explanation for the tendency of the agrarian movement to go off on a quest for some monetary panacea. And, when the trend of prices eventually changed, after the defeat of the Populists in their last campaign, there was seeming confirmation of the impression that the farmer could be called off from his political activity by no more than a few cents' increase in the price of his wheat. Prices did rise after 1896 and agrarian politics did subside. A golden era for agriculture preceded the First World War. It was a period of both favoring prices and political calm upon the land.

Much else in the farmer's list of grievances was of an economic character, even when his reaction was primarily political. It was never a sufficient program, for either the Grange or the Farmers' Alliance, simply to raise the prices listed in the nation's market places. The crystallization of discontent came with the stiff charges exacted by railroad and elevator operators. It came when overextended farmers arrived to discuss the scaling down of their debts and met only the detached obduracy of finance. It came with a growing suspicion of the trusts, the makers of plows and fertilizers, the providers of jute, and the processors of cotton. The transition from complaint about financial exaction shaded imperceptibly into the accusation of powei. When the imposition of high charges by corporate organs of wealth could be linked with stories of bribed legislators and purchased domination of the agencies of government, the only remedy seemed to lie in the conquest of political power by the farmers themselves. And so it was that motivation which was obviously economic in character led to political action.

Looking backward from the year 1900, this much perhaps was clear. The immediate sources of the recent discontent were largely economic. When the pressure of prices relaxed, the agrarian movement faltered. The political means of the movement had been indicated to the farmer by his exploiters' use of political means. The near majority position of farmers suggested the evolution of a political party. The economic explanation goes far in accounting for developments in the second half of the nineteenth century. It passes over the imponderable element of the agrarian political tradition with its distrust of power, but still the explanation is persuasive.

Looking forward from the turn of the century, however, would it have been possible to foresee the course of agrarian organization, given only a knowledge of the economic setting in the years to come? It is worth looking briefly at some of the major economic features of twentieth-century agriculture to see what might be expected from these alone.

Perhaps the largest feature is the declining relative position of farming. This decline, indeed, had long been under way. In the 1870's, half of the working population was engaged in agriculture. In the 1920's the fraction dwindled to a quarter and less. This represented a steady contraction during both the last quarter of the nineteenth century and the first half of the twentieth.[2] There was no significant difference between the two periods in the rate of change. What is impressive is the point reached in the decline. This minority position was established in the nineteenth century, but it was hardly obvious; it was clear to all early in the twentieth century.

This shrinkage of the farming sector of the population was dramatic to a nation whose outlook was deeply rooted in agrarian tradition, but even more dramatic was the disappearance of the once "inexhaustible" new lands of the continent-wide expanse. It was in 1893 that Frederick Jackson Turner noted the ending of the frontier, the line whose most significant feature was that it lay "at the hither edge of free land."[3] In the twentieth century there was still land to be found, occupied, and cultivated. Yet the era of free or nearly free land was past. The vision of westward movement in quest of independence and a new life was henceforth without substance for more than a few of the nation's farmers.

The sense of the frontier had been a mental trait of agrarians first and foremost, more so even than of the John Jacob Astors, the James J. Hills, and all the imperialists of commerce. John Taylor of Caroline gave an emphasis to the frontier and the once abundant lands of the continent that was only slightly less striking than that of Turner. Indeed, it is probable that the frontier had its strongest intellectual effect upon the quality of agrarianism. The frontier provided much of that connection between democracy and agrarianism which has been so nearly peculiar to America—how much it would be difficult to say. Nevertheless, the time arrived when this presupposition of the historic agrarian democracy—cheap abundant land—

became invalid; from this time onward, the problem of agrarian democracy became more difficult.

Attempts have been made to give a continuity to this tradition of yet-unoccupied land. The Reclamation Act of 1902 should be seen in just this setting. Its purpose was not merely to open up more land to cultivation or to develop the West; it was as much to give opportunity to the landless of the nation's common people. Hence came the limitation on the number of acres for which water could be provided to a single farm. Land is still being "reclaimed" in these terms. Even at a point midway in the twentieth century, water is flowing for the first time into the largest reclamation projects yet constructed. However, all the projects built and those yet to be conceived cannot provide the continuity in the land tradition of the frontier which once was sought. It has been estimated that 99,000,000 more acres of cropland will be needed by 1975 to feed the growing population.[4] To meet this requirement, improved technology must be the principal solution. New productive acreage on this scale cannot be found.

Technology, indeed, is the key to most of the economic aspects of modern agriculture. The transformation that took place here began before the Civil War. Its large-scale effects, however, came afterward and are still arriving. Earth-breaking machines and equipment for the planting and harvesting of grain provided the first great surge of farm mechanization. By 1900 the combine, most impressive of all farm machines, had been in use for more than a decade. Machinery, however, was but the most dramatic aspect of a many-sided technological change just beginning to affect farming on a large scale. Systematic experimentation amid the conditions of American agriculture was given a strong stimulus by passage of the Hatch Act of 1887, which established the agricultural experiment stations with federal assistance. From this there flowed a stream of new crops, new strains, new techniques, and even new concepts of farming.

As the twentieth century advanced, the rate of improvement accelerated and to the score of technology were added not only great numbers of improvements in plants and machines, but whole new classifications of scientific land use and new ways of processing and using farm products.[5] It is not possible even yet to see which of the many innovations that have been made or are still in process of development will prove to have the most sweeping effects. It would have been impossible in the early part of the century, for example, to visualize the increase of productivity resulting from the single item of hybrid corn. This one development, which began its sweep of the corn belt in 1937, offered the prospect of a one-fifth increase in the nation's most valuable crop without increase of acreage or labor. Nor could the impact or the extent of the introduction of the farm tractor have been visualized. Even recently, expert predictions of the numbers of tractors that would be forthcoming have been gross underestimates.[6]

This was Juggernaut in an almost mythological sense. The entire technology of agriculture was machine-like in its advance. Although at times farmers seemed sluggish in their acceptance of improvements—certainly the spread of the new technology came more tardily in farming than it did in industry—there was no organized resistance of workers to its adoption. The new machines, plants, fertilizers, and all the new developments were looked on as undiluted goods. Worship of the machine has not lessened with the passage of any decade. Indeed, there is every reason to believe the careful and emphatic statement of a contemporary student, that the forward surge in farm technology is still in its early stages.[7]

Although the blessings of technology were in themselves beyond question, much of the Jeffersonian dream had already come beneath its wheels. Decisions to use the new devices increased the dependence upon that commercial and industrial world of towns and cities which the early agrarians so mistrusted. It was dependence not alone for the devices themselves but for all the things of life which once were fashioned upon the farm and in the home. Farmers had freed themselves in part from the blind natural forces of storm and insects only to become increasingly the victims of the equally blind forces of market fluctuation. This was to be seen more certainly in the 1920's than it had been in the 1890's. One token was that in the 'twenties the term "farm problem" was taken as synonymous with "surplus"—and in a world that had yet to solve the Malthusian problem.

The most immediate effect of the improved technology has appeared in the productivity of agriculture. By the index of volume of farm output per worker, there was an increase from 100 in 1870 to 151 in 1900 and to 321 in 1945.[8] In terms of the ability of one farm worker to support other people, in 1870 one farm worker supported fewer than six, whereas in 1945 one farm worker was supporting more than fourteen.[9] Here was solid ground for the expectation that farmers would continue in the status of a shrinking minority.

The relative decline in the position of agriculture was more than a matter of population, however. Approximately one-fifth of the national income originated on farms in the 1870's, when half of the working population was engaged in farming; but little more than a tenth of the national income so originated in the 1920's, when a quarter of the population were farmers. And this decline has continued.[10] From this condition it might be expected that the farmers' sense of grievance would remain alive.

Continuity characterized all the aspects of agricultural development so far considered; no sharp break intervened between the nineteenth and the twentieth centuries. The relative decline of the farming population, the growing limitations on new land, the advance of technology, and the dwindling of agriculture's share in the national income, all were tendencies of the Granger and the Populist periods as well as of the twentieth century. There was a break, perhaps, when farmers ceased to be an actual majority, and another break when the frontier disappeared. Yet the real difference between the periods before and after 1900 lay in the degree to which all these tendencies had progressed. It lay also in the belated realization by farmers of their diminished role in modern life.

Taking agriculture as a whole, the only economic factor to which immediate political force could be assigned in the transition from one century to the next was the reversal of the trend of prices, but this could hardly serve as the sole and adequate index of agricultural organization in the twentieth century. The most that could be said is that the voice of farmer protest would still be heard and there would be no more serious attempts to form a political party composed only of farmers.

Agriculture, however, is not and never has been a single monolithic interest in our society. We have always known differences among farmers of different regions, different crops, and different incomes. The differences in the forms of political organization have been determined principally by the manner in which economic differences have been resolved. Jefferson successfully combined plantation farmers and frontiersmen in his party. The Populists brought cotton growers and wheat producers together. In such terms, then, does the economic structure of agriculture give any further indications of the character of modern farm organization?

Although the passage of time might slowly lessen the heritage of bitterness from the Civil War, it could not erase the differences of climate and natural resources between the regions. Cotton continues as a Southern crop; wheat is characteristically Western. Inevitably such differences must offer problems of the first magnitude to organization. When prices of major crops move in different directions or at greatly different rates, a difficult problem for organization may be expected. Thus, during the 'twenties the price of cotton showed a pattern different from those of corn and wheat. The first years of the 'twenties were evil times for both corn and cotton growers, less so for wheat producers. However, the price of cotton recovered quickly and even regained its wartime position. In 1926 it plummeted. The prices of corn and wheat were less erratic. Less divergence appeared thereafter, and in 1931 and 1932 all three shared the common disaster.[11] Since these are major crops we might expect to find that the early 'twenties would see the formation of a common front of Southern and Middle Western farmers, but that its bonds would be loose until 1926 and that organization would suddenly expand in the 'thirties.

The very process of reasoning in this example, however, suggests that the problem is more complex. Regionalism is in no small part a problem of different commodities. Although the major crops of corn, wheat, and cotton may appear to dominate the regional tendencies of farm movements, agriculture is in fact far more diversified. Each crop presents its own problems of price and each its own peculiar impulses to organization. Whether these result in commodity particularism or in general farm organization depends greatly on the degree to which their movement is parallel. As agriculture becomes more specialized, the intricacy of the relationships among commodity groups might be expected to increase.

The other dimension on which there are large differences within agriculture is that of class. In face of the lingering Jeffersonian vision it is easy to overlook the fact that these differences have always existed. One of the grimmest ironies of American history is that while our tradition of equality has some of its strongest roots in agrarianism, agriculture has been the scene of the worst outrages that tradition has ever suffered. Slavery was destroyed, however, and the farm movements that developed thereafter were founded on appeals to all strata of agriculture. The very success of the Populists in forging a mass movement of farmers contributed to revival of the Jeffersonian and Taylorian view of agriculture as an undifferentiated unity. It is true that farm tenancy, for example, was a problem in the last quarter of the nineteenth century.[12] Moreover, there have always been large differences between the great plantations and the hillside farms of the South, between large productive tracts and marginal units of the vestigial frontier in all regions. Yet the appeal of agrarianism in the late nineteenth century was to all farmers, and there was no organization on a basis of class *within* agriculture.

The assumption of unity in agriculture had no noteworthy challenges until the Great Depression. Occasional voices were raised to call attention to the plight of certain groups in rural life, but these were scarcely heard. Out of the census of 1930, however, a few facts emerged and were brought vividly to the national consciousness. The first of these was that one-half of the farms produced only about eleven per cent of the products going to market.[13] A second fact was the depth and extent of farm poverty. During 1929—by all but the most recent standards a prosperous year—one-quarter of the farms each produced less than $600 worth of products, including those used on the farm.[14]

The existence of these twin problems of low productivity and poverty among a large percentage of the farms has not been a short-run aberration. In the 'thirties the condition continued; the percentage of production by the poorer half of the farms remained very nearly the same. However, the fraction of all farms earning less than $600 a year rose almost to one-half.[15] The prosperity which began with the war years has done much to relieve the desperate character of farm poverty. Many farmers who were formerly dependent on the low return from their land now are able to earn livelihoods away from their farms. To the extent that they have done this, they have ceased to be farmers.[16] Yet there remain many farms to which the general prosperity has not brought a very high standard of living.[17] This is principally a reflection of the degree to which mechanization and technological improvement have by-passed[18] the small-scale and small family farms. At the other end of the scale, prosperity has brought great increases in income. This has been accentuated by the amount of nonfarm income going to the more prosperous group.[19] Whether the distance between poor and rich in agriculture has been growing is not clear; it is certain that the gap remains large.

"Agriculture" is not a simple homogeneous unit of the economy or of society. It includes many different groups with different problems. This is perhaps the economic fact of first importance for agricultural politics. It might be seen from a knowledge of economic factors that there would be impulses to organization of farmers, and that a purely agrarian political party would be an impossibility. However, the large economic tendencies gave little indication of the form that American farm organization would take. Which lines of division would be bridged? Which groups would be brought together? These were the major questions confronting agrarianism in the twentieth century. The answers lay outside the realm of sheer economic force.

3

NEW BEGINNINGS

As the twentieth century began, the greatest challenge to American capitalism in its most ruthless stage had been met and defeated. The weapons of challenge lay shattered and the organization dissolved while the leaders watched helplessly. Twice in the generation just past, mass movements had stirred and groped toward that sort of organization and activity which alone seemed to strike to the root of the evils they were pledged to destroy. The first of these movements had been the Knights of Labor, but this had failed before the nature of the problem had been revealed and it died just before reaching the maturity of a party. The second movement and by far the greater for the span of its meteoric lifetime was the Populist party. The two election years of 1892 and 1896 had marked the period of its greatest brilliance and thereafter the light swiftly faded to extinction.

What had been proved by the failure of the Knights of Labor and the Populists is today, perhaps, obscure; but the moral then drawn was that workers and farmers were inherently difficult to organize, and that any circle of unity about either must be of the smallest possible radius and must be drawn tight with the strongest bonds of immediate and obvious economic self-interest.[1] For the coming generation, farm and labor organizations were to travel similar roads—roads which took as their starting point this one moral.

Yet certain factors tended to lead farmers and workers in different directions. The most important of these was that farmers were proportionately a declining minority after having been a preponderant majority, whereas workers were a correlatively growing minority with the prospect of becoming the majority. The expecta-

19

tion would seem to have been that the one would decline to the status of a pressure group and the other would rise to the status of party. Yet the expectation has not been wholly realized.

A second factor derived from the very simple fact that the capitalism which was under attack was neither inert nor passive. It was, on the contrary, a highly active and seemingly coördinated body of politically alert men. Although the Populist threat had disappeared, the memory of it was still vivid in the minds of members of grain exchanges, heads of farm equipment trusts, and directors of banks. It is even likely that some of these glimpsed the possibility of enlisting organized agriculture or, rather, re-organized agriculture on the side of capitalism. Whether or not there was such a deliberate intention, few better means to accomplish the result could be imagined than the course that was followed.

The cry of challenge continued to be heard, yet the voice was different and gradually it became clear that new champions had arrived upon the scene. Agrarian mass movements had died with the old century.[2] Henceforth, farm organization was to be created anew, using some of the old materials but on a radically altered plan. It was a break with the past in that both purpose and means were directed to something foreign to the old organization.

The story of the first two decades of the twentieth century contains no little of the dramatic. Some of the details are not altogether distinct, but the outlines are clear. To trace this story it is necessary to glance back into the nineteenth century to seek the origins of that which emerged after 1900.

Among the cardinal points of the American democratic faith, education has always been given a place, one never well defined but nonetheless conspicuous. Throughout our history, education has demanded respect both as a means and sometimes even as an end of democracy.[3] It has been held up as a kind of Platonic guardian of the democratic order. Again, it has appeared as the holy vessel of all that is sacred and fundamental even to democracy itself. The concept of an inextricable linkage between democracy and education—always a source of confusion—has nowhere been more confused than in its application to agriculture.

The story properly begins with the passage of the Morrill Act in 1862.[4] This law utilized part of the great unexploited holdings of land for endowment of colleges "for the benefit of agriculture and the mechanic arts." The impulse behind the law was democratic, certainly. The great lands of the public domain, on which John Taylor had relied as the continuing base of agrarian democracy, could in no way more directly serve the democracy. Yet the act contained a twofold ambiguity. First, its purpose was not clear. Did "agriculture and the mechanic arts" mean two separate lines of education or did they merely indicate the breadth of the concept of agricultural education in the minds of the legislators? To put the issue more bluntly, did Congress intend education for farmers and mechanics or for farmers only? The question has obviously gained in importance as the proportion of "mechanics" has increased, and it is entirely likely that Congress did not anticipate this development. Yet it has been seriously argued that the act was intended to serve farmers only, and that mechanic arts were to be disseminated for their application to agriculture.[5]

The second ambiguity was more fundamental, though it is less easily stated. It lay in the general lack of agreement on the responsibility of education to democracy. Is it the part of education to satisfy whatever demands are made on it? Or does education have an obligation to observe goals and standards that are quite independent of these demands? The issue is large and often intangible, but it becomes urgent when applied to vocational education. Specifically, in agricultural education, should the colleges teach zoölogy or the care and feeding of farm animals? Should the agricultural colleges created by public act teach what the public wants or what the public ought to be taught? In a sense the issue was compromised when the act of Congress indicated that the goal was vocational education.

The agricultural colleges were established, and sought means to live with their dilemma. On the one hand, they taught common scientific and cultural subjects in an established tradition; on the other hand, they sought to prove their usefulness and to justify the faith that had created them by doing things obviously helpful to the farmers. The critics of the one side suggested that agriculture was not a proper subject for academic endeavor and those of the other side pointed to the lack of tangible results from the expenditure of such great resources. On the whole, the agricultural colleges were inclined to prove themselves on the practical level, but they were handicapped by the lack of practical disciplines which could be usefully taught. Only a few among the growing numbers of agricultural academicians cried that the choice had been wrongly made. Among the leaders of these was S. W. Johnson, of Yale University, who insisted that "the sole way of accomplishing the almost impossible double task of gaining respect in the eyes of the practical farmer and the hostile educator is by accomplishing the single task of gaining one's own self-respect first."" This certainly could be done only by giving first place to the proper ideals of education itself.

By 1900 the agricultural colleges were on their way to self-respect. Thirteen years earlier they had banded together as the Association of American Agricultural Colleges and Experiment Stations. This was in the same year in which the Hatch Act was passed establishing the agricultural experiment stations.' Of the two events, the latter was the greater, for out of the work of the experiment stations and their association with the colleges came a science and a discipline that could be usefully taught in agriculture. The lesson was brought home that the greatest practical usefulness issuing from the academic halls is the derivative not of an impulse to perform services and odd jobs assigned from the outside but of the determination to solve basic problems set by the academicians themselves.

Yet, now that the colleges had something to teach and discoveries to hand on to practical farmers, an attempt was made to silence the critics by persuading farmers to revise their ways. In the last decade of the nineteenth century, state legislatures were persuaded to provide funds for farmers' institutes, to which farmers were invited to hear lectures by the professors and to learn new methods. In 1903 Congress began federal participation in the program. Pamphlets were issued by the experiment stations on all manner of topics, and fairs became educational enterprises. Given that agricultural education and research had some light to shed, it was only legitimate that attempts should be made to disseminate the knowledge where it would do the most good.' All this had a highly respectable origin in the movement for scientific agriculture which began in the eighteenth century.

This was the foundation on which the new organization of agriculture took place. The agricultural education movement in itself offered no impulse to organization, but it had something invaluable to offer organization when the impulse appeared from external sources. What this contribution was only gradually emerged, and in a somewhat later period. Yet one thing was abundantly clear from the beginning: agricultural education was politically "safe." No important educational figure had played a significant part in the Populist movement. Education tended toward evolutionary gradualism, and agricultural education tended toward a particularly slow form of gradualism. Educational leaders were oriented toward natural science by training and by proclivity. They regarded themselves as nonpolitical and it may be hazarded that as a group they strongly partook of the ideological suppositions of the existing economic order. Although educational leaders occasionally expressed distaste for this trust or that, on the whole they believed that farmers should play the part of mediators in the conflict between capitalists and workers.[9]

The uncertainty of agricultural education about its own goals tended to enhance the political conservatism of the movement. Yet this very uncertainty led by a curious route to a course of essentially political action. To see the directions and the turnings of this route it is necessary to consider the personality of the man who was by most accounts the dominant figure in American agriculture during the first decade of the century.

Dr. Seaman A. Knapp was in 1900 already advanced in years and had behind him a distinguished career as a college president and a farm and land-company business manager. It is clear that he had force of character as well as a high grade of intelligence. Although the accounts of the man and his work tend to be rather deferential, it is certain that he had a strong streak of practical idealism.[10] In the course of developing and selling a tract of land in Louisiana he learned that it was not sufficient to discover the best methods of farming; it was necessary also to convince prospective buyers of the advisability of these methods. The Louisiana venture led to his development of a new strain of rice, an accomplishment which helped bring him the presidency of the Rice Growers' Association of America. The problem of persuading others to follow his methods was more difficult. Farmers show perhaps their strongest conservatism when it comes to the adoption of new methods of farming. Knapp found that neither word of mouth nor the printed word was adequate to carry conviction. Actual demonstration in the soil proved necessary. The success with new techniques of rice culture in Louisiana was such an object lesson.

All this was in Seaman Knapp's background as he began the task of convincing Southern farmers of the advantages of diversified farming. Partly as the result of his efforts, the Department of Agriculture (the Bureau of Plant Industry) established demonstration farms to show in practice how the new methods worked. Publicly owned farms were regarded with skepticism, however, even when they appeared to be successful. Knapp sought the help of the leading citizens of Terrell, Texas, in raising money for a different type of demonstration. Since the crop was cotton, and the Mexican boll weevil was rapidly destroying much of the region's economic hope, it should not have been difficult to stimulate experimentation. The businessmen of Terrell started the work going by offering a guaranty to one farmer if he would follow the Knapp methods. Fortunately, the experimenting farmer prospered even under adverse conditions, and payment of the guaranty was unnecessary.

To Knapp, however, the significant fact was that he had found a means of convincing farmers on their own land. This appeared significant also to his friends in the Department of Agriculture. Knapp was put to work in the war upon the boll weevil. Funds for his pay were found out of various appropriations, but the mainstay of the emergency program that developed was a special appropriation to fight the weevil. Knapp's task was to multiply his Terrell performance throughout the cotton region. The method was that developed in Terrell, the community demonstration farm.[11]

To carry this idea to the multitude of communities afflicted, a large number of individual agricultural missionaries were required. Thus came about Knapp's "social invention,"[12] the county agent system. The term "county agent" is a contraction of "county agricultural demonstration agent," for which the alternative, "county farm adviser," is sometimes preferred.

Within a few years this emergency program blossomed into a cause. After the initial participation of the Department of Agriculture in 1903, the most important element of support came from the Rockefeller-endowed General Education Board. The orientation of this organization was very different from that of the Department of

Agriculture. Unlike the department, which was interested principally in meeting a particular agricultural crisis, the board had a
large concern with the educational problems of the South. The entry
of the General Education Board set a highly respectable stamp of
approval on demonstration work *as education.*

Few events could have been more disturbing to the already
divided sensibilities of the region's agricultural colleges. Demonstration work was originated not by the colleges but by groups outside their walls. Moreover, the new technique was rapidly gaining
substantial support. Although Knapp's farm lessons were orthodox,
his teaching methods went considerably beyond what the colleges
had attempted with their institutes, exhibits, and pamphlets. The
infusion of Rockefeller money into this rival educational venture
was at best unsettling, and skepticism passed readily into opposition
to the demonstration ventures in Texas.[13] The colleges' sense of frus-
tration was aggravated by the spreading involvement of the federal
government and local businessmen in the program.

In 1909, three years after the General Education Board started
its contributions to demonstration work, the Association of American Agricultural Colleges and Experiment Stations set up a special
section on "Extension." This belated recognition of Knapp's work
intensified the conflict within the colleges, just as they had begun to
win that self-respect of which S. W. Johnson had spoken.

"Extension," in the beginning, is a deceptively simple idea—to
extend more convenient forms of the educational program to those
to whom regular courses of instruction are not available. However,
hidden complexities soon develop. How far shall the convenience
extend? In reaching out to new groups, new problems and interests
appear. To how many of these shall facilities be extended? One of
the immediate problems is that of practical education, which inevitably leads to a conflict between education and its substance.[14] This
happened in the work of the agricultural colleges which was aimed
at early reform of the methods of practicing farmers. With all good
intentions, the General Education Board exerted an almost intoler-
able pressure on the colleges to engage in activities beyond their
hitherto agreed-on scope. Many agricultural educators came to
share the judgment of the more impatient pragmatists of their communities—that agricultural education was failing to meet a chal-

lenge so long as the colleges refrained from taking up the Knapp type of demonstration.

These tendencies converged in a general point of view that was more at variance with the democratic tradition than the various groups sharing it realized. To the colleges, to the government, to the county agents, to the local businessmen, and to others yet to be considered, the farmer was a figure to be lifted out of the mire of his own ignorance and backwardness. To all engaged in Extension work and its variants it must have been exasperating to encounter so much difficulty in winning any response from the man whom all joined in praising as the backbone of society.

The problem of the farmer gradually assumed new proportions as the realization grew that the destiny of the nation was to be increasingly industrial. The rarely challenged Jeffersonian vision of the agrarian-based republic seemed to be going by default. Some such vague philosophic impulse prompted President Theodore Roosevelt to appoint a commission to look into the condition of rural life. In a letter asking Liberty Hyde Bailey to accept the chairmanship of the commission, the President stated, "No nation has ever achieved permanent greatness unless this greatness was based on the well-being of the great farmer class, the men who live on the soil; for it is upon their welfare, material and moral, that the welfare of the rest of the nation ultimately rests."[15]

The appointment of the Commission on Country Life was a landmark. Neither the findings nor the recommendations of the commission were dramatic. However, its appointment in a period of general prosperity that extended to the farms provided documentation of the peculiar hold which the agrarian dream has had upon America, even as the unreality of that dream was becoming obvious.

A large part of the commission's response was given over to affirmation. For example:

Upon the development of this distinctively rural civilization rests ultimately our ability, by methods of farming requiring the highest intelligence, to continue to feed and clothe the hungry nations; to supply the city and metropolis with fresh blood, clean bodies and clear brains that can endure the strain of modern life; and to preserve a race of men in the open country that, in the future as in the past, will be the stay and strength of the nation in time of war, and its guiding and controlling spirit in time of peace.[16]

The report dealt also with the tendency of rural youth to move to town, one of the factors which had prompted appointment of the commission. The report did not advocate any steps to counter this tendency nor even condemn it.[17] There was, as a matter of cold assessment, no going back to the agrarian dream. Aside from the relative decline of the farm population, however, the commission did discover certain disturbing facts about country life. Here the group deserves credit for considerable insight in regard to the problems of rural life: first, tenancy; second, "The farming interest is not as a whole receiving the full rewards to which it is entitled"; and third, the farmer is "disadvantaged" when he deals with other business interests and therefore needs governmental protection.[18] The farmer's problem was the problem of "the separate man." Several lesser but noteworthy observations were made on the need for rural highways and for soil conservation. All in all, the commission managed to put its finger on some of the most important characteristics of twentieth-century agriculture.

Having analyzed the problem, and even originated a catch phrase of some force, "the separate man," the commission concluded its report with a reliance on education. "Everything resolves itself at the end into a question of personality."[19] Solution of the problem involved (1) taking stock of country life, (2) nationalized Extension work, and (3) a campaign for rural progress. "Rural teachers, librarians, clergymen, editors, physicians, and others" were to unite with farmers for the fulfillment of the program. Actually, the only tangible recommendation here was for nationalizing "Extension," which by this time meant the sort of demonstration work developed by Seaman Knapp.[20]

The inconsistency between the commission's analysis and its recommendations may have been the product of the peculiar faith in education which pervaded the time. It may also be that there was a genuine difference of opinion among the board members.[21] The report spoke well of "voluntary associations" (apparently coöperatives), the land grant colleges and experiment stations, and the churches. The churches shared with forest conservation (this was clearly the work of the ubiquitous Gifford Pinchot) the honor of special chapters. Yet, for all this mixture of special topics, the recurrent theme was that the farmer "usually stands practically alone against organized interests."[22] Withal, education, in this case demonstration work, was the solution offered.

The pressures upon the colleges increased. The impact of the report of the Commission on Country Life was similar to that of the participation of the General Education Board in the demonstration work.[23] Perhaps if these had been the only pressures and if the question had been merely a straightforward issue of devising the best means of carrying the doctrines of enlightened agriculture to the farmers, a compromise might have been reached. However, other pressures of a different character were being applied.

The first of these was from the federal bureaucracy. It is a significant fact that the most profound modifications of relationships among governmental bodies in our federal system have come about in agriculture. As a result, political scientists have found these relationships a fertile area for the study of administrative structure. From the Land Ordinance of 1785, through the Morrill Act and the Smith-Lever Act to the present, the public administration of agricultural affairs has been conducted in a manner that has steadily altered the relationships between federal, state, and local bodies. Inevitably, the close ties between localities and the Department of Agriculture have involved the latter in political movements. With all the best intentions of remaining neutral, holders of responsible positions in the department have been compelled to handle political questions. While the activities of the bureaucrats can scarcely be said to have dominated the development at any point, neither has their influence been negligible.

Before 1900 the department was hardly a force of consequence. The colleges had been fearful of its influence when the Hatch Act was passed establishing the experiment stations.[24] This, however, had proved an unjustified fear and the act was, as it turned out, one of the bright rays of hope falling on the colleges. The department came to employ increasing numbers of men who had come from the colleges, either as graduates or as teachers and research workers. By the end of the first decade of the twentieth century, this group amounted to what has been called the department's "characteristic personnel."[25] It might, perhaps, have been expected that this infiltration of the department by the colleges would result in an orientation of the department toward a college point of view. This, however, is to overlook the reorientation of college-trained personnel to the government's point of view. Many people have commented on the heady sense of influence that is gained by entry into government work from the halls of learning. The sudden realization occurs that from a government post it is possible to put into practice some of the lessons taught from the lecture platform. This may be largely illusory, but it is a psychological factor of some importance. Moreover, as we have seen, there was no clear-cut college view.

Nevertheless, the interests of the department during this time lay in education.[26] With this interest and with the colleges' own uncertainty of purpose it was almost inevitable that the department should emphasize practicality, that is to say, the Seaman Knapp type of demonstration work. This, in fact, had occurred almost from the outset. Knapp had had special assistance from the department during his early work in Texas and in his larger campaign against the boll weevil. The department had administered the funds contributed by the General Education Board.[27] Moreover, the department seemed impatient, at times almost contemptuous, in regard to the results attained by the colleges.[28]

Thus the substance of official opinion was strongly one-sided in its influence on agricultural education. The quasi-public body of the General Education Board, the public inquiry of the Commission on Country Life, and the bureaucracy of the Department of Agriculture agreed in emphasizing education as the solution to the farm problem and concurred in an estimate that the colleges were failing in their job. But there was more to the picture than this.

It will be recalled that Seaman Knapp found his most important support at the outset from the businessmen of the towns. The money guaranty in Terrell, Texas, came from this source. Seeking this type of support became one of the cardinal principles of "farmers' coöperative demonstration work," as the new medium of salvation came to be officially described.[29] The coöperation of the town business community was perhaps the crucial element in the success of the method. Given the assumption that the farmer was benightedly reactionary in his technology, the problem was one of "persuasion," which at times was rather loosely interpreted. A highly effective means of convincing his flock, Knapp found, was refusal by the town merchants and bankers to grant credit except on condition of coöperation with Knapp or his agents. Accordingly, he took care to see that these strategically placed citizens were members of his committees.[30]

This readiness of small businessmen to coöperate with the farmers spread to the larger units of business and its associations. The concern of big business for the welfare of agriculture was not, it is true, altogether new. The argument had always carried weight that the prosperity of, say, a railroad was dependent on the prosperity of its territory. The much-maligned railroads had already undertaken to coöperate with the agricultural colleges in arranging farm trains which passed through rural areas showing educational exhibits. It was natural, then, that the railroads should support the idea of farmers' coöperative demonstration work. Here and there other groups perceived the advantages of the Knapp plan and gave it backing. One of the most helpful acts was Julius Rosenwald's offer of $1,000 to each of the first one hundred counties to employ a county agent.

By the end of the decade, the Knapp plan had come to resemble a definite movement. Coöperative demonstration work and the county agent so far had been emergency and Southern phenomena. However, the idea gradually crystallized, in the Department of Agriculture and in business, that the program should be made permanent and extended nationwide. From 1909 onward the movement rapidly gained momentum. The Commission on Country Life was but one feature of the movement. The focus of nearly everything done after 1909 was the passage of federal legislation to formalize and nationalize the county agent system.

It is impossible to list all the business firms and associations that were active in the movement. One of the most energetic groups was that of the bankers. Credit for the initial impulse toward legislation was taken by the Illinois Bankers' Association, whose agitation began in 1910.[31] The American Bankers' Association had taken an interest in the farmers' plight to the extent of appointing a committee on agriculture in 1909. In 1911 this became the Committee on Agricultural Development and Education.[32] The 1913 convention of the association made the committee a "commission," which took as its continuing purpose to establish rapport between the farmer and the banker. Its existence continued after the passage of the

Smith-Lever Act, and in December, 1913, it started publication of an attractive monthy bulletin designed to help bring about the desired *rapprochement.*[33]

The motive of the Bankers' Association was a frank mixture of altruism and self-interest; there is no point in emphasizing the one against the other. The bankers' desire for farm prosperity was without question real. As the agricultural committee reported in 1913:

> The majority of the members of our committee have devoted their time to the more essential question of developing educational features, both in schools and on the farms, to enable the farmer and his family to live a broader and happier life and develop the business in which they are engaged to the highest state of efficiency, thereby making them more successful producers, a better credit risk, and a more contented and prosperous people.[34]

The interest in "a contented people" accorded well with the desire to remove the grounds for a historically well-founded apprehension: "Nearly all farmers welcome the coöperation of bankers in furthering their interests, as bankers welcome the farmers in aiding them to secure a scientific system of currency. We all have to work together, and no interests ought to work together more than bankers and farmers."[35] Underlying the determined efforts of the association was the feeling that "the banker has been misunderstood."[36] The program for agriculture included good roads, soil fertility, and education. Education meant coöperative demonstrations and county agents. This was the positive alternative to dissent and radicalism which the bankers held out to the sometimes misguided men of the soil.[37]

The National Implement and Vehicle Association also took a special interest in the farmer's welfare. Here, again, the principal preoccupation was education of the farmer, by coöperative demonstration. One of the important bodies of this association was its Agricultural Extension Committee, which published under its own auspices articles by D. F. Houston, Secretary of Agriculture, Harcourt Morgan of the Tennessee Agricultural College, Tait Butler of *The Progressive Farmer,* and B. F. Harris of the Bankers' Agricultural Commission.[38] The farm equipment makers, who had received their share of castigation from rural rabble rousers, had a clear incentive to attempt to improve public (or at least farm) relations. John Deere and Company and the International Harvester Company employed well-known agricultural academicians as their part in the movement.[39]

Various corporations, generally the trusts which had been attacked in the Populist days, undertook to demonstrate their interest in rural welfare by supporting the coöperative demonstration movement. Especially active among the railroads were the Great Northern (Extension work was a particularly strong interest of James J. Hill), the Pennsylvania, the Rock Island, and the Nashville, Chattanooga and St. Louis. In 1910, chambers of commerce, boards of trade, and related organizations in New York, Philadelphia, Chicago, and Baltimore formed the Council of North American Grain Exchanges. The Universal Portland Cement Company, the American Steel and Wire Company, Wells Fargo and Company, the National Association of Retail Merchants, the Western Retail Lumbermen's Association, the Southwestern Lumbermen's Association—all were among the interests which recalled the days of Populist wrath and which were to be found participating in the movement to save the farmer.[40]

In a sense, the group was fairly diverse, but it nevertheless had a remarkable coherence. Moreover, its program was both tangible and in accord with the temper of the time. Since legislation was the definite objective of the movement, organization became inevitable. This appeared in the National Soil Fertility League. The League was sponsored by some of the most prominent leaders of the period: James J. Hill, Champ Clark, William Jennings Bryan, Henry Wallace, Samuel Gompers, and J. M. Studebaker. For the most part, the League was conceived by businessmen and regarded itself as a business group. Its president, H. H. Gross, described the League as made up of "nearly all the leading transportation companies and large numbers of financial institutions and manufacturing concerns."[41] The organization referred to its members as "businessmen."[42] The purpose of the League was frankly to secure passage of the Lever bill. According to the testimony of Gross, the first draft of this bill was drawn in the League's office.[43]

The history of the moves that culminated in passage of the Smith-Lever Extension Act of 1914 is a fairly good reflection of the forces and dilemmas which have been surveyed here. The colleges' association was almost from the start in favor of national appropriations for Extension work. In 1909 the association presented a plan with this aim, specifying that the money appropriated should go only to the land grant colleges and that the idea of Extension should be broadly conceived." It is not altogether inaccurate to say that the colleges wanted a monopoly on the money released for all forms of agricultural Extension and complete, unfettered autonomy in its spending. The practical incompatibility of the two aims was sensed by few in the association. Had the realities of the situation been more vividly presented to the colleges, perhaps the final compromise might have been avoided. In the event, the colleges gained their first objective and lost their second: the money came to their hands, but autonomy was denied.

In the early stages of the bill's history, one of the primary issues of the land grant colleges was revived. The legislative proposals included several that went beyond agricultural education. They were vocational education bills in that they provided for instruction in trades and industries as well as in agriculture. These bills, the Dolliver and the Page bills, gained the support of organized labor. This, however, was very nearly the extent of the support for these bills in competition with the narrower Lever bills."

One of the striking facts about the history of the Smith-Lever Act is that, at a time when a broad conception of vocational education was possible as a basis for the forthcoming legislation, when the colleges might have acquired an important ally in their own cause, the Association of American Agricultural Colleges and Experiment Stations turned its back. Its 1910 convention, after engaging in a cautious discussion of the trades and industries provisions of the Dolliver bill, finally decided to oppose them. The reasoning was that these provisions would divide the money appropriated and the land grant colleges would lose their control of the program." It is difficult to escape the feeling that the association and its member colleges had again failed an important test.

Despite the ambiguous stand taken by the colleges through their association, the impression grew that they were opposed to a program which many other elements of the community were supporting. H. H. Gross appeared before several meetings of the association to attempt to generate more enthusiasm for the program, and in 1913 the Secretary of Agriculture came on the same mission. The interpretation put upon the attitude of the colleges was that they were jealous of Knapp's work simply because they had not originated it. The colleges' own Extension work—the farmers' institutes, the pamphlets, the itinerant lecturers, and so on—was regarded as absurdly ineffectual (as perhaps it was) and as standing in the way of widespread and sustained operation of the really important county agent system.[47]

There was, however, a growing uneasiness among the colleges. Although the official actions of their association indicated that the issues were by no means clear, a fairly eloquent minority had identified some of the implications of the stand taken by the association. In 1909, H. J. Waters of Kansas told his fellows, "It has been a fundamental mistake to assume that the duty of the experiment station is solely or even principally to benefit the farmer directly."[48]

In 1911 President W. H. Jordan made this the focal point of his address:

The gravity of the situation is augmented by the fact that the agricultural and business interests of the country, alive to the value of our work, are now proposing to us what we shall do and are urging upon us, not only efforts of our own, but our active support of new efforts that are outside our province, but to which we are expected to sustain relations of advice and aid. These suggestions, which sometimes are almost equivalent to demands, are certainly made in the spirit of good will and helpfulness and are worthy of our most respectful and careful consideration; but it is seriously to be doubted whether popular conceptions of the aims and methods of education and inquiry are a safe basis on which to establish the policy that shall dominate the work and influence of either the college or the station.[49]

These warnings were perhaps the best which the colleges ever received. They were brushed aside, however. The child, coöperative Extension, was already born and there was nothing to do but adopt it.[50] One more implication had yet to be drawn. It related to the increase of political control and the way in which this control would be used. Realization of this came late, in 1913, when the crucial hour had already passed. Dean Eugene Davenport could hardly have foreseen the exact manner in which the new law would operate, but his words at the 1913 meeting had a prophetic quality:

The inevitable result of the department's concerning itself intimately with local conditions is to attract the attention of unscrupulous politicians, who will find therein a powerful means of advancing their own personal interests. Given four or five thousand local agents scattered among the farmers of all the congressional districts and under the practical control of a department which depends for its very life upon annual appropriations by Congress, all operating under the interlocking scheme of the new Lever bill, and we should have constructed and at work the most gigantic political machine ever devised. That it would be used, there is abundant evidence already at hand.[51]

The choice was made by the colleges, and by their acquiescence the Smith-Lever bill was passed. It would have passed, in all certainty, even over their opposition. However, without their active participation, coöperative Extension would have appeared in a different guise. Certainly its political character would have been more apparent.

The first effect of the decision came soon after the passage of the act. A "Memorandum of Understanding" went out from the Department of Agriculture to the colleges. To lay hands on the money, the colleges must assent to a plan of reorganizing their own establishments, must engage not to spend less than 75 per cent of the money on Knapp-type Extension work, and must submit to supervision and control by the Department of Agriculture. Now, at last, the meaning of the choice was beginning to be understood.[52] There was dismay, but too late.

The other effects were already emerging from the shadows.

4

The HEIRS of POPULISM

What had become of the embattled farmer? Had his breed died out in the last titanic struggle of Populism? Or had his appearance upon the political field of the 'nineties been only an apparition? What magic had been worked to exorcise him from that field?

The breed had not died out, though perhaps it was declining, for the "boundless" lands of the continent had now been bounded. The words of Turner in 1893 continued for a full generation to seep into the national consciousness, carrying with them a deepening realization of what the presence of a frontier had meant to the nation. Henceforth the dream of John Taylor was finally and forever relegated to nostalgia; the unity of the nation in a free and upright agriculture moved further with each day into the company of past utopias.

Certainly the decade of the 'nineties had had many of the qualities of a nightmare, but the agrarian challenge of that time had been anything but insubstantial. Just as the farmers' grievances had been real, so too had his program. It would be untrue to say that at every point his program struck at fundamentals, yet equally it would be untrue to say that it entirely missed them. The strength of the reaction against the program and the lasting memory of the programs of the 'nineties as shown in the trusts' paternal solicitude for the farmer during the two decades that followed are good evidence of the strength of the Populist threat.

In the Klondike and on the Rand dramatic events were releasing

forces of a strength as yet little appreciated—forces which were
to render much of the farmer's old program obsolete. The discoveries of gold in quantity stripped the "free silver" campaign of its
meaning. The mystery, if any, lay in the operations of the business
cycle. Insensibly, prices of farm products (which, when low, are
always clear portents of farmer resentment and zeal for organizing
among his kind) moved upward. Moreover, paternalism was leagued
with what now passed under the name of education. There is little
point in comparing the strength of this influence with that of return-
ing good times; both worked toward the same effect.

For all this, however, the first two decades of the twentieth century
were not a time of complete vacuum so far as farm organization was
concerned. The tradition of the old Alliance did not pass once and
for all with the demise of that organization. From Texas, the veri-
table spawning ground of agrarian political movements, missionaries began to go out across the Southland in the name of a new
society, the Farmers' Educational and Coöperative Union of America, the Farmers' Union as it soon came to be known. Perhaps more
than any other farm group, it provided continuity in the tradition
of farm protest. The founder of the society, Newt Gresham, was "an
official relic" of the old Alliance, for which he had been an organ-
izer.¹ The summation of the purposes of the Farmers' Union was at
once a plagiarism and a rededication of the spirit of the Alliance:
"To garner the tears of the distressed, the blood of martyrs, the
laugh of innocent childhood, the sweat of honest labor and the
virtue of a happy home as the brightest jewels known."² In such
statements—and for all that the taste of today greets them with
amusement, they were the product of deep feeling—one may sense
again the temper of the 'seventies and the 'nineties. Yet this was the
twentieth century; the Farmers' Union was founded in 1902.

There was more than this efflorescence of Southern fundamen-
talism, however, in the program of the Farmers' Union. The first
of its purposes, "to secure equity," was a concept that looked backward as well as forward—to the "just price" and to "parity" alike.
The second purpose struck more deeply, "to discourage the credit
and mortgage system." This, with the determination "to eliminate
gambling in farm products by Boards of Trade, Cotton Exchanges
and other speculators," indicates a preservation of the old temper

of mind which insisted that definite and tangible spiders be found in the webs which had been spun about the simple men of the soil.' The members of pits and bankers' associations had reason, indeed, to feel that the farmer was basically untamed and ready again to prepare insurgence. And if the presidents of railroads were omitted from the anathemas of the Farmers' Union in its statement of purposes, they were included in its legislative program under the determination to seek laws strictly and narrowly defining physical valuation of railroads (as well as of telegraph and express companies) for purposes of rate regulation.

All were authentic echoes of the old Populism. But even here there were important differences in the applications. The constitution of the Farmers' Union, for example, clearly indicated the organization's suspicion of money-changers and speculators. Anyone "engaged in banking, merchandising, practicing law, or [who] belongs to any trust or combine for the purpose of speculating in agricultural products or the necessities of life" was ineligible for membership.' Newspaper editors were a doubtful category; they were eligible, however, if they took a special oath. Whatever may have been the understandable setting of the restrictions, their most important meaning was that even this first inheritor of the Populist tradition had finally and thoroughly gone over to the view that farmers were a *class*. Whatever its roots in the less-corn-and-more-hell aspects of Populism, it was a tacit repudiation of the Taylorian view of the universality of agriculture as a political base for the nation.

The class strategy of the Farmers' Union was, perhaps, implicit in other features. From the beginning, the Union maintained cordial relations with organized labor. Union publications carried the union printers' label; fraternal delegates were received in conventions from the American Federation of Labor. These gestures may have been results of a sense of genuine community with labor, but it is more likely that they were merely overtures for alliance. Community and alliance are not the same: the one aims at a common program; the other is mere logrolling. Of less apparent importance in the early stages of the organization, but of more in later years was the fact that among those eligible and welcome were tenants.

The real and obvious break which the Farmers' Union made with the past, however, was tactical. The moral that would never fail to be drawn from what seemed the debacle of 1896 was that farm organizations must under no circumstances be drawn into politics. That is to say, they must have no commitments or responsibilities in the work of parties. On this point farm organizers were virtually unanimous. For the Union farmers, salvation lay, it seemed, in the definition of a program and in the single-minded enforcement of that program by whatever pressures to which legislatures were sensitive.

Necessarily, this new tactic became more successful as the program was more rigidly and narrowly defined. Thus, the choice of tactic itself implied intensification of the class basis of organization. The more homogeneous the class, the narrower and more specific its demands could be and the more fully could these be met. The Farmers' Union, oddly, may lay claim to have inaugurated the tactic among farm organizations. What this specifically foreshadowed was emphasis on prices. And this, too, is to be found in the statement of the Union's purposes.

The Farmers' Union, like its great predecessor, the Farmers' Alliance, has been a regional organization for most of its history. In the first decade of its existence, its center of gravity lay in the South. Then this gradually shifted northward to the prairie states. It was the familiar pattern of collaboration between cotton farmers and wheat farmers. By the end of the First World War, the states between the Rockies and the Mississippi and above the Arkansas had surpassed the Deep South in Farmers' Union strength.

The Farmers' Union laid claim to an ultimate constituency, "a floating membership," of 3,000,000.[5] This, however, was but the dream. The membership in 1910 was something like 120,000; at the end of the First World War it had risen to 140,000.[6] All in all, the Farmers' Union has not in itself been a moving force in our political life, but it has had great importance as an irritant and a stimulant for more important forces.

Another representative of the old agrarian tradition was the Grange. Its claims of continuity were clearer and its ancestry more remote in origin. Yet, whatever the truth of its historical identity with the crusading organization of the 'seventies, it was obvious that some change of spirit had long since taken place. The bitter taste of political defeat still lingered and the after-sensation was kept vivid by the failure of the Alliance. Organizational survival remained as the Grange's ultimate goal.

True, the Grange had a platform for the farmer membership and a program to be recommended to the legislatures. For the most part this was direct and specific. Federal appropriations for highway improvement, a parcel post system, postal savings banks, the Great Lakes waterway, election of United States senators by direct vote—these were characteristic planks in the platform. So far as the traditional demands of farm organizations went, a general statement referred vaguely to the Interstate Commerce Commission and "equitable" revision of the tariff. There was just a hint here of the old antagonism to the "interests," as there was in the demand for "laws protecting legitimate business enterprises and punishing business criminals."[7] This last was too ambiguous, or perhaps too bold; it was withdrawn from the program the year after it appeared and did not return.

As the European war slowly engulfed the years, the Grange acquired two new preoccupations, peace and prohibition. These were embraced with all the steadfastness of which rural Protestantism was capable and which the organization reserved for moral issues but continued to deny to such mundane farm concerns as agricultural credit.[8]

Even such political issues as these seem out of place in the proceedings of the Grange during the first quarter of the century. The greater love of the organization was for its ritual, its apostrophes to Ceres, Flora, and Demeter, and all the harmless mumbo-jumbo of its pseudo-Masonry. If something beyond was to be undertaken, it was far better that this should be in the nature of practical coöperation, in self-help by groups in buying and selling. Yet the pressures grew through the war years for a legislative representative in Washington, D.C. These were resisted with vigor when the suggestion was made in 1919 that the Grange join the National Board of Farm Organizations to exercise a farmer vigilance over the national Congress. The Grange stayed out of this lobbying venture, but soon established its own representative instead.

The survival of the Grange as an organization was due perhaps less to its own caution than to the fact that its constitution allows considerable decentralization; hence there is a wide range of opinion among Grange organizations in different states. During the First World War, for example, a group became known as the "insurgent" Granges of Washington, Maine, Pennsylvania, Kentucky, Colorado, and Oregon.[9] This group urged the establishment of a Washington lobbyist. By the end of the war, the National Grange was preëminent among farm organizations in membership, with a total well stabilized above the half million mark.[10] Dr. Kenyon L. Butterfield, writing in 1921, found it necessary to protest that "contrary to occasional statements . . . the Grange is not dead."[11] The protest was justified, but perhaps it was too loud.

The third heir of the old agrarianism was at once the truest and the strangest of the lot, the Non-Partisan League. Here was the stoutest and most violent of farmers' tribunes. Nowhere, either in the 'seventies or in the 'nineties, in the South or in the West, were "the interests" so bitterly denounced as they were by the League in the years from 1915 to 1920. No spokesman for farmers ever singled out the bankers, the grain dealers, and the railroads with more bitter invective than did the self-anointed leaders of the League. Here, with undisguised rancor, was a class organization with a class program and a class strategy. The last was no less than the capture and use of the machinery of the state. The now classic grievances of banker usury and gross exploitation by elevator companies were met head on by a number of plans for state ownership and operation.

The plans were carried out in the home of the League, North Dakota. The organization, founded in 1915, had swiftly carried the whole state into a maelstrom of bitterness and controversy out of which it is difficult even today to extricate issues from personalities.[12] However, as the organization spread to neighboring states, the splendid adaptability of the program and organizing plan to the special conditions of North Dakota failed to meet requirements of organization strength as they had at home. In 1920 the League claimed a membership of 200,000 in thirteen Western states. This would have been strength indeed, but figures of this sort are unreliable, and a dispersion through only thirteen states is slight for a body with pretensions as a national organization. On the larger scene it ranks best as a symptom.

Of the other farm organizations, the American Society of Equity was the most interesting. Founded in 1902, it had ambitions to become a national body, but its strength remained regional, being concentrated in Wisconsin, North Dakota, and Minnesota. Its program was built more definitely around farmer control of prices than that of any other group.[18] The original plan of the group was the most simple conceivable, but could have operated only if the society had been the sole representative of all commercial farmers. As things were, it shifted emphasis to coöperatives. Its history was marked by factionalism. The practical importance of the society was that much of the Non-Partisan League leadership emerged from its ranks. The most memorable statement from the society was, "What the farmer wants to produce is not crops, but money"[14]—a reminder that was prophetic for the twentieth century.

For the rest, it is possible only to list the Gleaners, the National Dairy Union, the Pennsylvania Rural Progress Association, the National Conference on Marketing and Farm Credits, the National Milk Producers' Federation, the Farmers' Equity Union, the Farmers' Mutual Benefit Association, the Farmers' Social and Economic Union, and the Farmers' Relief Association.[15] And this is incomplete.

On the face of things, it would seem that in the first twenty years of the century the farmer was organized and that the keeping of the agrarian tradition was in numerous and capable hands. The hands were perhaps too numerous, but constant efforts were made to focus their energies in Washington. The Farmers' National War Council gave way after the armistice to the Farmers' National Council. It would not have been unreasonable to assume, in 1919, that the various units of organization among farmers could be brought together in the grand concert of a revived agrarianism of the old order.

In some of its aspects, however, the revival was tending away from the old spirit. First was the implicit abandonment of the presumption of universality in farm organization as a political base for the nation. No longer could the nation be pictured as fundamentally agrarian, even by the dreamers. Second was the increasing importance of coöperatives in the programs of the organizations. Third was the new intensification of emphasis on prices. Each one of these changes implied a narrowing of the public interests of organized agriculture; each involved a sharper conception of farmers as a particular class. These were changes in degree, though, and, such as they were, implied no break with the past. The old hostility to the interests consorted well with the evolving programs. The cries and the language of Populism could still be heard, but increasingly they were linked with strange associations from the industrial age— hatred of organized labor, xenophobia, and antisemitism. If a new prophet of this decaying Populism had been named, Henry Ford would have been the leading candidate.

In truth, the membership figures of all the revived agrarian organizations could not be added up and a movement discovered. The societies, the unions, the leagues, all the groups of wheat growers, cotton producers, tobacco planters, and others were mere fragments and were not to be welded together on any pattern inherited from the old Farmers' Alliance. The job of fusing the farmers into a political power was being preempted by another organization, one to which the old tradition was not so much opposed as irrelevant.

5

The AMERICAN FARM BUREAU FEDERATION

An observer traveling through rural America in the years between 1902 and 1919 might well have reported a ground swell of spontaneous organization among farmers. He might have noticed, first, a little band of men gathered about one of their kind, but one who had some of the marks of success and the gift of persuasion. The setting might be an open field, a shady spot beside a barn, or the interior of a warehouse. Everything would suggest informality and naturalness of procedure.

As the observer found the scene duplicated and reduplicated, however, he would discover that the appearance of spontaneity was a highly artful creation. The central figure, the county agent, even before the passage of the Smith-Lever Act of 1914 was a public figure and increasingly a public official. He was paid and his job lay precisely in the activities around which the group was organized. If a moral were to be drawn here, it would be that organization even at this elementary level is not the product of either chance or natural propensity.

This would be too trite to set down were it not for the fact that it was denied, and strenuously, before an inquiring committee of the national Congress. The committee, a body not normally concerned with problems of agriculture, had experienced—apparently with surprise and certainly with no little sensitivity—the full force of a pressure campaign. Since the campaign was being conducted

44

in the name of the farmers of America, the committee launched an irascible investigation into the validity of the claim. The investigation, after a brief pursuit of false scent, discovered the track and thereafter concentrated on learning the anomalous facts of farm organization in the twentieth century.[1] These hearings may be taken as the debut of the major political force of modern agriculture, the American Farm Bureau Federation.

The theory that ultimately developed from the investigation was that the American Farm Bureau Federation was a new and spontaneous growth which had suddenly appeared in 1920. This theory was not unequivocally upheld; it represented the best of only one of two desirable worlds. Yet the theory is worth examining, since it continues to have official standing. To do this it is necessary to look not only at the information given to the House Committee on Banking and Currency but that which was regularly made available year by year before 1920.

The central figure of the period was undoubtedly the county agent. Nearly every question that arose in the hearings before Congress or that was discussed in print revolved about the position and activities of the agent. The period preceding the 'twenties was that of his greatest political effect, but he has not ceased to be a controversial figure.

The county agent derived his support and maintenance from a variety of sources, which at first were exclusively private. Then, public agencies were increasingly drawn into the work and provision of funds for his pay. The Smith-Lever Act explicitly permitted continuation of the system of paying the agent from separately administered public and private funds. This was based on the precedents of gifts from the General Education Board, Julius Rosenwald, and business firms in the first decade of the century. Just how an agent could successfully resolve the problem of his divided responsibility when he was an employee of the federal, state, and county governments as well as of a private association should have been an obvious question in 1914.[2] There is little indication, however, that any responsible officer saw the problem until much later.

The spread of the county agent system is a highly significant feature of organized agriculture in the present century. It has been hailed as a "movement" and is often spoken of as if it had been spontaneously generated. The element of truth in this view derives from the fact that the Smith-Lever Act neither created the system nor made it permanent. Both had been accomplished before 1914. At the time of the passage of the act, governmental agencies (state and federal) were already spending $1,600,000 on the work, and 881 agents were established in the field.[3] The graph of the number of county agents during the first decades of the system indicates a steady rate of increase between 1907 and 1917. In 1914 the shape of the curve changed but little, and the change appears as a slight flattening.

The real change of gradient came in 1917, when the system received the benefits of special war appropriations. Under the conditions of forced growth through these appropriations, the number of agents reached a point well above 2,600 in 1918. By the end of the first decade of operation under the Smith-Lever Act, the number of county agents stood at 2,251. The system had spread to approximately three-quarters of the agricultural counties of the nation. Thus, the combined effect of the Smith-Lever Act and the wartime programs was, in quantitative terms, roughly to double the size of the system.[4]

For the rest, however, the passage of the Smith-Lever Act introduced important innovations. First, it regularized the county agent system. Second, it reduced the status of the land grant colleges as participants in the "movement."[5] Third, it established the halls of Congress as focal points in questions relating to agricultural Extension. In short, the Extension movement was more than a spontaneous development.

The official conception of the work of the county agent has always been one of education. Somewhat paradoxically, however, every report of the program has brought forth masses of statistics on the numbers of farms controlling insect pests, feeding balanced rations, culling herds, planting improved seeds, and so on. The goals of the program are measured almost exclusively in the language of technical productivity. Thus, there has been strong incentive to achieve the quickest and most extensive application of approved methods. Even with a staff as large as that of the county agent system, it is impossible to reach all commercial farms and to reëducate their sometimes backward proprietors directly. For this reason, from the time of Seaman Knapp onward, county agents have been instructed to work with the leaders and with groups of farmers.

In practical terms this meant that the agents were required to provide organization among farmers as the first step in their own operations. The New York state director of Extension listed the reasons for the agents' organizing drive thus: "(*a*) It multiplies effort—especially self-help effort. (*b*) It establishes close contact with localities. (*c*) It makes leadership most effective. (*d*) It provides a clearing house."[6] On the basis of this sort of official reasoning, the county agent became the publicly paid organizer of the American Farm Bureau Federation.

The county organizations which the county agents built up about their operations followed no preconceived plan.[7] So far as there was thinking on the problem in the Department of Agriculture, it was probably contained in the definition of such an organization by one of the directing officials: a body "to coördinate and correlate" the work of all farm organizations. It was to be "nonpolitical, nonsectarian, nonsecret" and to represent "the whole farming population."[8] The words "nonpolitical" and "nonsecret" suggest the department's mistrust of existing farm organizations. Later, as the department's share in fostering a new farm organization came under criticism, the point was elaborated that the previously existing organizations were improper vehicles for the county agents' message.[9] However, the explanation probably included an element of rationalization.

The name chosen for the local organizations formed by the county agents derived in a curious way from the early business leadership of the county agent movement. The Binghamton (N.Y.) Chamber of Commerce in 1911 set up a bureau of its own organization to sponsor a county agent. This quite reasonably was listed as the "farm bureau." This business group was acting under the initiative of the traffic manager of the Lackawanna Railroad, and using the idea of W. J. Spillman, who suggested that a county agent be employed by the private group.[10] For some reason the name was adopted by the Department of Agriculture as applying to any coöperating county organization.[11] The choice probably is an indication of the conception of the farm bureaus as public bodies which prevailed in the department at the time. Certainly, the name has caused no little confusion in regard to the status of the Farm Bureau—confusion which has operated to the benefit of the organization generally.

One of the best-documented facts about the Farm Bureau movement is that it was a direct outgrowth of the county agent system. All the instructions to agents from the department were based upon the assumption that the first part of the agent's work would consist in organizing farm bureaus.[12] Department officials made numerous statements taking credit for the movement. C. B. Smith, for example, said, in 1921, "I do not believe it is going too far to say that the United States Department of Agriculture and the office with which I am connected is responsible for the development of farm bureaus in this country."[13] As early as 1915 the department called for Farm Bureau participation in the financial and other arrangements of the county agent system.[14] Perhaps the high point in department fervor for the "movement" came in 1919, when Secretary Houston called on farmers to join or form farm bureaus in order to stop bolshevism.[15]

The official view of the position of the farm bureaus before 1920 provided a central place for the land grant colleges. The college Extension director was presumed to be the active director of all county agents in the state. Approval of appointments, administration of the whole plan, in fact all the lines of authority, seemed to lead to his desk, with only minor threads of responsibility extending from there to Washington. The state Extension director had the authority to give "orders" to individual agents.[16] On paper the scheme seemed to obviate the apprehensions of the colleges and to insure against overcentralization of the program in Washington. As his part in the Farm Bureau activities of the county agent work, the college Extension director provided sample constitutions, by-laws, membership cards, suggestions for Farm Bureau papers, and so on. Moreover, he often sent trained organizers to assist local groups.[17] The plan was well calculated to foster the illusion that the colleges were the controlling powers of the movement.[18]

There were, however, a few realists among the college leaders and a considerable uneasiness prevailed at their meetings. The colleges' association, at rather an early stage, voted against permitting agents to handle organization funds.[19] In 1919 and 1920 the college repre-

sentatives were preoccupied with a problem of which the department still seemed to be unaware. The local farm bureaus had
already begun to federate on a state basis, and in 1920 the federation of these federations was consummated. This development
posed the problem of relationships in unmistakable form. At the
next two conventions of the colleges' association a series of papers
were read on the general question, What should be the relation of
the county agent to the Farm Bureau and of the college to a state
Farm Bureau federation?[20]

Perhaps the most striking insight into the program came from
Dr. Clarence Ousley of Texas:

> It seemed to me, from the brief allusion to the subject in the paper by Dr.
> Galloway, that this Bureau movement was a scheme whereby a progressive
> body of farmers took advantage of the department and college in order exclu-
> sively to utilize the services of the county agent. If that is what the bureau
> means, then it is an unwholesome movement. The whole tendency of agricul-
> tural education is to benefit the man who is already progressive. It does not
> reach the man who is in most need, the neglected man, who neglects himself,
> who does not seek knowledge, and to whom the colleges and the department,
> through the county agent, should go as a missionary.[21]

This was a good example of the sort of light which the colleges could
cast on the problems of the farmer. When it came to taking action
on the problems which the college representatives now saw, however,
something less than decisive measures were adopted. The conventions recommended coöperation between colleges and farm bureaus.
At any rate, the colleges deserve credit for seeing the problem, if
unwillingly.

The complexity of the pattern of relationships spun about the
county agent was increased as numerous state legislatures adapted
their codes to the new Extension work. Most of the new legislation
was passed to enable counties to make appropriations for support
of agents and their work. Considering that the Department of Agriculture and the colleges were laying great stress on Farm Bureau
organization, it was not unreasonable that twelve or more states
should have specifically named county bureaus as the legal coöperating agencies in Extension work.[22] Most of these laws were passed
before the drive to federate the local bureaus was well advanced.

Sometimes explicitly and sometimes implicitly, these laws made the farm bureaus legal representatives of the county governments. Some county Farm Bureau heads were integrated with the budgetary establishments of the counties. Beyond this, the laws formalized the connection between the county units and the colleges by providing that the college Extension directors should be the state administrative heads of the local programs.[23]

The entry of the United States into the First World War placed a premium on production and accelerated the organization of farm bureaus by county agents. The number of agents was swiftly increased, and the amount of money available to their activities was greatly expanded by the Emergency Food Production Act of 1917.[24] This was the period of mushroom-like growth in the numbers and membership of county farm bureaus.[25]

The period of expansion and preoccupation with wartime problems of production coincided with that of several significant developments which tended to be overlooked in the wartime confusion. The first was the increasing commercial activity of the agents. As the local farm bureaus discovered that the agent was their servant rather than their leader, they put the agent to work doing the office and managerial work of coöperatives. A common example of this was in fertilizer purchasing. The "fertilizer trust" had long been disliked by farmers, and the availability of the agent's services provided a means of retaliation which soon evoked protest from established dealers. This became, in fact, the first point of genuine controversy over the county agent system.[26]

The second major development was the increasing momentum of the drive for federation. The first state federation, that of Missouri, had been formed in 1915; Massachusetts and Illinois followed soon thereafter. The central nucleus of state federation, however, was formed during the war years. By the end of the war, ten such groups had been organized. The next step was obvious.

The third change was a shift in the nature of the relation between the county agent and the local Farm Bureau. Although the agent had organized the bureau and was regarded by the governmental agencies as an educator and a leader, he could not maintain himself in this role.[27] According to a questionnaire in 1919, agents in nine out of nineteen states studied were listed as "managers" of local farm bureaus.[28] Not only was this a probably declining proportion, but the very title suggests that the agent was being relegated to a bureaucratic role in the private organization. This process of the assimilation of a public official into the service ranks of a private association was somewhat paradoxical in that the proportion of public funds for his support was increasing. Whereas originally the agents were supported privately, by 1924 the proportion of public funds had increased to 93 per cent.[29]

At the end of the war, then, the foundations were well laid for national organization. Farm bureaus had spread over most of the agricultural counties of the nation and the movement toward state federation was well advanced. The movement had in its hands the free services of a willing bureaucracy. It was generally feared that the farm bureaus were merely pliable tools in the hands of the Department of Agriculture and the land grant colleges. Underlying all this was a collective Farm Bureau membership of more than 400,000.[30]

A preliminary meeting was called by the president of the New York federation early in 1919. The objective as stated by the president of this meeting was to create an organization "thoroughly representative of agriculture throughout the entire United States," and to mobilize "the strongest farmers of the nation."[31] Despite the absence of any convincing reference to education in the aims of the proposed organization, C. B. Smith of the Department of Agriculture gave his approval.

The organization meeting took place in Chicago a year later. Delegates from thirty-one states were present. If there was any doubt in regard to the probable direction the federation would take, it was resolved by the speeches at the meetings. The objectives mentioned were clearly economic and political: "To keep control of our food products" until they get to the consumer, to stop any policy "that will align organized farmers with the radicals of other organizations," to "stabilize the nation," to "put agriculture into proper relationship with the rest of the world."[32] The organization was completed, after some wrangling over regional claims, a few months later. Officers were chosen (including a "Washington representative") and voted handsome salaries.

It would be difficult to learn from an examination of the program of the American Farm Bureau Federation that it originated in an educational movement. The aims did include some that were listed as educational, but the substance of these is confined to the first: "To create in the urban mind a better conception of the Farmer's relationship to other units in the social and economic structure." The actual objectives were those listed under the heads "legislative" and "economic."[33]

The federation opened its Washington activities in a bold and energetic manner. Numerous bills were taken under the wing of the office, and on at least one occasion congressmen were asked to report to the federation lobbyist just how they had voted. It is scarcely remarkable that even hardened representatives were startled by these tactics. There were rumblings through the first two years of the operations of the office, and then Congress retaliated with an investigation.[34]

Mr. Gray Silver, the Washington representative of the federation, may have been naïve ("I am a farmer from Apple Pie Ridge") when he testified on the Hill. On being asked by the committee chairman (L. T. McFadden of Pennsylvania) whether the county agent was the nucleus of the county farm bureaus, Silver answered in the negative. On being pressed about the organizing activities of the agents, he replied that he had never known of an agent—"as recognized under that name"—to be an organizer for the Farm Bureau "so far as the Farm Bureau direct is concerned." All instructions to the agents, so far as Mr. Silver was aware, came from the colleges.[35]

The chairman thereupon tried a new tack and asked whether the Farm Bureau was a governmental agency. The answer this time was categorical: the Farm Bureau was a voluntary organization. This was the crucial point of the investigation. The committee had a copy of a speech made by the department's C. B. Smith in which the statement was made that "the farm bureau . . . is practically a public institution; essentially a sub-college of agriculture."[36] The contradiction was glaring enough to prod the committee into discovery of abundant evidence that local farm bureaus and federations both owed their existence to the Extension organization of the department.[37]

By the time this had been established, the president of the national federation, J. R. Howard, was in the witness chair. When asked whether he considered the county agent a governmental employee, he answered, "a semigovernmental employee."[38] There have been few clearer statements of the federation's claims upon the agents than this. With an apparent sense of shock the committee extended its inquiry to uncomfortable lengths, but little could be added to the self-assured statements of the federation president. It would be wrong to suggest that Howard came off second best. The term "public institution" is still applied to the Farm Bureau so far as its claims on the county agents are concerned; at the same time, the organization has been able to establish its claims as a voluntary society for all other practical purposes. It is definitely the best of both worlds.[39]

The Department of Agriculture now found itself in a position curiously similar to that in which earlier it had helped to place the land grant colleges. Like the colleges, which had assumed that they were being given new governing powers in agriculture, the department seems to have believed that it was merely extending the range of its own functions as it developed the county agent system. The mantle of education had served to hide the nature of the movement not only from the world at large but to a lesser degree from the colleges and the department as well. To the extent that the two last sensed the character of the movement, they were inclined to condone their own part in its fostering for the reason that both successively felt themselves its masters.

The involvement of the department, however, was rather more uncomfortable than that of the colleges. The formal responsibility for creation of the Farm Bureau Federation rested rather too obviously upon the Department of Agriculture. The line of escape from this responsibility relies upon the ingenious theory that the year 1920 marked a sharp break with the past. The farm bureaus built by government officials were, so the theory goes, purely public bodies. When the state federations were formed and particularly when the national federation abruptly materialized, a new situation suddenly appeared. The federations were not public bodies, and government officials now had a nice line of demarcation to observe. The theory has been made somewhat difficult to hold by the unfortunate history of official statements of the department and the frankness of federation officials. However, it seems to have given comfort to the people in the department.[40]

The practical aspects of the situation in the early 'twenties did necessitate some kind of departmental action. In 1921, Dr. True, as head of the States Relations Service,[41] reached an agreement with President Howard by which the activities of the county agents were to be limited. The farm bureaus were to continue to contribute funds for the maintenance of agents and to join in the work of Extension. But county agents were not to organize farm bureaus, operate membership campaigns, solicit membership, receive dues, handle Farm Bureau funds, edit Farm Bureau publications, or manage Farm Bureau activities.[42] It was an interesting bargain, if in no other respect than that its terms had to be repeated in a formal order from the Secretary of Agriculture a year later.[43]

6

TRIAL
and ERROR

The time into which the American Farm Bureau Federation was born was one of economic paradox. The nation quickly emerged from the problems of postwar economic readjustment to enjoy the greatest period of prosperity yet seen. The farm population, however, was largely excluded from the benefits of recovery. For agriculture the postwar decade was a period of depression which merged into the catastrophe of the 'thirties. When the slogan "Food will win the war" had been coined, casual assurances had been given that the increased production could be advantageously sustained in time of peace. The needs for relief in food abroad justified these assurances for more than a year. In 1920, however, the depression began. Its most critical phase extended through 1923. Thereafter, the situation began to improve, though very slowly.

This was the first agricultural depression since the 'nineties. Judging from the experience of the nineteenth century, a resurgence of agrarian organization might have been expected. Certainly, the Farm Bureau Federation seemed the most likely of the various candidates for the role of organizer. To the unobservant, and even to the deeply implicated officialdom of the Department of Agriculture, there had been something Minerva-like in the sudden appearance of the federation. It might have been the working of destiny or of some obscure natural law which brought a vigorous organization of farmers into being just as the economic tide was turning.

This was illusion. The American Farm Bureau Federation was

55

formed well before the beginning of hard times, and its origins reached back almost two decades. It was the product not of depression but of prosperity. The greatest successes in organization had occurred during one of the periods of greatest farm prosperity. The organizing campaigns of the federation only added a superficial layer to the solid base which had been laid by the county agents.[1]

The Farm Bureau Federation did not become a mass movement in any sense. Its membership peak for the whole of the depression period, 466,421, was reached in 1921. Very quickly thereafter it declined to a fairly stable 300,000.[2] This failure to continue its growth is rather odd, for the Farm Bureau was now the dominant farm organization. Times were hard and the farmer had as keen a sense of his grievances as ever. The reasons for the decline of the Farm Bureau are in part obvious and in part obscure. The first and most comprehensive point is that the Farm Bureau had no desire to become a mass organization. The best evidence for this is the widespread requirement of high dues: $10 annually was a common figure, and $15 was not unusual. Compared with trade-union dues, these were not high. However, farm bureaus did not have so strong a hold upon their members as the trade unions had upon theirs. Moreover, a cash outlay of $10 represented a substantial item to farmers, a large part of whose income consisted of a living drawn directly from the products of the farm. Certainly, this requirement excluded subsistence farmers.[3]

The disinclination to become a mass movement was perhaps implied by President Howard when he stated, "I stand as a rock against radicalism."[4] While Secretary Houston had been too liberal in giving credit to the Farm Bureau for stopping "bolshevism" in 1919, something like this does apply for the early 'twenties. The Farm Bureau during this time behaved "responsibly" and made none of the demagogic appeals which might have stimulated the growth of the organization. In a large sense, the conduct of the Farm Bureau through the great depression can be regarded as the substantial return on the investment in concern for agricultural welfare which business groups had made in the preceding period. These groups may not have understood the exact significance of their own steps, but their measures were effective in diverting farm organization away from "radical" channels.[5]

The Farm Bureau Federation was a major political power from the first year of its formation, but the character and purpose of the organization[6] remained in process of formation throughout most of the period of agricultural depression. The educational aspect of the farm bureaus suffered a sharp and immediate diminution as the local organizations federated. This change, however, was more apparent than real; its dramatic quality derived mainly from the illusions hitherto cherished by the department and the colleges. There had been, it is true, a lively controversy at the organization meeting of the national federation over the issue of a program of commercial coöperatives plus legislative action—advocated by the Middle Western delegates, versus a strictly educational program— sponsored by the Eastern and the Southern delegates. The Middle Western group had the greatest strength, and much of its program was adopted. It is an interesting fact that this dispute over policy was paralleled by disputes on the basis of representation and the amount of dues.[7]

The decision to operate through Congress was acted on with a vigor and an effectiveness that have seldom been equaled. In May, 1921, a group of senators met at the Washington office of the Farm Bureau.[8] This meeting resulted in the formation of a "farm bloc," which became an object of consternation in the early 'twenties. There is every reason to believe that the organization of the bloc was uniquely the achievement of the Farm Bureau Federation. Gray Silver acted as the group's secretary and mentor on what "the farmer" wanted. The bloc was avowedly nonpartisan and, since its members constituted a controlling majority of the Senate Committee on Agriculture, it was a great threat to party machinery.[9] The bloc, later joined by additional senators, eventually included a total of twenty-two.

More important than sheer numbers on the Senate floor, however, was the discipline which the Farm Bureau Federation provided. Its Washington office sent out questionnaires on legislative policy to the state headquarters, which distributed them among their member- ship. The results were tabulated in the Washington office by con- gressional districts. The material thus refined proved invaluable in persuading reluctant members of the legislative group to accede to bloc discipline.[10]

This display of lobbying virtuosity brought results. Packer and stockyard control, regulation of grain exchanges, extension of the War Finance Corporation's powers to lend money for export of farm products, limitation on immigration, tariffs on farm products, legalization of farmers' coöperatives—these were among the achievements claimed by or for the farm bloc. It is notable that some of these measures had been objectives of farm organizations for many decades. In view of this fact, it seems overgenerous to give complete credit to the 1921 bloc. However, the burst of farm legislation in the early 'twenties has probably been surpassed only in the period of the early New Deal. By any reckoning, farm bloc performance must be counted as a remarkable show of strength.

Portentous though the years 1921 to 1923 were in Congress, this was not a revolution that had occurred. The leader of the farm bloc, Senator Kenyon, was given a judgeship and the congressional group thereafter gradually lost force. There was no attempt to re-form the organization, and in the Sixty-eighth Congress the farm bloc as a tightly knit group was gone.[11]

The experience of the first few years as a national force may perhaps have been too heady for the new federation. Certainly, it was rather too strong a threat to the party system to be received passively. Party regularity could not be allowed to succumb so readily to a freshman lobby.[12] The entrenched Republican party, once the initial panic over the formation of the farm bloc had passed, asserted its hostility, or at least its indifference, to the power of the Farm Bureau and denied farm demands.

Whether or not the Farm Bureau had overreached itself in Washington, a more fundamental reason existed for the receding tide of legislative success after the first few years. The organization had not yet defined its purpose. The quick success of the farm bloc in passing many of its measures may have contributed to its decline. Gray Silver had given the following list of Farm Bureau interests when the Senate group had met at the Farm Bureau office: commodity financing, personal credits, legalization of coöperative marketing, readjustment of freight rates, tariffs, taxation, and packer regulation.[13] This was in itself a diffuse list. As the major items were passed, the fighting strength of the group necessarily decreased. If the group were to develop a general program, it would be in process of becoming a political party, thereby diluting the strength of Farm Bureau control and making it less effective. For a time, indeed, there seemed some danger that enough senators would seek admission to the bloc to give it a majority. Silver feared this development just because the group would then extend its interests and would become "harder to control."[14] Thus, until the Farm Bureau had adopted a narrowly focused program of its own, there was good reason for discontinuance of the congressional farm bloc.

One obstacle to the formulation of the necessary program was that the Farm Bureau Federation had not been formed around an idea but around a bureaucracy. Neither leadership nor membership was committed to any central core of doctrine. In fact, the history of the Farm Bureau suggests that the organization has been not an originator but a broker of ideas in farm policy. Second, serious lines of cleavage existed within the organization. This had been apparent at the organizational meetings in the very beginning. The Farm Bureau spoke in the name of all the farmers of the nation, but the farmers of different sections wanted different things. The problems of Southern cotton differed from those of Middle West corn. This was a long-standing problem to which not even the Farm Bureau had a quick and easy solution.

The principal alternative to seeking legislation from Congress lay in coöperatives. Almost every farm organization has at one time or another made coöperation, whether for purchasing, processing, or marketing, a central aim. Coöperative marketing became one of the first objectives of the Farm Bureau Federation.[15] So long as the anti-monopolistic restrictions of the Sherman Act remained unqualified (except by the ambiguous Clayton Act), the program necessarily involved legislative action. Action on this was a conspicuous achievement of the congressional farm bloc. Self-help through coöperation, however, seemed to at least one faction of the Farm Bureau leadership—that of J. R. Howard—to be the remedy for the dramatic decline in prices which commercial farmers were experiencing, and almost an end in itself.

The Farm Bureau, which had not yet assumed the role of farming's unique spokesman, took the leadership in calling a conference of grain growers in 1920. Representatives were sent from most of the farm organizations, but the National Board of Farm Organizations withdrew in a controversy over control of the new growers' body.[16] A year's gestation brought forth the U. S. Grain Growers, Inc., a coöperative sales agency to which members were to be bound contractually. It did not have a successful history and the Farm Bureau Federation was happy to be relieved of the association. Similar, though less grandiose, ventures were inaugurated in livestock, dairy products, wool, cotton, fruits, and vegetable marketing.

Definite commitment to coöperative marketing as the major organizational purpose came after the end of the farm-bloc phase of Farm Bureau activity. Howard, retiring in 1922, managed to pass the presidency on to his supporter, O. E. Bradfute of Ohio. "Service through coöperative marketing" became the slogan of the Farm Bureau Federation. Here, it would seem, the federation had at last found its function. Although the development of coöperative marketing was far removed from the educational goals out of which the organization had ostensibly derived, the course was intrinsically reasonable. The county agents had been active from an early date in forming and managing coöperatives. The department had looked benignly on coöperation among farmers. Moreover, it was a form of direct action on the preoccupying problem of prices.[17]

It is conceivable that the Farm Bureau Federation might in time have developed into the central association of marketing coöperatives, but this would have implied a much smaller role than was originally envisaged for it. It is altogether likely that the coöperatives, under Farm Bureau leadership, would have followed separatist tendencies not unlike those of the international unions in the American Federation of Labor. The coöperatives, in point of fact, have displayed this trait under their own diverse associations.[18] Without some central financial or equivalent control by the Farm Bureau, it is difficult to see how the bureau could have stemmed the strong tide toward autonomy which would have developed.

In any event, the wisdom of taking coöperative marketing as the central Farm Bureau objective was questionable, for a parallel organization, the National Council of Farmers' Coöperative Marketing Associations, was being conducted by Aaron Sapiro.[19] The Farm Bureau elements attending the Sapiro conference sought to limit the activities of their rival. Being unsuccessful in this, the federation hired Sapiro as legal adviser on coöperative marketing.[20]

The personality of Sapiro proved a source of dissension and eventually he was forced out of the organization.

The Farm Bureau Federation was thus faced with the necessity of resolving a group of separate but closely related conflicts if it were to continue. A jurisdictional conflict with the rival Sapiro organization was particularly serious, since the Sapiro group had numerous adherents among both membership and leadership of the Farm Bureau. Moreover, there was a grave split in the Middle West, heartland of the Farm Bureau, over the place of coöperatives in federation policy. Different state federations were committed to different policies. Howard had apparently come to look upon coöperatives as the peculiar mission of the federation and, to a lesser degree, his views were paralleled in Ohio.[21] Howard's choice of Bradfute as his successor was a recognition of this affinity. Even inside Iowa, Howard's own base, the tide was running strongly against the coöperative emphasis.[22] The real center of opposition, however, was Illinois, which has always been the pivot of the national organization. In 1925 the Illinois Agricultural Association (the Illinois Farm Bureau) nearly left the national federation, but compromised with a resolution calling on the federation to "purge itself of all evil influences that seem to exist at this time."[23] A similar and allied movement was strong in Indiana.

Another problem was that of regional cleavage. The South, although not so strongly organized by the Farm Bureau as was the Middle West, represented an indispensable component of the federation if it were to be what it claimed, the spokesman of agriculture. The cotton coöperative association had apparently gone over to the Sapiro organization, and, more important, was cold to the rising ideas of McNary-Haugenism. Any solution of farm surplus which exploited foreign markets and was built on tariffs ran head on into two stubborn facts: cotton was already exported in larger quantities than most crops, and tariffs were traditionally disliked in the South. Moreover, the federation's vice-president, Edward A. O'Neal of Alabama, was actively opposed to the coöperative emphasis. His strongest reason was probably suggested by the statement of the Farm Bureau historian that coöperatives had proved of little help in maintaining the membership of either state or national organizations.[24]

Some of the complicating side issues were in part policy and in part personality. The Grain Growers, Inc., had degenerated into a commercial venture which was being exploited by the early bureaucracy of the Farm Bureau, as represented by Gray Silver and John Coverdale, first secretary of the federation. This problem and the entire controversy over the position of coöperatives in the Farm Bureau scheme of things were confused by a palace controversy between Henry C. Wallace and Herbert Hoover over the distribution of marketing functions between the Department of Agriculture and the Department of Commerce.

The American Farm Bureau Federation thus was faced with a dilemma. On the level of method, a choice had to be made between commercial action and political action. Commercial action had been disastrous to farm organizations in the past. Political action, on the other hand, appeared even more dangerous; the disaster of 1896 had not been forgotten. On the level of policy the choice was between service to coöperatives and pressure for surplus disposal legislation. It was, of course, abstractly conceivable that both policies could be followed concurrently. To a minor degree this has been done. There was nothing contradictory *in the policies themselves*. However, the survival and growth of the organization depended on its establishment as the farmer's spokesman in some unique manner. This implied a focusing of energies and a primary, if not exclusive, emphasis on one policy. In effect, then, the Farm Bureau was confronted with a major crisis.

The crisis extended through 1925. The trend of things was, however, foreshadowed in the convention which began the critical year. The meeting in December, 1924, effectually increased the power of the Middle Western element by adding two members from that region to the executive committee of the national federation.[25] The resolution of the remaining questions came with the convention of 1925. The final eclipse of coöperative marketing was brought about by the combined forces of the Illinois group, E. A. O'Neal, and representatives of the mountain states. This alliance easily triumphed over the Ohio and Eastern elements to elect Sam H. Thompson, of the Illinois Agricultural Association, as president. O'Neal continued as vice-president.[26]

The upheaval of 1925 was in large part a matter of personalities and rivalries in leadership.[27] Yet the battle had been fought on issues of policy, and the clear-cut victory of the legislative element provided solutions to many of the organizational problems of the Farm Bureau Federation. It meant that the federation had found a purpose. The question of method followed necessarily.

The program to which the federation was now committed had exceptional merit from the standpoint of the organization. It was simple, apparently easily understood, and direct. It consisted in securing passage of the McNary-Haugen bill. If there were complexities within the bill and its plan, this was no concern of the federation, since the program was readymade and even had a readymade and irresistible slogan, "Equality for agriculture."

Like nearly everything for which the Farm Bureau has ever stood, the McNary-Haugen plan did not originate from within its own ranks. The idea had been brought to the Farm Bureau office as early as 1921 by its originators, George N. Peek and Hugh S. Johnson of the Moline Plow Company.[28] The idea in its essentials was to obtain a government guaranty of prices of farm products. This was to be founded on the one method of governmental interference with the price mechanism that had the approval of tradition, the tariff. To "make the tariff work" for agriculture, farm surpluses were to be exported at world prices, while domestic prices were to be maintained at an acceptable level. The inevitable losses in such an operation were to be met by one of varying schemes for scrip, debentures, or domestic allotments. The scrip and domestic allotment plans put levies on the marketed units; the debenture plan relied on customs revenue.

This approach to the problem of low prices found influential support long before it became the central tenet of the Farm Bureau Federation. Peek was indefatigable in sponsorship of his own plan. More important, the plan was on the way to becoming a department measure.[29] Winning the support of the state Farm Bureau Federation preceded national federation support by several years. However, passage of the McNary-Haugen bills was thought to depend on the formation of an effective combination of commodity groups. Wheat growers had been among the first enthusiasts. Corn producers followed. Cotton planters joined the movement in the later 'twenties as their prices fell.[30]

Several results flowed from the decision to adopt McNary-Haugenism. The first and more obvious result was that the Farm Bureau was henceforth projected more openly into the arena of party politics. The very strategy necessary to the success of the surplus-disposal bills was a small-scale replica of that involved in the success of a national party at election time.[31] More clearly than this, it made necessary direct approaches to the parties themselves. Since the farm bloc had been dissolved, it was imperative that some kind of commitment be obtained from the regular parties. However, Coolidge twice vetoed McNary-Haugen bills, and Hoover was in disfavor with the dominant Farm Bureau faction. The result was that the moderately favorable 1928 plank of the Democrats was sufficient to draw open support from the organization. In supporting a party policy—a policy which was neither its own work nor particularly satisfactory in substance—the Farm Bureau was in effect acknowledging its own weakness as a pressure group. This was a confession that the making of policy yet remained a party matter. It was a position which the leadership of the Farm Bureau did not relish.

The second result was that by accepting the already framed program of McNary-Haugenism as its own, the Farm Bureau accepted a mold within which its own development was to take place. For the McNary-Haugen bills implied a very definite view on what "agriculture" consisted of and a theory about the ills besetting it. On the whole, this view was consistent with the predispositions of the Farm Bureau, but it was a narrower and more limiting concept than that with which the federation had started. The theory about the ills of agriculture referred, in this decade, to "the farm problem." Statements on this problem were much the same whether made by the agricultural academicians, the bureaucrats, or the National Industrial Conference Board. The "farm problem" was simply the complex of problems facing the commercial producers of crops with large surpluses.[32] By narrowing its focus to these groups, the Farm Bureau was doing much to define its own future.

The fight for the McNary-Haugen plan was lost. Even with Farm Bureau organization of the forces behind the plan, the presidential veto proved an insuperable obstacle. The show of strength made in the party dickerings brought no more than a membership to the

Farm Bureau president on a Federal Farm Board, which the federation regarded as impotent. Meanwhile, the federation's own membership had declined.[33] Thus there were serious grounds for questioning the line of development which Farm Bureau policy had taken. And yet this development had laid down one of the bases of a strong organization.

7

SUCCESS

In the early 'thirties the very survival of the American Farm Bureau Federation was threatened. Although the federation claimed to be "the voice of organized agriculture,"[1] it remained but one of three general farm organizations. Despite unusual organizational advantages over its rivals, it had entered an almost disastrous stage of decline. The record of accomplishment after the spectacular days of the first congressional farm bloc was negligible. Its assault on the party system had been an admitted failure. Finally, and most seriously, the federation had compromised itself by collaboration in the Republican farm policy. It is doubtful whether the Farm Bureau could have refused to accept representation on the Hoover Farm Board without loss of prestige. Yet the facts remained that the Farm Bureau had participated and that the board was a failure.

By this time it had become clear that the American Farm Bureau Federation must find its place as a general farm organization. The rationale of its organization required that its function be broadly framed to appeal to different sections and different commodity groups. The early emphasis on coöperatives had not brought strong central organization. Instead, it had meant commodity particularism. Once the Sherman Act restraints on coöperative marketing had been removed, there was little to hold the various groups together. Moreover, the coöperatives already had their own federation. At best, coöperatives offered only the sort of auxiliary strength that friendly benefit systems give trade unions.

The sectional aspect of the problem was almost as apparent. The strength of the federation in 1930 lay overwhelmingly in the Middle

66

West.[2] In commodity terms, its strength was corn-hog. The secondary focus was the South and cotton. Here, however, the power of the Farm Bureau was meager. Federation leaders had repeatedly noted that much of the opposition in Congress to the domestic allotment scheme supported by the Farm Bureau had come from the South.[3] There were outlying Farm Bureau strongholds in California and New York, with the dairy states of the Northwest perhaps also to be considered as outlying.

Thus the problem facing the Farm Bureau was fundamentally similar to that regularly before the major parties: to forge an intersectional alliance of two or more major regional interests and to pick up whatever outside incidental strength was consistent with the basic alliance. For the Farm Bureau, the basic alliance was obviously that between cotton South and corn-hog Middle West. The first step in framing it was taken when Edward A. O'Neal of Alabama was made president and Charles Hearst of Iowa vice-president.[4] The selection of O'Neal was not justified by the relative actualities of strength; it was, rather, a manifest of the policy to be followed in the future. The addition of Earl Smith of Illinois to the directorate somewhat later was perhaps a recognition that the primary center of Farm Bureau power must always be the corn belt.

This strategy, hardly more than an outline before the days of the New Deal, was laid down in 1931. It appeared at a moment when the crisis before the Farm Bureau was perhaps at its gravest. The membership figures reflected the first serious impact of the depression and the failure of Farm Bureau legislative policy. In 1931 there was a drop of 45,000, and eventually the size of the Farm Bureau was cut in half.[5]

The occasion which made the elevation of O'Neal to the presidency of the federation possible was the decision by the organization to support the Federal Farm Board. President Sam Thompson resigned as an officer of the Farm Bureau and joined the board at President Hoover's request. It meant recognition of the federation as a power in agricultural politics, something which the leadership may well have felt to be almost a necessity at the time, but the decision was hardly a pleasant one. As the Republican party substitute for farm legislation demanded by the federation and other organizations, the Federal Farm Board could not be presented as the achievement of the federation. Moreover, any hopes that had been pinned on the Farm Board as a means of raising agricultural prices were waning. The board chairman confessed that the job could not be accomplished without control of production.[5]

The situation of the Farm Bureau as one of numerous farm organizations was less than comfortable. Assuredly, however, the National Grange was no great threat. Its leadership had had a legislative program since the early 'twenties and had one now.[7] Yet there was little likelihood that the Grange would acquire, or even seek, any great increase of influence. The consistent conservatism of the Grange, secure in the belief that it had found a reliable basis of organizational survival, was stated by one of its presidents thus:

> The Grange has seen more than fifty farm organizations—State and National—rise and fall. It has gone through four great major depressions, and periods of boom and collapse, drought and bumper crops, and still moves forward because the soul of the Grange is its ritualistic side, and its emphasis is on moral and spiritual ideals.[8]

Such an organization might prove to be pallbearer to the Farm Bureau but never usurper.

The Farmers' Union was quite different. The Union had been through some of the same troubles which had plagued the Farm Bureau, particularly the conflict between coöperative and legislative emphasis. The legislative policy had won out in 1929. The stronghold of the Farmers' Union had been the wheat country of the Great Plains. However, there was a significant Farmers' Union in Iowa, which was first among Farm Bureau states in 1930.[9] The president of the Iowa Farmers' Union, Milo Reno, was also head of the Farmers' National Holiday Association, a group which sometimes became involved in incidents bordering on violence.[10] More alarming to the Farm Bureau than the dumping of milk upon the highway was the strong opposition to both the Farm Bureau and the Extension Service aroused by the Reno organizations, which organized a campaign to cut off public support for the county agents and to persuade Farm Bureau members to resign.[11] The farm holiday movement was perhaps the radical edge of the Farmers' Union in this period, but it was not repudiated by the parent organization.[12] In fact, the leadership of the Farmers' Union conceived of the organization as still standing in the old Populist tradition, militant and aggressive.[13]

In this situation the most rankling taunt was that farm relief had failed because the farm organizations could not agree on what they wanted.[14] Aside from its obvious element of truth, it underlined the failure of the Farm Bureau to make good on its claim of being the unique spokesman for agriculture. Moreover, the increasingly widespread belief in the truth of the charge represented a peculiar threat to the Farm Bureau, since it, more than either the Grange or the Farmers' Union, was committed to the role of legislative agent to the farmer. Accordingly, the new O'Neal regime attempted to form a united front with the other general farm organizations. Three meetings were held in 1931.[15] These efforts bore fruit early in 1932, when the big three organizations reached agreement on a legislative program.[16] The agreement was vague on the crucial point, how to raise farm prices. However, it did call for anything—whether the debenture plan or the equalization fee—that would work to control surpluses. Beyond this, the program denounced the sales tax, an unequal tariff, and speculation; it favored money stabilization (i.e., inflation) and Philippine independence.

The leaders of the Farm Bureau Federation took credit for the new "unity."[17] In point of fact, the agreement was not much more than a façade. The Grange was lethargic and the Farmers' Union was suspicious. However, the Farm Bureau was encouraged to enlarge the scope of the movement at the head of which it had placed itself. Representatives of fourteen farm organizations met in October.[18] Whatever the differences among the various groups, the fact of the meetings was of the first importance. The Farm Bureau was quick to appropriate and exploit the advantage.

The structure thus built before the national election endured through the critical period when agricultural policy was being formulated for the New Deal era. Early in 1933 the organization of the National Agricultural Conference was completed. The effect for the Farm Bureau was to make its own leader, O'Neal, more conspicuous than before. Again in 1934 the conference met and drove for its common objectives, but this time the Farmers' Union was a discordant voice in the general harmony. Thereafter the conference usually went its way without the Union.

Nevertheless, the spokesmen of the Farm Bureau were able to rejoice over the successful passage through an exceedingly difficult time. It now mattered little that John Simpson was talking about "fake farm organizations";[19] the claim of the Farm Bureau was good that "the organization stands at the pinnacle of its power and influence in national affairs. The advice and help of our leaders are sought in the highest councils of our nation. More and more the Farm Bureau is looked to for leadership as the spokesman of organized agriculture."[20] What the Farm Bureau had been unable to accomplish by direct organization among farmers it had managed by adroit manipulation of other organizations. That is to say, it had solved an immediate problem of its own internal life by action in its external affairs.

The first fruits of this external policy appeared even before inauguration of the new administration. Roosevelt sent Morgenthau, Tugwell, and W. I. Myers as his representatives to the conferences of the Farm Bureau in December, 1932.[21] Here was assurance that the "voice of agriculture" would have some kind of a say in measures to come.

More interesting (and more obscure) is the part that the Farm Bureau played in the selection of the new Secretary of Agriculture. According to the semiofficial historian of the organization, O'Neal exercised a veto on the plan to give the post to Morgenthau.[22] At any rate, the choice of Henry A. Wallace seems to have been thoroughly acceptable to the Farm Bureau. Wallace had been one of the witnesses summoned to Washington the previous year to testify on a measure sponsored by the organization.[23] Policies of the Farm Bureau had been supported by Wallace's editorial page, and the Wallace family was regarded, at least retrospectively, as a firm supporter of the Farm Bureau by the faction now in control.[24] Very early in the life of the new administration O'Neal announced, "I regard Secretary Wallace as the farmers' right bower in the Farm Bureau's program. He has coöperated with us 100 per cent . . . we believe he will continue his coöperation."[25]

The agricultural program that emerged early in 1933 was claimed by the Farm Bureau as its own. In one sense, the claim was justified. The Farm Bureau gave its support to the legislative program of the early New Deal in agriculture. In another sense, however, the claim was misleading. The previous convention of the federation had passed a set of seventeen resolutions in the legislative area. The program ran from a demand for "honest money" through the guaranty of bank deposits, economy in government, and the St. Lawrence waterway. The resolution on the agricultural surplus was far from definite.[26] The farm mortgage problem and the monetary panacea seemed to loom larger in Farm Bureau concern at this time. Yet the general trend of future policy was already fairly clear. Roosevelt had favored the domestic allotment plan during the campaign, and opportunism, if nothing else, would seem to have suggested Farm Bureau support for this device.[27]

The evolution of the ideas that went into the scheme is usually traced to W. J. Spillman, with contributions from John D. Black and M. L. Wilson. In any assessment of the factors which determined Farm Bureau policy, a large share of importance must be attributed to personal influence with the New Deal leadership. Certainly, M. L. Wilson and Rexford Tugwell strongly supported the adaptation of the domestic allotment idea to the legislative program of the new regime.[28] The other fundamental idea in the evolving farm program, "equality for agriculture," with a base calculated on the years 1909 to 1914, came from George N. Peek and Hugh S. Johnson.[29] Significantly, all but one of these men had a part in the administrative history of the new farm program.

In the fluid time of 1933 this personal element was a source of uncertainty in the equations of power. The program that was coming out of the actionist New Deal might well take surprising turns. The Farm Bureau had a measure of security in having supported the program outlined by Roosevelt during the campaign and in having secured a degree of commitment from the conference of farm organizations. Yet the Roosevelt farm contingent held divergent tendencies and the farm organizations were far from united. The latter fact was demonstrated first. In the last session of the lame-duck Seventy-second Congress a bill was brought up embodying the essentials of the later Agricultural Adjustment Act. O'Neal, the first witness called, claimed to represent some fourteen farm organizations, including the Grange and the Farmers' Union.[30] The united front survived this claim, but the bill nevertheless failed. When the new Congress met, the rift in the unity of the conference suddenly became obvious. Taber of the Grange gave unqualified support to the program, but Simpson denounced it. Simpson's objections were not in themselves important except as they indicated a return by the Farmers' Union to insistence on its own particular variant.[31]

The Agricultural Adjustment Act passed in May.[32] The basic plan had been chosen. Production was to be restricted on a quota related to previous acreage planted. The inducements were subsidies drawn from a variety of processing and other taxes. Although the act itself was complex, the plan was simple—and little more than the plan had been decided. The conflicts of agricultural politics shifted to the more obscure fields of administration.

George N. Peek, the first administrator of the Agricultural Adjustment Administration (A.A.A.), has said, "The farm organizations had little to do with the program."[33] This statement by one of the main participants must carry some weight. However, the issues as seen by this effective but blunt and unperceptive man tended to revolve about the controversy within the Department of Agriculture between the "liberal" group and the "agrarian" group.[34] In no small degree, this controversy was a matter of personalities. The "liberal" group looked to Tugwell for leadership. The "agrarian" group was the older element which had come to look upon the department as its peculiar property. It would be difficult to single out any individual as its head. Perhaps Chester Davis came as close as any to the position of leadership.

Many of the differences between the two factions lay in the fact that the liberals were a city-bred group and lacked the homespun mannerisms of rural America. Anyone who has spent much time about the department is aware of the degree to which the protective coloration of rustic ways is cultivated in the offices of the vast buildings on the Mall. Failure to achieve this coloration is itself ground for suspicion.

The issues were finally reducible to the question of who was to receive the benefits of the A.A.A. program. Necessarily, they involved the structure of power which was essential to the Farm Bureau. The climax of the conflict came in the "purge" of 1935. The immediate issue was a legal interpretation relating to the share of tenants in A.A.A. payments.[35] The issue was genuine, but it was mingled with other genuine issues and with matters of personality. The picture, dramatic though it was, did not show the underlying problem of power and administrative structure.

To understand the part of the Farm Bureau in the A.A.A. program it is necessary to consider again the relationship between the Farm Bureau and the Extension Service. Although economy in government had repeatedly been favored by resolutions passed at Farm Bureau conventions, the saving was never envisioned as applying to the expenditures of the Extension Service. O'Neal "personally polled" the Senate Committee on Agriculture in 1931, attempting to gain increased appropriation for Extension.[36] A similar battle to fight cuts in Extension appropriations took place in 1932.[37] At the same time, the Farm Bureau was seeking to tighten the relationships between the colleges, the Farm Board, the Department of Agriculture, the Extension Service, and itself.[38] O'Neal and Charles Hearst of the Iowa Farm Bureau took Henry A. Wallace along with them to call on C. W. Warburton, director of Extension, to argue for the use of county agents in presenting to farmers "the way in which different types of economic policies affect agriculture."[39] To the Farm Bureau, an administrative structure which held so little place for the Extension Service was far from satisfactory. The trouble rested, in all probability, in the independent status of the Farm Board. Despite the presence on the board of a Farm Bureau representative, the board was insufficiently responsive. What was needed was a "complete coördination" of the board with the other agencies.[40] This implied a larger role for the Extension Service.

One of the most important Farm Bureau purposes in the legislative drive of 1933 was to correct the administrative structure of the previous era. An independent board had proved rather too susceptible to congressional influence.[41] The device for inaugurating the new program was at hand in the Extension system. O'Neal made this one of his points of emphasis in a visit to the White House with Wallace:

Where is there an agency that is so close to the grass-roots, and that has so much influence with the real people? [i.e., as the Extension Service and the land grant colleges] ... I was strongly against any political administration of the act. Anything savoring of such an administration would be fatal.[42]

O'Neal's distaste for "political administration" of the A.A.A. was paralleled by the desire of administrative heads to obtain exten-

sive participation in the program. The latter derived in part from a
fear that the price effects of the program would be limited by an
inadequate response by producers. There was also, however, a genuine and widespread belief that local involvement of the farmers
themselves in questions of administration was the essence of democracy. Accordingly, the administration developed an elaborate plan
for consulting "the real people":

> First, after having studied the situation to determine how an adjustment
> for corn and hogs might affect incomes of farmers, the A.A.A. held a series
> of regional conferences participated in by representatives of agricultural
> colleges and by farm leaders in the present program. In these conferences,
> the various alternative directions which a program might take were dis-
> cussed. The gains which farmers might expect to realize through the alterna-
> tive plans were assessed, and the desirable adaptations of the plans to the
> particular conditions of different regions were considered. The farmers and
> state representatives at the conferences expressed themselves on all points
> involved freely as did the representatives of the A.A.A. and gave their
> opinions as to whether farmers in their regions wanted a program for 1935,
> and if so, what kind of a program they wanted.
>
> The second step was the referendum taken among corn and hog farmers,
> following discussions sponsored by the farmers' production control asso-
> ciations, and committees. In the actual voting, no record was kept of indi-
> vidual votes and no questions were asked as to how any farmer had voted.
>
> After the votes had been tabulated, and the majority will of the farmers
> was known, the third step was a meeting in Washington at which representa-
> tives of control associations, general farm organizations, the State colleges
> and the A.A.A. worked out the program in detail.[43]

The central feature of the plan was the county production control
association. The local association had not only the duties outlined
above, but the assigning of quotas and the checking of compliance
through local committees as well. Obviously, all this required a
staggering amount of organization work. For wheat producers alone,
there were 1,450 of these associations.[44] By the end of 1934 there
was a total of more than 4,200 county associations.[45] In the first year
of the A.A.A., 70,200 local farm leaders were trained.[46]

From the standpoint of the Department of Agriculture, only one
agency could accomplish the task quickly—the Extension Service.
Most of the educational activities of Extension were shelved, and

agents were directed to turn their efforts to the organization of the A.A.A. program. The A.A.A. itself developed an organization, but this was confined principally to Washington.[47] The real reliance was upon the county agent. Many of the agents became secretaries of the local associations.[48]

The result for the Extension Service itself was a new lease on life. A new enthusiasm followed from the "enlarged field of service."[49] More tangibly, the A.A.A. provided the wherewithal for expansion of the agency. Funds were transferred to Extension and new personnel were employed. Geographically, the blank spaces in the map of the nation by counties were quickly filled.[50] The period of decline of the Extension Service had come to an end; it now maintained a genuine "action" program and, moreover, had gained an improved claim to leadership at the local level.[51]

The building of an administrative machine for the A.A.A. was not the accomplishment of the Extension Service alone, however. The officers of the Department of Agriculture recognized the farm organizations as consultative organs in themselves. In addition, the Farm Bureau responded to the organizational desires of the department and joined the campaign. When the A.A.A. was first set up, the Farm Bureau sent word to the state federations to decide whom they wanted to administer the act in their own states. In many communities the local farm bureaus "literally took over" the task of organizing the A.A.A. committees.[52] Thus, by exploiting the sudden opportunity given by government willingness to act, the Farm Bureau succeeded in making the A.A.A. its own in administration as well as in policy. There was more than mere braggadocio in the statement that "the Farm Bureau and the A.A.A. are inseparable."[53]

A membership campaign was conducted by the Farm Bureau to parallel the intensive organization of farmers for the A.A.A.[54] The new vitality among county agents, the exhilaration of attaining favorable legislation, and the assurance of a benevolent attitude in the department combined to make the campaign a success. Membership rose both spectacularly and steadily through the years of the first A.A.A.[55] The organization of commercial producers in A.A.A. control associations almost necessarily redounded to the advantage of the Farm Bureau, not only because the bureau had been alert in capitalizing on its part in legislation and its close ties with the Extension Service, but also because the federation was an organization of commercial farmers.

This was most apparent in the South, where the Farm Bureau had a peculiarly pressing problem of organization. The very necessity which had brought O'Neal into the presidency—that of cementing a regional alliance between the Middle West and the South— required that the Farm Bureau display greater strength in the South. The membership of even the largest state Farm Bureau in the South was only about half that of the seventh largest state federation elsewhere in 1934.[56] The gravity of the problem undoubtedly helped to overcome the distaste of the national leadership for identification with the special commodity legislation for cotton and tobacco to supplement the A.A.A.[57] The federation was already alive to the dangers of "commodityism," but the risks were worth the prospective gain in prestige for the organization in a key area.

The gains in the South came somewhat slowly, since a large amount of formative organization work was necessary. However, by the end of 1936 results became apparent. In that year the Southern region made the largest gain. A special organization department was set up and a mass campaign was directed throughout the South. County agents, who were generally freer in that region than elsewhere from legal restrictions on outside organization work, were stimulated to form farm bureaus and sign up the beneficiaries of the new government programs.[58] During this period some of the local farm bureaus became adjuncts of the county agents rather than the other way about, as in the normal situation.[59]

When the A.A.A. program went into operation in the South, some of the results of this organizational history became apparent. During the famous "plow-up" stage of the program, stories of fraud and influence by the Ku Klux Klan circulated. A system by which payment checks were diverted to creditors of actual farmers was openly arrived at in consultations between government officials and the local participants in this grass-roots democracy. Tenants were generally excluded from benefits paid from A.A.A. funds, despite their greater relative personal sacrifice to the program.[60] The explanation lay mainly in the fact that, as one group of observers noted, "the Agricultural Adjustment Administration organized its program under the direction of the planters themselves."[61] The county agents and the Farm Bureau were the means of organization. This was the essential background of the discord in the Department of Agriculture which erupted in the 1935 "purge."[62]

This, then, was the pattern established in the early years of the New Deal. The Farm Bureau had succeeded in identifying itself with the legislation. By the decision to use the Extension Service in administering the A.A.A. the department had helped to identify the Farm Bureau with the administration of the program. The results had been, on the one hand, a vast increase in the strength and influence of the Farm Bureau and, on the other hand, a great financial boon to the type of farmers who were the natural clientele of the Farm Bureau.

The A.A.A. was struck down in the Supreme Court on January 6, 1936.[63] The crisis thus precipitated affected not only the Department of Agriculture and the whole New Deal but the welfare of the Farm Bureau as well. On January 9 the national board of directors met in special session. On January 10 the Farm Bureau leaders presented a program to a conference of farm leaders summoned by Secretary Wallace. On January 11 the conference adopted a soil conservation plan embodying the essentials of the old A.A.A. On January 14 the executive committee of the Farm Bureau drafted a proposal to go before the National Agricultural Conference on the following day. Approval was obtained there, and in the short span of seven weeks the A.A.A. was legislated back into existence.[64]

The action was swift and incisive, but there were uneasy moments, nevertheless. In the Senate hearings on the new measure, Earl Smith served as spokesman for the Farm Bureau and, as in 1933, presented the program as that of all farmers and farm organizations. Yet, when E. H. Everson of the Farmers' Union appeared, the old cost-of-production scheme was brought forth as the Farmers' Union plan. Even Taber of the Grange went off on an independent tack.[65] The unity of the farm organizations was far from impressive. However, the Farm Bureau program prevailed without great difficulty.

Local administration was reorganized under the new substitute for the old A.A.A. Whereas previously the local control associations had been based on particular commodities and had numbered more than 4,000, now the local groups were consolidated into "county agricultural conservation associations." There were now only 2,711 of these.[66] This change represented a clear organizational gain for the Farm Bureau on three scores. First, administrative organization was now general and not broken along commodity lines. Second, it paralleled the local Farm Bureau structure. Third, it was more amenable to direction through the county agents. In the South the county agent automatically became secretary of the local association; elsewhere, "in most counties in nearly all States, county agents . . . [were] elected to this position."[67] The effectiveness of the system for Farm Bureau purposes was attested in the following summary:

> Out of 169 members of the State Soil Conservation Committees, in states where the Farm Bureau is organized, a total of 117 are Farm Bureau members, and in a number of states, 90 per cent or more of the county and township committeemen are Farm Bureau members. This shows the extent to which the Farm Bureau is furnishing leadership of the Soil Conservation program.[68]

The distribution of financial benefits under the new act was not greatly unlike that under the old.[69]

The Soil Conservation and Domestic Allotment Act of 1936 was admittedly a stopgap. Despite Farm Bureau consultations with experts on constitutional law, there was much doubt in regard to the chances for the act in the Supreme Court. Moreover, an extensive series of problems had grown out of the existing system. Even the men who were strategically situated in the Department of Agriculture felt that restriction of production meant an "economy of scarcity" and was out of accord with the long-range goals of the New Deal. The soul searchings that went on at this time were at least in part the result of a desire to resolve the dilemma of restricting production of food when starvation was at large in the world.

In February, Secretary Wallace called a conference of farm organizations to help frame new "permanent" legislation.[70] Far more than the presentations of 1933 and 1936, this was a Farm Bureau undertaking. As O'Neal frankly explained to the Senate committee, "The farm organization leaders were asked to draw the bill and the Farm Bureau employed Mr. Lee and Mr. Lee worked with the Department and advised with experts and economists in the Department in order to work up this draft of the bill for the farm leaders."[71]

O'Neal, Earl Smith, and other familiar Farm Bureau witnesses carried on the campaign in both houses. That in the Senate was generally smooth, but in the House it ran afoul of the operations of Charles Holman of the National Coöperative Milk Producers' Federation. The issue was the apparent possibility under the new act that Southern producers might use land diverted from cotton to engage in dairying. Again, a rift appeared in the unity of the farm organizations on whose behalf, presumably, the Farm Bureau leaders were arguing. This resulted in the revelation that all the Agricultural Conference members who worked on the Southern part of the bill were Farm Bureau men except one who was head of the Southern cotton coöperative organization.[72]

The act which finally passed in 1938 incorporated most of what the Farm Bureau had asked, including soil conservation, acreage allotments (voluntary, with benefit payments), commodity credit loans, marketing quotas, crop insurance, and parity payments. The provision for marketing quotas incorporated the referenda device and storage loans in quota years. For practical purposes the loan system under the Commodity Credit Corporation was the immediately important part of the act. It quickly became a legal fiction for direct subsidy of commercial producers. For the rest, the act was sufficiently complex to confuse those who had doubts in regard to its merit.[73]

With the passage of the 1938 act, the Farm Bureau had accomplished its basic legislative program. At the same time it had established itself in a position of preëminence among farm organizations. In a review of Farm Bureau history before 1939, the statement was made that "practically all the important movements for the benefit of agriculture which have been developed during the past twenty years received their original public impetus from the Farm Bureau."[74] The claim was somewhat larger than the record justified, however one interprets the phrase "for the benefit of agriculture." Nevertheless, by 1938 the situation had changed. The system of power had been built and consolidated. The Farm Bureau was in a position to formulate its terms and enforce them. The act of 1938 represented just such an accomplishment. The statement in the same review was quite true: "Alone of all the national farm organizations, the American Farm Bureau Federation fought unremittingly for the passage of this act."[75] Moreover, the Farm Bureau was in a highly favorable position in the administrative scheme of this, the main body of agricultural policy.[76]

In the achievement of power during the 'thirties the Farm Bureau surmounted some obstacles so successfully that their existence tends to be overlooked. The most important of these was what O'Neal and others labeled "commodityism." In one sense it was the same difficulty that had been at issue in the conflict over coöperative marketing in the 'twenties. It was hoped that this problem would be solved by the elevation of O'Neal to the presidency. His selection set the seal, so to speak, on the long-desired interregional alliance. It is significant that the comment appeared soon after O'Neal's inauguration that, until the Farm Bureau's formation, agriculture had been bound by "sectionalism and commodityism."[77] The statement as it stands is untrue for the long term. The great historical agrarian movements had surmounted the difficulty. Yet for the period preceding the Farm Bureau's ascendancy it was true. The failure of the organization in the later 'twenties was the failure to gain the support of cotton producers.

"Commodityism" was not eradicated by any single measure of the Farm Bureau in the 'thirties. It continued as a recurrent problem. Its appearance in the supplementary acts for cotton and tobacco has already been noted. It appeared in the Marketing Agreements Act of 1937, which permitted "orderly marketing" of milk, fruits, and vegetables. The Farm Bureau supported all these measures for the simple reason that the commodity groups were too strong to be resisted and it was better to placate than to antagonize them. Perhaps there was an issue of "commodityism" in the addition of scattered crops to the A.A.A. list of seven "basic" commodities in 1934 and 1935. The additions brought the total to fifteen.[78] This was undoubtedly a continuation of the conflict among commodity groups which had appeared in the original conference called by Secretary Wallace in 1933.[79] An issue of "commodityism" involved the powerful milk coöperative group in the 1937 hearings on the "permanent" A.A.A.

The Farm Bureau repeatedly attempted to give assurance that it was the organization to represent all commercial groups.[80] The head of the Wyoming Farm Bureau told Western cattle and wool growers, who had stayed aloof from the Farm Bureau, that their own association alone could not get the results offered by the Farm Bureau.[81] It was much the same with various other groups. The argument was not wholly convincing, however. The narrowly focused commodity organizations had a peculiar strength deriving from their own narrowness of structure and purpose. To take an analogy from the world of labor, a small craft union of highly skilled workers can often make gains for its members through the craft organization that would be impossible if those particular workers were submerged in a large general union. The "threat of commodityism" was still vivid in 1939.[82] At the convention of that year, special conferences were held on commodity problems.[83] It was recognition, perhaps, that, strong as the Farm Bureau had become, there was no final solution to the issue of "commodityism."

A second although lesser problem appeared momentarily on the horizon in 1935. The A.A.A. and the Farm Bureau together had promoted the organization of farmers into local control associations. These were plainly intended as "public" associations, but the analogy to the origin of the Farm Bureau as a "public" auxiliary of the Extension Service was fairly obvious. O'Neal early warned that established farm organizations must be used in A.A.A. operations instead of creating new ones.[84] In May, 1935, the fears of Farm Bureau officials seemed to be in danger of realization. The secretary of a Texas control association issued a call for a convention of state organizations to be held in Washington. Although Wallace and Chester Davis took steps to head off the movement, some 4,500 farmers accompanied by 100 or so county agents did come to the capital. They made a protest against the current drive of processors to destroy the processing tax, and then dispersed. A memorandum from Davis ended the episode.[85]

The incident nicely symbolized the relationship which meshed the Department of Agriculture, the land grant colleges, the Extension Service, and the Farm Bureau. The county agent was made to play a political part, yet his activities were conducted at the end of a leash. The same control which was exerted over him extended in some degree to the other public bodies involved. Increasingly the control was vested in the Farm Bureau. The able leadership of the bureau was, in all likelihood, aware of the significance of the administrative structure. Use of the Extension Service in administration of "action" programs was one of the points which O'Neal took up with the President in 1933.[86] It was consistently a matter of high policy with the Farm Bureau throughout the formative years of the A.A.A.

At the same time, the Farm Bureau leadership was careful to ensure the continuance of its own influence with the Extension Service and the colleges. In 1933 O'Neal appeared, as he often did, before the convention of the colleges' association. He reminded his hearers that it was the Farm Bureau that had really fought for their appropriations.[87] The provision of funds for the Extension Service from the A.A.A. was further evidence that coöperation with the organization program carried its rewards. The passage of the Bankhead-Jones Act of 1935 under Farm Bureau urgings was perhaps the best demonstration that the federation was the real source of this financial support for the colleges. This act authorized regular appropriations on an enlarged scale for research and Extension. The Farm Bureau could be counted on to fight for the authorized appropriations.

Although the benefits to the colleges were both substantial and assured, the costs of the act were heavy. Even in the crisis-ridden days of the early A.A.A., members of the association had misgivings. It was noted in 1934 that "the Agricultural Adjustment Act has imposed, at least for the time being, certain responsibilities which cannot, even with the most liberal classification, be termed educational."[88] Already new doubts were being voiced.[89]

Yet these were minority dissents. The relationship between the Farm Bureau, the colleges, and the Extension Service became closer rather than otherwise, and in 1936 the Farm Bureau reported that it was more intimate than ever before.[90] The bureau had enough assurance of this affinity to insist regularly upon "coördination" of all efforts in agricultural administration, with the Extension Service as the coördinating agent.[91] Inevitably, the bureau was violently opposed to the recommendations of the Brownlow Committee of 1937, which would have increased the conservation activities of the Department of the Interior.[92] More interestingly, the Farm Bureau opposed the Bailey and the Cooley bills of 1940 and 1941, which would have "decentralized" agricultural administration by placing it in the hands of the state directors of agriculture.[93] Although the bills would have given a token to the grass-roots theory which the Farm Bureau has sedulously advocated, the plain fact was that here the organizational interest of the Farm Bureau lay with the federal Extension Service rather than with the state agricultural departments.

As for the Extension Service itself, its leadership remained content with the fruits of its association with the Farm Bureau.[94] It is difficult to say whether the Extension heads continued to believe that their activities were primarily educational or whether they conceived that they actually shared in the political power which they had served to build. If the latter, the words of B. H. Crocheron should have come as a shock:

During this and previous administrations it [Extension] has acted as chore-boy for the Federal Government and for the farmers' organizations. Those who believed this policy would bring to Extension vast resources and power have been mistaken. The nation has given the credit to the bureaus that have been helped and not to the great outstanding agency, Agricultural Extension, which has done the helping.[95]

What might have been added was that the power accrued to the Farm Bureau.

8

The FARM
SECURITY
ADMINISTRATION

Although the Triple A represented the main stream
of agricultural policy in the New Deal era, an almost wholly new
current entered farm affairs in that period. This current was embodied in the Farm Security Administration. A few of its sources
can be discovered in the familiar springs of farm policy, but the
principal streams by which it was fed came from outside the bounds
of dominant agricultural interests.

"Agricultural policy" over the years preceding the depression
had come to mean an area of controversy in which prices were the
central issue. As the economic crisis deepened, agricultural credit
came to share somewhat in the concerns of farm leaders, educators,
and administrators. Yet it is remarkable how rarely the agricultural
spokesmen exhibited any awareness of problems outside these two
orbits. The Commission on Country Life of the time of Theodore
Roosevelt had perhaps been the last attempt to look upon the problems of farming and of farmers in general. The main orientation of
public policy lay in the discovery of methods of efficient production
and their diffusion. True, various regulatory and other auxiliary
activities combined to swell the tasks of the government with regard
to agriculture. Here and there, discussions were held on tenancy,
corporation farming, and soil conservation, but the attention attracted to them was hardly such as to suggest that these were proper
concerns of agricultural policy.[1] The most significant fact, however,

was that the important agricultural organizations did not seem greatly concerned with any problem other than that of prices.

When the new administration took office in 1933, one of the most pressing problems was sheer relief. Both the energy with which the problem was attacked and the confusion in methods form chapters in a familiar story. Poverty and acute distress were to be found everywhere, both in cities and on farms. The administrative structure, swiftly thrown together, was one of multiple agencies, overlapping jurisdictions, and chaotic action.

Strangely enough, the vast (for the time) establishment of the Department of Agriculture and its auxiliaries had little part in this strenuous activity. It was tacitly admitted that the department's custodianship of the country's agrarian foundations did not extend to the direct relief of poverty upon the land. The engrafting of the Extension system upon the agricultural bureaucracy and its development during the almost two decades of its existence had created the presumption that all problems of farming and rural life lay in the department's province. By the very structure of the Extension Service, the old obstacle of the state-federal relationship to national action in the local sphere had been circumvented. By the activities of county agents throughout the country, the educational limitations upon their duties had been cast aside. The Extension system was, indeed, the long arm of the department going out to nearly all the farming counties of the nation, in touch with the problems of farmers everywhere and ready to help in all their troubles. And yet that arm did not reach out to the poor.

The great task of providing care for the distressed[2] fell to emergency agencies. Of these the one which carried the most importance for subsequent developments in rural life was the Federal Emergency Relief Administration. The changes which swept through this agency were many and kaleidoscopic and cannot be recounted here.[3] One change, however, was of great importance. This was the early shift of emphasis from immediate relief to long-term rehabilitation. In itself, the change was a recognition that the problems with which the emergency agency was dealing were more than transitory. In 1934 a program of loans to distressed farmers was added to the system of outright doles. It did not supplant direct relief, but rather supplemented it, and was combined with grants when these were required for individual recovery. This was the origin of "rural rehabilitation," which eventually found its way, willy-nilly, into the Department of Agriculture.

A second device that appeared in the early New Deal derived from sources that could more properly be described as agricultural. This was the idea of subsistence homesteads. It originated in part, no doubt, from the somewhat spontaneous back-to-the-farm movement.' This movement was deplored by farm leaders. More important was the urging of M. L. Wilson, a reflective "farm leader" who had played an early part in the development of the Extension system and who had great influence on Roosevelt and his farm advisers. The idea had apparently been suggested to Wilson by the success of some private projects in Utah, and at the meeting with the president-elect in which the plan for the A.A.A. was discussed, he brought forth the homestead scheme; it met with Roosevelt's approval.'

The new administration, then, adopted the subsistence homesteads idea and made it a matter of public policy. Unlike other parts of the new rural program, authority for which was often vague, the subsistence homesteads scheme was given a definite legislative base. It is characteristic of the origins of the New Deal program on rural poverty that this authority was placed not in the new agricultural legislation but in the National Industrial Recovery Act.' In part, this was a reflection of the belief that homesteads would help relieve urban poverty. In all likelihood, however, the absence of enthusiasm in the Department of Agriculture or among the external farm groups was equally important. This inference is supported by the fact that administration of the homesteads was placed in a special division of the Department of the Interior. Thus, the seeds of New Deal policy on rural poverty—rural rehabilitation and subsistence homesteads—were both germinated outside the Department of Agriculture.

Administration of these two projects was transplanted on April 30, 1935, to a new agency, again one that was independent of the Department of Agriculture. This was the Resettlement Administration, headed by Rexford Tugwell, who was concurrently Under Secretary of Agriculture. Tugwell thus served as a link between the established agricultural hierarchy and the new rural programs. However, the choice of Tugwell emphasized the divergence of the new agency's programs from the rest of agricultural policy; while within the house of agriculture, he was definitely not of it.[7]

The life of the Resettlement Administration was short and spectacular. The problems which confronted the agency were many and difficult to integrate in a coherent administrative scheme. Just to list them will indicate their lack of unity: resettlement, rural rehabilitation, settlement from urban areas, soil erosion, stream pollution, seacoast erosion, forestation and reforestation, flood control, loans to purchase land and equipment by farmers, tenants, croppers, and farm laborers, and migratory labor camps (the first federal public housing).

The administrative materials for the new agency came from three sources: rural rehabilitation from the Federal Emergency Relief Administration, subsistence homesteads from the Department of the Interior, and land policy from the Department of Agriculture. These divisions had become going concerns and had developed their own points of view. As the new agency grew on top of these three units— which it did in dramatic fashion—the possibilities for confusion became nearly unlimited.[8] Almost continual reorganization characterized its internal life.

Nevertheless, the Resettlement Administration represented the development of a fairly coherent point of view on the problem of rural poverty. As its name suggested, the agency concentrated on the detrimental effects of cultivating submarginal land. To take farmers off land that should be used for pasturage or forests and to reëstablish them upon good land that would support a decent standard of living—this was the ideal solution of the agency. The limitations of the approach are now obvious: they were the limitations upon the availability of good land itself. However, it is probably unfair to condemn the agency on this score, since its life was short and it did contain tendencies which led in other directions as well. The emphasis was important in one regard, however. This was its evocation of an old tenet of the American creed, the belief that the small independent landholder is the backbone of the nation. So far as this aspect of the Resettlement Administration's program was emphasized, the agency was standing firmly upon an old tradition.

This concern for the small landholder was reflected during this period by a drive to secure federal legislation to reduce farm tenancy. In 1935 Senator John H. Bankhead sponsored a bill for this purpose which passed the Senate but failed in the House. Various outside groups devoted their energies to dramatizing the problem and making it known. Their success was sufficient to persuade both political parties to include statements on tenancy in their platforms. Soon after the election, the President appointed a special committee to study the problem.[*]

The Resettlement Administration had come under sharp political attack, partly because of the personality of Tugwell.[10] In order to save the program, Tugwell resigned, and the agency was transferred bodily into the Department of Agriculture. This shift, which preceded the report of the President's Committee on Farm Tenancy by six weeks, was but the preliminary to a general reorganization which came with passage of the Bankhead-Jones Farm Tenancy Act of 1937.[11] This act, which was designed, at least in the eyes of some, to place a legislative foundation under the entire program dealing with rural poverty, emerged from Congress primarily as an act to assist farm tenants to become landowners. It authorized short-term loans for rehabilitation and a program for retirement of submarginal land. It carried no appropriation for the rehabilitation program, and the appropriations for the other two functions were small. As the foundation for a long-term program dealing with the problem of rural poverty, the act was disappointing. Soon after the passage of the act, the Secretary of Agriculture abolished the Resettlement Administration and created the Farm Security Administration (F.S.A.) to take its place.

This complicated history of bureaucratic organization and reorganization has a meaning that goes beyond the search for sheerly efficient media of administration. A big issue was at stake: the establishment of a federal program directed to the problem of rural poverty as part of the nation's public policy. It is fairly clear that there was little hope for the development of such a program within what might have appeared the logical part of the federal establishment, the Department of Agriculture. Initiative for such a program came from neither the department nor the external organization to which the department looked for its own support before Congress. The program had to be nurtured outside the department, and then, when the political climate appeared threatening to the life of the program, it was brought into the department in which superficially it appeared to belong. This was, in general, the logic of the often bewildering series of changes in the administrative structure of the program. The appointment of the President's Committee on Farm Tenancy, the resignation of Tugwell, the movement of the Resettlement Administration into the Department of Agriculture, the Bankhead-Jones Act, and the creation of the F.S.A. were all parts of a coherent plan to establish the program on rural poverty.[12]

This administrative history has a number of interesting features. First, the program did not originate with the usual farm sources. Second, it grew large very quickly. Third, the success of a relatively few liberal New Deal leaders in starting the program is remarkable. Their achievement was made almost wholly without organized support outside the administration. Because of the lack of powerful external organization, much in the program had to be carried on without specific congressional sanction. Fourth, the decision to place the program in the Department of Agriculture was something of a Hobson's choice; the program might not have survived as long as it did without this compromise.

The F.S.A., then, became the heir to a large number of the programs for rural welfare which had no support from established agricultural organizations, private or public. It also inherited an administrative organization that had matured without great loss of the zeal which had characterized the Tugwell period. The F.S.A. operated much more quietly than the Resettlement Administration—and on a larger scale. The administrative structure of the F.S.A. was built on direct lines of authority extending from the county supervisor, through the state heads and regional chiefs to the administrator. In this regard it was in marked contrast to the Extension Service. Local advisory committees were utilized to assist F.S.A. supervisors, but, except in one small program, these committees had no administrative powers until the last years of the agency. Since the program of the F.S.A. was in reality a diversified group of undertakings—it might be called a poor man's Department of Agriculture—it is necessary to glance at its different parts.

The program greatest in magnitude and significance was rural rehabilitation.[13] It is no exaggeration to say that most of the agency's emphasis went to this one program.[14] First, it was politically expedient. The program was less spectacular than the resettlement schemes and involved smaller individual expenditures (although the total amount spent was much larger). Second, it was more flexible and more readily adapted to individual needs. Third, it was more effective in dealing with poverty-stricken farmers.

Although rural rehabilitation became exceedingly complex in itself, the basic idea was simple: it is better to make needy families producing and self-supporting than to give them mere relief. As the problem was analyzed by the F.S.A. after the program had become well matured, many farm families had failed because of their lack of knowledge; they didn't know how to farm. Second, one-crop farming was too prevalent; there was too little "live-at-home farming." Third, many families could not change over to efficient methods for lack of money to buy tools, seed, and livestock.[15] To meet these problems, loans were made to selected farm families whose operations were then supervised. Each "client" family was required to make a plan for its own guidance. The Farm Security supervisor provided assistance in the formulation and execution of the plan. The techniques of farming were simply those which had long been taught by the Extension Service. The evil of one-crop farming had, in fact, been one of the primary lessons of Seaman A. Knapp.

Much of the activity of the F.S.A. was thus an extension of the department's traditional efforts in education. In this sense there was justification for the frequent remark by F.S.A. personnel that if the Extension Service had met the challenge within its own sphere of interest, the F.S.A. might never have been created. In another sense, the heavy emphasis of the F.S.A. upon education represented the "agriculturalization" of the rural poverty program. The change of direction in the program after the Resettlement Administration had entered the Department of Agriculture was indeed toward assimilation with other agricultural programs. However, too much should not be made of this shift, since a large part of the F.S.A. program remained independent, and the personnel of the F.S.A. tended to remain outsiders even when within the department.

In addition to the supervised loans made under the rural rehabilitation program, small grants were sometimes made. The making of grants, as well as the supervision exercised by the supervisors, represented a sharp break with established loan agency practice. The justification was both ample and obvious. The purpose was not credit but rehabilitation, and rehabilitation was an alternative to relief. Yet there were those who refused to regard the F.S.A. as anything but a credit agency. To them, F.S.A. operations were unsound. For all this, the loans made by the agency did not in the outcome represent any grave outrage to banking standards. A large percentage of the money loaned has been repaid with interest.[16]

Within the rural rehabilitation program, farm debt adjustment and tenure improvement ranked almost as programs in themselves. For the many parts of the Western states in which lack of water was a problem and the great undertakings of the Bureau of Reclamation gave no help, a water facilities program was carried on by the F.S.A.[17] The F.S.A. also helped to organize marketing and purchasing coöperatives. Many of these received loans to get their operations under way. A special category of coöperatives consisted of medical care plans. Since most of these offered increased income to rural doctors, it was possible to secure the endorsement of the medical associations.

Another major program of the F.S.A. was farm ownership. It originated with the Bankhead-Jones Act. This was again a loan program, although it was closer to the concepts of traditional banking practice than was the rural rehabilitation program. Loans were authorized for forty years at three per cent interest to enable selected tenants to buy family-size farms. In this requirement that the farms be of family size, the F.S.A. was made the formal custodian of the old tradition. The farm ownership program was limited in scope and accounted for but a small fraction of the total effort of the F.S.A.[18] Yet, because it had the best legislative foundation and because it invoked an ancient shibboleth, it was the program on which the F.S.A. was most frequently defended.

The program which came to be best known was that of the resettlement projects. Although these comprised only nine per cent of F.S.A. financial undertakings, they were later made to appear as the whole program of the agency. In many respects the projects were the most interesting part of the entire effort. Taken as a whole, they were an attempt to discover some means of curing the ills of rural life that went beyond establishment of a few families on small farms. In themselves the projects were of slight importance. As experiments on varied lines they might have been extremely useful in casting light upon the problems of agricultural policy. Realization of this possibility was not permitted.[19]

Three of the projects, the Greenbelt communities, were experiments in suburban housing and community development. Some were attempts to settle stranded industrial workers in communities where part-time farming could supplement their income. Others were attempts to bring industrial establishments to the country. A hosiery mill was built to provide employment for rural workers on one project. In most of the projects, however, the existing patterns of large-scale farming, of both plantation and corporation types, were adapted to coöperative organization. As such, they were as much within the native tradition as coöperatives designed to serve the business purposes of buying and selling. They strongly suggested some of the early American coöperative communities; yet the enemies of the F.S.A. likened them instead to Russian *kolkozes*.

Most of the resettlement projects had been started in the days of the Federal Emergency Relief Administration and the Resettlement Administration. The F.S.A., for most of its history, moved away from the approach implicit in the projects. One reason was that most of the projects were not going well. Many had been poorly planned or hastily started. Because of the relief emergency, the membership of the communities was not carefully chosen. Moreover, the unreasoning prejudice aroused by the projects was used by enemies of the F.S.A. to discredit the entire agency. Although the F.S.A. showed some inclination to reëxamine the approach during the 'forties, its own emphasis on the family-size farm played into the hands of its enemies. The projects have generally been set down as complete failures. Yet they were concrete evidence of a genuine attempt to find some solution to the rural dilemma that would be more effective than rehabilitation or tenant purchase.

The F.S.A. program on agricultural labor included the operation of a chain of migratory labor camps, chiefly in the West.[20] The purpose of these camps was frankly the treatment of symptoms. Even in its limited objective of providing "a minimum of shelter and sanitary facilities," the program was grossly inadequate in scale. Despite its inadequacy, however, the program was far more significant than its relative position in the list of F.S.A. expenditures indicates.[21] It was the potential nucleus around which in time there might have developed an entirely different program devoted to the welfare of agricultural labor—that unacknowledged part of the rural population which had little prospect of settlement on family-size farms.

These various programs of the F.S.A. diverged from each other perhaps more than those in the agency appreciated. Each of the approaches necessitated an experimental attitude in administration. The rural rehabilitation program led to the creation of new kinds of coöperatives. The suspicion that rehabilitation was not reaching those who were most in need led to an experimental program in selected distressed areas.[22] The resettlement projects led to experiments with methods of prefabrication in building, and as a result the agency was given tasks that were seemingly unrelated to its principal mission. It became one of the builders of defense housing during the war. It was given the thankless chore of salvaging rural communities disrupted by the abrupt military occupancy of large tracts of farm land. It administered the early stages of the wartime farm-labor program under which Mexican workers were brought into the United States. The dynamic character of the agency tends to justify the belief that in time a really effective program on rural poverty might have evolved from its many-sided efforts.[23]

In general, the F.S.A. was the residual legatee of nearly every human problem of rural life that was not solved by increasing the prices of a few "basic" commodities. To no other place in the federal establishment, least of all to other agencies in the Department of Agriculture, could such problems be assigned. The F.S.A. welcomed the responsibility. One of the remarkable—and unfortunate—features of the organization was that its programs were carried out under vague and scattered fragments of legislative authority.[24] This permitted flexibility of operation, but it made the whole agency an administrative adventure. It may be said that this was an example of a familiar pattern of bureaucratic aggrandizement. Such a statement would be inaccurate; other agencies which might have assumed the responsibility in fact did not. Moreover, assumption of these particular responsibilities carried its dangers. The fate of the F.S.A. is sufficient evidence of this.

The sheer fact that the agency held the torch of rural welfare was its major significance—not that this method or that was employed. The chief critic of the family-size farm idea has suggested that the F.S.A. embodied the New Deal revival of "the Jeffersonian ideal" (i.e., the family-size farm).[25] This is thoroughly to misunderstand the significance of the F.S.A. program. Whether or not the family-size farm is the sole means of curing the ills of rural poverty, support of it was an expediency forced upon the agency by the political circumstances in which it developed. Purchase of family farms for tenants was a possible method of assisting some of the rural poor, and it was employed.

The problems of rural poverty in which the F.S.A. became involved were themselves exceedingly varied. They varied, first, by regions. It might almost have been possible to organize the work of the agency by regions and thereby to have achieved much the same approach to its problems. The most distressed area of the nation was, of course, the South. In the words of President Roosevelt, the South presented "the Nation's number one economic problem—the Nation's problem, not merely the South's."[26] As a result, the F.S.A. was heavily oriented toward the South. Many on the agency's staff were Southerners. This focusing of energies was also reflected in the distribution of rehabilitation funds: 38 per cent of all borrowers were located in twelve Southern states.[27]

In the South, economic distress was particularly severe among the Negroes. In the bleak picture of discrimination against Negroes in the South, as Gunnar Myrdal saw it, one of the few bright spots was the fact that Negroes shared in the F.S.A. program to a degree almost corresponding to their proportion in the population.[28] Success in achieving this degree of fairness in administration required no little political courage.

The problems of the South were not limited to those arising from the racial issue. Low standards of health, of education, of housing, of farming practice were to a peculiar degree Southern problems. The F.S.A. made some kind of attack on most of them. The point of importance here is not so much that the F.S.A. was energetic and alert in attacking these problems but that, in so doing, it directly antagonized powerful organized interests. This may be illustrated by the crusade of F.S.A. workers to cure one of the worst characteristics of cotton farming, the practice of planting the crop right up to the doorstep. In teaching its "clients" to plant gardens and to shift to dairying as a means of livelihood, the agency was earning the displeasure not only of landlords who favored exploitative methods of farming but also of the commercial dairy interests of the North.[29]

A second regional concentration of F.S.A. efforts was in the Great Plains area, where drought and dust storms during the 'thirties had caused acute suffering, on the scale of a national disaster.[30] Payment of emergency rehabilitation grants under the F.S.A. centered almost wholly in the Great Plains area. Loans were made also to coöperatives in order that they might buy grain elevators whose operators had failed. Again the agency incurred the hostility of important interests—the large private grain dealers of Minneapolis.[31]

The most serious effects of migrancy were felt in areas having heavy seasonal demands for field labor. In California, where the problem has always been at its worst, there was a long-standing tradition of exploiting farm workers. By seeking to alleviate the degraded conditions in which these workers moved, the F.S.A. appeared to be impairing the system by which the shifting army of farm labor was kept docile and cheap.

This catalogue of political liabilities of the F.S.A. was serious.[32] However, it was almost insignificant compared to the scale of the problem of rural poverty. Out of the activities of the F.S.A. and the many special studies of rural life in the 'thirties, a few great facts emerged: first, the depth and extent of rural poverty; second, the low level of productivity of the poorer farms.[33] It was apparent that rural poverty was not only grave but that it was a long-term problem and not merely a product of the business cycle. The farmers who were most afflicted, moreover, were generally excluded from the benefits provided in the principal schemes of agricultural policy. And, from the standpoint of economic efficiency, too many people were trying to live on the land.

The policy of the F.S.A. was open to serious doubts arising from these implications. So far as it sought settlement on the land, the policy had limited application. So far as this succeeded, there were questions whether it was not restricting farm income and adding to rural unemployment. These questions grow pale, however, before the fact that the F.S.A. had as its potential burden the welfare of a part of the farm population which at times approached one-half.

Measured on this scale, the effort was pitifully inadequate. In the absence of other efforts, though, the F.S.A. (together with its predecessors) represented the greatest innovation in agricultural policy since the passage of the Homestead Act.

The major dilemma of the F.S.A. was that it had to administer a welfare program within the framework of agricultural policy. In this it never succeeded. Since the size of the F.S.A. programs was small alongside the whole problem, the economic conflict was not significant. Politically, however, the dilemma was important. To this, attention must now be turned.

9

ATTACK

In mid-1941 the Farm Security Administration came under an attack that has seldom been equaled for bitterness. By mid-1943 the F.S.A. was dying; by the end of 1946 it was dead.

The story of this attack is one of the bleakest in the history of agricultural politics. In itself, it constitutes one of the most important pages of that history. The struggle seems in retrospect to have been conducted behind a veil of obscurity woven out of superficial complexities and war distractions. The battle was fought over seemingly trivial matters of administrative organization. However, that alone cannot explain the virulence of the assault; its meaning was much deeper. And yet the paradox remains that administrative organization was the crux of the entire battle. This was frankly, even bluntly, stated, and the attack was subtle only in the sense that the import of administrative form was grasped by few outside the circles of the antagonists themselves.

The American Farm Bureau Federation was the agency which destroyed the F.S.A., and bureau leadership directed the attack. Auxiliaries were marshaled into the battle, but it nonetheless remains true that this was a Farm Bureau campaign. Accordingly, it is important to trace the attitude of the Farm Bureau in the period preceding the outbreak of hostilities.

In its official publications the federation has occasionally taken credit for the F.S.A., although it has avoided the claim of outright sponsorship.[1] When Farm Bureau responsibility for the death of the F.S.A. is mentioned, the response is that F.S.A. was simply "a good idea that went wrong"; the bureau had no fault to find with the intentions of the agency or even with the people who supported it or benefited by it. The F.S.A. had become a wastefully administered bureaucracy which was imposing upon the people in need of its help; the Farm Bureau intervened only when the situation became serious. As a matter of fact, however, the bureau did not actually begin its campaign from outside the federal bureaucracy until 1941. The F.S.A., before this, had been under constant pressure to conform to the peculiar outlook of the Department of Agriculture, and to a degree it had conformed. What happened in 1941 was not that the F.S.A. had become hostile to the ways of the department or the farm leaders, but that the Farm Bureau found this moment opportune for attack. The F.S.A. by this time had traveled a long way in its own "agriculturalization." The family-size farm was becoming increasingly its central tenet.

Actually, the Farm Bureau had never been a supporter of the F.S.A. in any sense. Before the creation of the F.S.A., the Farm Bureau had not played any significant part in calling attention to the prevalence of rural poverty except as it was useful to do so in securing government support of prices. The struggle which culminated in the "purge" of 1935 and the entrance of the Resettlement Administration into the Department of Agriculture involved little effort by the Farm Bureau as an organization. Not all the moves made in this period are visible now, but it is likely that events were influenced by pressures which were partly generated from sources close to the Farm Bureau and that the change in the status of the Resettlement Administration was made in anticipation of more drastic action. For a time, the concession of placing the problems of rural poverty in the care of the Department of Agriculture was adequate.

O'Neal was one of the members of the President's Committee on Farm Tenancy. His inclusion in this group, which he can hardly have found congenial, was perhaps made in the hope that he might be persuaded to lead the American Farm Bureau Federation toward a socially enlightened policy for agriculture; if so, the hope was doomed. O'Neal refused to approve the report of the committee without qualification. His statement was restrained and contained no general condemnation of the findings or the plan. However, in view of later developments, his statement is significant. He made six points; the first three require quotation in full:

1. The law should be administered by the Secretary of Agriculture through the directors of extension in the various States, who will carry out the provisions of the act under rules and regulations prescribed by the Secretary.

2. Administration in county or region should be by an appointee of the Secretary, selected from a list supplied by the director of extension in the State. All appointees should meet qualifications set up for county agents in the State.

3. To pass on the eligibility of applicants for aid under the proposed law in each county or region, a nonsalaried committee of three members should be appointed by the Secretary from a list supplied by the extension director. In case the Secretary is unable to select a full committee from the first list submitted, he should be empowered to ask for additional names. All committee members must be men whose chief interest and experience have been in agriculture. This committee should be permanent and should act in an advisory capacity to the local administrator and the director of extension.[2]

The remaining three points were that assistance should be confined to worthy young farmers who were unable to get credit from other agencies, that tenants purchasing farms under the plan should get title at an early stage, and that loans from the Secretary should be permissible only in the period before transfer of title. In his letter, O'Neal added, "I have grave doubts that credit can carry the burden of such a program."

When the Bankhead-Jones farm tenancy bill came up in Congress, the Farm Bureau parade of witnesses usual in hearings on agricultural legislation was absent. The Farm Bureau was represented only by a letter from O'Neal. It took but a single page in the record. O'Neal urged such a law despite his belief that "a fair price system" would do more than anything else to prevent loss of farm homes through foreclosure. He then repeated verbatim the points made in his statement to the President's committee.[3] Thus the Farm Bureau would not support the bill; neither would it openly oppose the bill.[4]

This position, taken on what proved to be the blueprint for the F.S.A., was consistently maintained by the Farm Bureau during the next few years. The F.S.A. did not have the approval of the Farm Bureau; when the showdown came, the first three points stated by O'Neal in 1937 were the ones which the Farm Bureau sought to establish. At the same time, the statement contains no hint of the strong hostility that was to appear in 1942 and 1943, after the F.S.A. had been in existence for a number of years. Articles on the F.S.A. appeared occasionally in the Farm Bureau's chief publication, and these were quite objective. As late as July, 1940, the organization included in the agricultural platform which it offered to both political parties a recommendation that rehabilitation of farm families and help for tenants and migrants should be continued by the F.S.A.[5] This was perhaps the high-water mark in Farm Bureau tolerance of the F.S.A.

Any responsible person who took this statement as being meaningful, however, was disappointed. The Farm Bureau was willing that the recommendation should go into political platforms, but it was not willing to give the political support which this seemed to imply. When Farm Bureau delegations appeared before congressional appropriation committees they gave no support to F.S.A. appropriation requests. This was true in both 1939 and 1940. On the whole, the Farm Bureau was merely indifferent to the F.S.A. during this period.

In 1940, however, Farm Bureau leadership was increasingly uncertain of its relationship with Secretary Wallace and, indeed, with much of the Department of Agriculture. The F.S.A. continued as a large unit of the department; it was clearly outside the Farm Bureau sphere of influence. The department was making strenuous efforts to instill vitality and independence into the county committees charged with production control and planning.[6] Wallace and "liberal" elements in the administration succeeded in getting a reorganization of the independent agencies dealing with farm credit which brought these into the department in a more centralized administration. The previous decentralization had been amenable to control by elements friendly to the Farm Bureau. This last was probably the precipitating issue that decided the Farm Bureau leadership to wage a campaign to remake the Department of Agriculture.[7]

When the annual convention of the Farm Bureau met in December, 1940, the usual list of resolutions was revised and the first two places were given to national reorganization and state administration. The former was a plan that would deal with most of the so-called "action" programs. The latter was a commendation of the Extension services of the land grant colleges as administrative agencies. One of many points under this heading was the recommendation that the Extension Service should be responsible for the home and farm management phases of the F.S.A. programs. Another heading covered farm credit. Independence in administration was the objective sought here. The last specific recommendation under this head was, "We favor placing the loaning activities of the Farm Security Administration as a separate Department under this Board."[8] This was the declaration of war.

The attack was opened in 1941 with a full-scale offensive on the Department of Agriculture at the crucial appropriation hearings. The Farm Bureau leadership was well aware that its influence was stronger in the House than in the Senate; so the opening battle was fought solely before the former. The most favorable ground for Farm Bureau purposes would have been the House Committee on Agriculture, but this could not be chosen because the wartime situation forbade consideration of any new farm legislation. The Senate committees, whether on Agriculture or Appropriations, were less favorable to the Farm Bureau than either House committee. The House Committee on Appropriations was accordingly the best possibility at hand, and the Farm Bureau concentrated upon it.[9]

The campaign of 1941 was the most ambitious of the entire period. O'Neal brought in a total of fourteen state Farm Bureau heads, each with a set speech and a point to make. Among them, they presented a coherent statement of the Farm Bureau plan for reorganizing the Department of Agriculture. Since the Farm Bureau was striking for complete victory at one blow, the full story of the year's campaign properly belongs in another chapter.[10] What is relevant here is that the plan for breaking the F.S.A. in two was forcefully stated: the farm and home management services should be given to the Extension Service and the loaning functions should be given to the Farm Credit Administration.[11]

In this the Farm Bureau overreached itself. The House subcommittee refused to be made the vehicle for such a sweeping change. In terms of narrow objectives, however, the Farm Bureau scored a success—the achievement of getting a rider to the appropriation bill effectively keeping F.S.A. personnel out of Civil Service. This was an important step, for the federal government was then undergoing a rapid reorganization in preparation for war. Experienced government workers were in great demand in the new agencies, and many incentives were offered people in the older agencies to take new jobs. Moreover, the Ramspeck bill, which authorized presidential "blanketing-in" of workers outside the Civil Service, was under consideration. It was expected to result in Civil Service status for almost all government personnel still unprotected; those in the F.S.A. shared this hope. When the rider forbade such action, agency morale plummeted and many resignations followed. This is precisely the sort of tactic by which an alert pressure group can accomplish far-reaching results in an inconspicuous manner. Here the effect was seriously to cripple the F.S.A.

The Farm Bureau also engaged in widespread efforts to generate support for its plan. O'Neal mentioned "a great many discussions in groups and regions; South, Midwest and East and all around."[12] Wherever possible, other organizations were brought into the campaign. The Washington office of the Farm Bureau requested the state organizations to seek out evidence to be used against the F.S.A. This was apparently the result of a decision made after the large-scale attempt had failed, to strike for a narrower objective. The material gained in this manner was inadequate and seems to have consisted mainly of vague complaints that nevertheless yielded a few tactical hints.[13]

Although the decision had been made to concentrate on the F.S.A., the Farm Bureau leadership was unprepared when its opportunity came in December. The Byrd Committee, a joint committee on reduction of nonessential governmental expenditures, began its hearings at this time. The F.S.A. was one of the first agencies summoned to justify itself before the committee. The initial hearing went off quietly and without any display of congressional skepticism. The watchful legislative department of the Farm Bureau, however, quickly improvised a course of action. The very purpose of the Byrd Committee gave an excellent clue to the most promising line of attack. But the Farm Bureau lacked ammunition for the purpose.

The national convention of the Farm Bureau met just before Christmas. The resolutions passed were somewhat different in form from those of previous years in that they had to deal with wartime conditions. However, they placed curtailment of nondefense spending in a conspicuous place. The administrative program was unchanged, although it was stated less concretely. There was no mention of the F.S.A.[14]

In January, 1942, the inner circle of the national board of the Farm Bureau met and directed O'Neal to seek out the material needed for a hearing before the Byrd Committee. He, in turn, ordered the legal staff of the national organization to investigate F.S.A. operations. The general counsel, Kirkpatrick, sent six investigators into eight different states, with instructions to get what they could quickly. O'Neal specified the types of information to which they should pay special attention:

1. Check organization and policies of F.S.A. coöperatives.

2. Large socialized farming projects.

3. Solicitation of clients for rural rehabilitation loans and farm tenant plans.

4. Grants of money to improve status of delinquent borrowers.

5. Cases of excessive costs saddled on borrowers—unnecessary equipment, etc.

6. Cases of farm management programs in conflict with AAA or extension programs.

7. Excessive overhead expense in administration.

8. Duplication and unnecessary expense in Soil Conservation Service. Examples of high costs and results attained by Extension Service.[15]

Because of limited time, only the first five points received attention. Beyond this, the investigators were given to understand rather clearly that the objective was to find material on which criticisms of the F.S.A. could be based.[16]

The bureau's "investigation" of the F.S.A. took place between January 7, the date of the decision to make the search, and February 6, when the findings were presented to the congressional committee. The analysts sent to the Northern states had little success and O'Neal was not able to use their reports except to mention that the inquiry had touched the states mentioned. But the investigator sent into the Southern states, William G. Carr, a Chicago attorney, struck an area in which F.S.A. operations were more extensive. His report was made to carry the burden of the Farm Bureau charges. This was the substance behind O'Neal's confident assurance to the committee that "Our counsel, Mr. Kirkpatrick, has made a very complete study of this whole agricultural program."[17]

The Farm Bureau performance before the committee was opened with a flourish that indicated a flair for the dramatic. O'Neal, in his long career as impresario at congressional hearings, had acquired a good sense of the gestures likely to arrest attention. Accordingly, he introduced first a Southern judge who had discovered that F.S.A. supervisors regarded the poll tax as a legitimate item on the allowable list of expenditures in the farm and home plans on which loans were based. The point was made that the F.S.A. was paying poll taxes.[18] Thereafter, O'Neal had his audience well in hand.

After a tribute to the purposes of the committee, O'Neal began: "While we thoroughly agree that the activities under the farm-tenant purchase program and the Farm Security program should be drastically and severely curtailed, we believe that at least part of the work of these agencies [*sic*] should not forthwith be abolished."[19] However, most of the work of the F.S.A., he continued, was now unnecessary, and the remainder of its activities should be parceled out among other agencies. He then outlined the Farm Bureau case against the F.S.A. The charges must be summarized if the sweeping nature of the condemnation is to be appreciated. These were:

1. F.S.A. assignment of quotas of clients in order to spend funds appropriated by Congress "and to maintain personnel employed by the agency."

2. Solicitation of clients to meet quotas.

3. Burdening of clients with excessive loans.

4. Establishment of impractical collective farming projects.

5. Giving grants to enable repayment of loans "rather than using such funds to relieve destitution."

6. Use of renewal notes and variable payment plans to disguise low payment on loans.

7. "Flagrant attempts to build pressure groups to maintain congressional appropriations."

8. Instances of refusal to accept payment of indebtedness in full.

9. Rigid control of business and farming plans of clients.[20]

The evidence supporting these charges came mainly from the Carr report to O'Neal and Kirkpatrick. For the most part it consisted of a series of indefinite citations of individual cases supplemented by Carr's own summaries of public opinion in the states he visited. Thus, he found that the general public of Arkansas was against the F.S.A.[21] This discovery was made on the basis of a few days' visit.[22] Most of the material presented in the Carr report was hearsay, and even the number of examples cited was not impressive. Despite the evident unreliability of the material, a fact which much of the committee seems to have appreciated, the Carr "documentary material," as O'Neal called it, was inserted in the record.[23]

The remainder of the Farm Bureau evidence was in the form of articles and statements by F.S.A. employees. One news story quoted a statement by an assistant administrator to the effect that fee-simple ownership accounted for many of the ills of the American land.[24] Although much the same statement could have been found in the Report of the President's Committee on Farm Tenancy, the idea proved shocking to Congress in 1942 and 1943.[25] Even the ghost of the old antagonism to Tugwell was invoked against the F.S.A.

It is unlikely that the Farm Bureau case—a tissue of scattered instances reported in colored language and of large generalizations—would have been granted a hearing had it not been for the determination of groups in Congress such as the Byrd Committee, which were using the war situation to dismantle as much of the New Deal as possible, and the peculiar structure of the congressional committee system which permitted the rehearing of discredited charges before different bodies.

The Farm Bureau repeated the nine charges and the Carr material so extensively and so often that these came to acquire an aura of truth. After the Byrd Committee had seen and heard them, they were presented to the Senate Committee on Appropriations and the House Committee on Appropriations. These committees, which had to examine the requests of governmental agencies each year, were thus treated to reviews of the Farm Bureau material in both 1942 and 1943. The Senate committee had been fortunate that it had not been selected to serve as a sounding board in 1941. The Farm Bureau added little new material in support of its charges through these hearings.

Slowly, however, an organization was improvised to defend the work of the F.S.A. The list of groups was impressive, but frequently their spokesmen failed in the acid congressional test: they could rarely show that they were real dirt farmers. They ranged all the way from labor unions to the Y.W.C.A. Only one of these assorted groups can be said to have been truly effective—the Catholic Rural Life Conference, represented by a remarkable priest, Monsignor John O'Grady. Monsignor O'Grady made by far the most forceful and persuasive appeal in the entire round of hearings, asking not only the continuation but also the extension of the F.S.A.[26] His efforts were nevertheless insufficient to still the charge that the F.S.A. was communistic.

The campaign against the F.S.A. seemed to follow some developmental law of its own nature. Each time the attack was renewed before a different committee, the charges and the material with which they were supported were much the same. Yet the shortcomings (from the Farm Bureau point of view) of previous hearings seemed to dictate that the charges should be made more shrilly and that the recriminations should become more bitter. It was inevitable that personal hostilities should grow, but it was scarcely necessary that the Farm Bureau's dislike of the F.S.A. should extend to the latter's clients. This occurred.

As O'Neal and his assistants sought charges that would goad Congress to action, the emphasis insensibly was shifted. At first the Farm Bureau had taken the ground that F.S.A. clients were not receiving enough help, but by 1943 O'Neal was insisting that the latter should be cut off from any help. His argument was that the "2,000,000 smallest farms consumed on the average about one-half of the production of these farms and sent only $100 worth of products to market. This group produced only about 3 per cent of the marketed crops. They do not have the land, facilities, or labor to produce large quantities of food."[27] The statement was interesting not only for its dubious inference—this was contested by such authorities as John D. Black and Howard Tolley—but for the double indication of Farm Bureau awareness of the existence of rural poverty and Farm Bureau unwillingness that anything be done to relieve it.[28]

By 1943 the Farm Bureau had found allies who brought an important new set of reasons for the elimination of the F.S.A. The president of the Irrigated Cotton Growers charged that the F.S.A., in administering the program by which Mexican labor was brought into the United States under terms of a formal agreement signed by the two governments, had insisted that a minimum wage of thirty cents an hour be paid for cotton picking.[29]

The reverberations from the F.S.A. policy extended to the Old South. Oscar Johnson, president of the National Cotton Council of America, came before the same committee and testified that the F.S.A. was "impeding" the cost of production, lowering worker morale, threatening disruption of economic and social conditions and relationships, and promoting class distinctions, hatred, prejudice, and distrust. He presented a copy of a letter from Philip Murray to various unions urging support of the F.S.A. as evidence of "a direct tie-up between the C.I.O. and the F.S.A." If there was any doubt in regard to Mr. Johnson's meaning, this was removed by a resolution passed by the Cotton Council which he read:

> We contend that Farm Security Administration, as it now operates, with few exceptions is in direct violation of our position as stated above and that it threatens the foundations of American agriculture and, through their contention for a minimum wage per hour for cotton picking, threatens to disrupt a fair and satisfactory system that has successfully operated in the Cotton Belt for over 100 years.[30]

The outcome of the struggle was decided in the summer of 1943. The Farm Bureau's campaign before the existing committees of Congress resulted in the setting up of still another committee, a subcommittee, commonly known as the Cooley Committee, of the House Committee on Agriculture to investigate the activities of the F.S.A. The committee was in existence for more than a year and provided an open forum for all who cared to bring charges against the F.S.A.[31] The committee itself was amenable to Farm Bureau suggestions in its probing, and either was unaware of the objectives of the F.S.A. or was hostile to them. The investigation made by the committee was not characterized by any sense of proportion or, indeed, by any sense of the realities of rural poverty.

One of the inevitable results of this prolonged series of investigations was to build up a case for the prosecution, not merely because the prosecutors had been active but because grievances tended to pyramid. In this hearing, the voice of the National Grange was added to that of the Farm Bureau and its close allies. Curiously enough, the motivation of the Grange came as much from its hostility to the Farm Bureau as from any concern about the F.S.A. itself. The Grange had always resented the close relationship between the

Extension Service and the Farm Bureau. In the Farmers' Union defense of the F.S.A., the Grange saw a comparable relationship developing between the F.S.A. and the Farmers' Union. There was some truth in this view. The Farmers' Union had had representatives on hand at each one of the hearings to support the F.S.A. Ever since the accession of James Patton as president of the Farmers' Union, the affinity between the F.S.A. and his organization had been growing.[32] F.S.A. officials conferred frequently with Patton but never with O'Neal. Baldwin, in fact, mentioned that O'Neal avoided the F.S.A. office. Patton did not.

A real question exists whether the F.S.A. personnel deliberately attempted to "build up" the Farmers' Union. James Maddox, who was in a position to know what was going on, says that some help was given to Farmers' Union organizers in certain areas and that such assistance was discussed in one or two other regions. However, his judgment is that the F.S.A. hardly got beyond toying with the idea.[33] At any rate, it seems doubtful whether the friendliness of the Farmers' Union was an asset to the F.S.A. during its trial.

Whatever the truth of the matter, Albert Goss, Master of the Grange, believed that his organization suffered from the affinity existing between other farm organizations and segments of the Department of Agriculture. Accordingly, when he appeared before the Cooley Committee, he lashed out in both directions. He necessarily dealt most with the Farm Bureau–Extension relationship, but the net effect was to add the weight of the Grange to the Farm Bureau's campaign against the F.S.A.[34]

The purposes of the Farm Bureau were served in another manner by the succession of hearings. Each of those preceding the Cooley hearing were, so to speak, rehearsals for this, the showdown battle. There had been abundant opportunity to observe the relative effectiveness of the various charges. The accusations were substantially the same as hitherto, but the emphases were noticeably different. In the Farm Bureau presentation, first place was now given to the resettlement projects. The costliness of the projects, their numerous weaknesses of operation, and the analogy that could be drawn with the collective farms of Soviet Russia were stressed. Grouped with the projects were the more recent efforts of the F.S.A. to help many farm families which had been rendered homeless by military acquisitions of land. The F.S.A. had bought tracts of land to deal with this problem, and these purchases were presented as evidence of deliberate intention to evade the will of Congress that the resettlement project idea should not be extended.[35]

While the Cooley Committee covered virtually all the familiar ground as well as some that was new, the issue of the total objective of the F.S.A. was lost in that of the resettlement projects. Without question, the agency had been weakest in this part of the program. For one thing, Congress was antagonistic to anything that smacked of coöperative farming. Then, too, the F.S.A. for a number of years had lost faith and interest in some of its own projects. This was the clearest indication of the agency's "agriculturalization." The problem presented by military relocation had brought the entire issue of F.S.A.'s basic approach to the surface again, but the policy actually remained the traditional family-size farm. Moreover, few of the F.S.A. projects seemed to be operating successfully, although here the evidence is probably inadequate as a basis for judgment. The agency had unwisely arranged for ninety-nine-year leases of certain tracts. This was seized upon as the best possible evidence of F.S.A.'s contempt for the concept of fee-simple ownership of land. Accordingly, much of the committee's time and energy was directed to this phase of the F.S.A. program.

The hearing went beyond its predecessors in the degree to which scurrility was tolerated. The Carr "documents," which had been rejected by some of the previous committees, were brought forth again and O'Neal was asked leading questions which permitted further rehearsing of the old charges.[36] Perhaps the low point came when the committee appeared in Phoenix and gave hearing to the suggestion that the F.S.A. regional director, who had helped negotiate the labor agreement with Mexico and who was married to "a lady of Mexican extraction," by some curious theory of international relations thereby betrayed "communistic" leanings.[37]

The fate of the F.S.A. had been determined long before the committee made its report, but there is nonetheless some significance in the language with which the findings were clothed.

The committee has sought to determine whether or not those charged with the responsibility of administering the affairs of the Farm Security Administration have violated the true intent and meaning of the several

acts of Congress by virtue of which the agency has been permitted to function, and further to determine to what extent, if any, in the management of
the affairs of the agency, there has been a departure from traditional
American policies and well-established laws and customs.... [the F.S.A.
was] financing communistic resettlement projects, where the families could
never own homes, or be paid for all that they made or for all the time they
worked, and was supervising its borrowers to the extent of telling the
borrower how to raise his children, how to plan his home life and, it is
strongly suspected in some cases, how to vote.[38]

The committee found the F.S.A. guilty on two major counts
throughout: the F.S.A. was treating its clients badly; the F.S.A. was
doing too much for its clients. Although most of the discussion covered the resettlement projects and the labor program, the recommendation was for liquidation of both the projects and the rural
rehabilitation program (the labor program had already been taken
from the F.S.A.).

A number of features in this long series of congressional inquiries
are worthy of comment. First is their progressively degraded character. Second is the absence of any searching investigation into the
total operations of the F.S.A. or the guiding concepts of its administration. The latter certainly was needed. The F.S.A. had never
faced the basic dilemma of its policy. Binding people to the land
in a time of rapid technological change, whether by rehabilitation,
tenant purchase, or resettlement projects, could not insure a standard of living commensurate with that in other segments of the population for the large mass with which the F.S.A. had to deal. Some
F.S.A. operations had a definite odor of paternalism about them.
This the various committees caught, but they discussed it in such
terms that the merits of the matter could never be learned. Third
is the readiness with which the committees—and Congress as a
whole—allowed themselves to be manipulated by the lobbyists of
the Farm Bureau.

The F.S.A. disintegrated before the Cooley Committee was
through. The defense housing activities of the agency were transferred to the National Housing Administration in December, 1941.[39]
This was a reasonable change, but it did remove a highly specialized
corps of builders. A year later the F.S.A. was placed in the War
Food Administration headed by Chester Davis, a friend of the Farm

Bureau.[40] The labor program was removed, and a new law prohibited a minimum wage and housing or security of working conditions for government-transported American workers; funds were denied for additional farm labor camps, and immigration restrictions were waived.[41]

The 1944 appropriation for the F.S.A. was withheld in 1943 and in the fall of that year Baldwin resigned as administrator. Most of the policy-making staff followed. Frank Hancock, a former North Carolina congressman, was appointed to Baldwin's position and did his best to meet the requirements of the Cooley Committee and the Farm Bureau. One of the measures of his success is the swiftness with which he dispersed the agency's personnel. When Hancock was through, little was left of what Secretary Wickard had once called the "specialized zeal" of the F.S.A.[42]

The F.S.A. was formally ended late in 1946. Under the terms of an act passed in that year, the agency was liquidated and the Farmers' Home Administration was set up to carry on the "good" parts of its work. The successor had three functions: to continue the farm ownership program started under the 1937 Bankhead-Jones Act, to manage the water facilities program, and to make production loans. The first two had been parts of the F.S.A. program; the third was a former program of the Farm Credit Administration. The act specified that preference must be given to veterans. In practice, this has meant that the Farmers' Home Administration is primarily a veterans' agency.[43] The agency has given sufficient evidence of its reliability for Congress to entrust a new program to its care; it may now make loans to "bona fide fur farmers." Such is the resolution of the problem of rural poverty.

IO

The LARGE CAMPAIGN

The story of the life and death of the Farm Security Administration has a meaning that is quite independent of the currents that were to be found elsewhere in agricultural politics. This, after all, was the story of the greatest attempt to cope with the problem of rural poverty—perhaps the only significant attempt—in the nation's history. The program of the agency contained much that was wrong, much that was false, and more that was ill directed. In its energetic and chaotic way, however, the F.S.A. was an effective branch of government. Its program was meaningful in that it was addressed openly and often directly to the most critical areas of rural life. For a few years it gave an inkling of hope to the great regions of the rural poor that the government was not merely an instrument in the hands of the owners of plantations and corporation farms. If anyone was "to rescue for human society the native values of rural life,"[1] no stouter champion has ever been found than the F.S.A.

Destruction of the F.S.A. may well outweigh any other passage in agricultural politics. In the stream of events, however, it was only an episode. The attack on the F.S.A. was part of a larger campaign. It was a battle, one of many, in which tactical and strategic objectives were so intermingled that the gains and the losses cannot easily be assigned. The problem is partly one of orientation, partly of analysis, and also partly of fact.

Why was the F.S.A. attacked? One fairly coherent answer to this question was given in the testimony of C. B. Baldwin before one of the many congressional committees to which he was summoned in the early 'forties.

It is in this context and only in this context that the current fight to weaken the Farm Security Administration can be understood. The choice before the committee is whether the small independent farmer should be given an opportunity to maintain and improve his status or whether these large interests should be permitted to take advantage of the war situation to accumulate large land holdings and to make laborers out of farmers.[2]

This was in "the choice before the committee" indeed. "Large interests" probably were seeking to do just what Baldwin charged; some did have the objective of larger holdings in peace as well as in war. When the Farm Bureau marshaled the forces hostile to the F.S.A., it gathered up all who could be induced, and who could afford to come, to join the assault, and these included men like Oscar Johnson. Yet even here it should be recalled that the part of the attack which best fits the Baldwin analysis was that of Oscar Johnson, who spoke not for the Farm Bureau but for the Cotton Council.[3] And since this was, to a peculiar degree, a Farm Bureau attack, it is important to see how the Farm Bureau itself assessed the outcome. This can readily be given: *the Farm Bureau was bitterly dissatisfied.*[4]

Is there a conflict here? Why should the Farm Bureau be dissatisfied with success? Is the Baldwin interpretation wrong? Or was the Farm Bureau's role merely an incidental part of the attack? Was Baldwin carried away by his own oversimplification of the issue and by an exaggerated view of the importance of the F.S.A.? Was the Farm Bureau merely a puppet on the strings of sinister plotters in distant mahogany-paneled offices? Basically, the problem is a theoretical one and can be answered only in theoretical terms. First, however, it is necessary to examine the setting of the Farm Bureau's attack upon the F.S.A. and some of the other battles and victories of the larger war.

In the confusion of the early years of the New Deal, personalities played a larger part in politics, for the function of leadership had more scope and was more sought and relied upon. Hitherto obscure men—Hopkins, Ickes, and Tugwell—suddenly rose to positions of prominence and great influence. And, since the issues had not yet been defined, it was inevitable that the peculiarities of a George Peek should loom larger than the particulars of administrative form and structure.

The Department of Agriculture's "purge" of 1935 was the early stage of the war. Although one could seek, and perhaps discover, the hand of the American Farm Bureau Federation in this opening battle, it would be an error to assign to it a large responsibility for the outcome. The personalities were too important and as yet too distinct from the structure which was being built. In the larger sense, this was the sheerly ideological phase of the struggle. The lines were drawn, not on the orders of officers of the line, but by the play of natural sympathy and the often intangible, even unreasonable, pulls of dimly seen class interest. This contributed to the uncertain state of the decision. Some prominent men were cut off from the Department of Agriculture, but the Resettlement Administration and other New Deal agricultural programs went on unchecked. The battle was decided as it was fought—in personalities.

Yet, in these first few years, issues were emerging and gathering about the personalities who monopolized the headlines. A suspicion arose in 1936 that the Agricultural Adjustment Administration was not the undisputed possession of the Farm Bureau. Again this was cloaked in personalities; strange young men—and others not so young—found their way into the lesser, but still important, places of the administrative structure of the agency. Their technical services were necessary, but they remained guilty of the crime of not having emerged from the cornfields. It was hardly surprising that goals were discussed along the Mall which were unheard of in the halls of the land grant colleges.

Something else, too, had happened. The Department of Agriculture no longer contained all the farmer's part of the government. By what appears to have been sheer instinct, decisions were taken to establish new programs outside the department. The formation of the Resettlement Administration has been discussed. So important a venture could not be entrusted to the leadership of the established rural order. But this was not unique. The Soil Erosion Service had been set up in 1933 in the Department of the Interior with Public Works Administration money. Ever since the days of John Taylor of Caroline, the catastrophic fact of soil erosion had been written large upon the land. The meaning of the fact had had its interpreters—Taylor, Pinchot, Bennett, to name but three of the greatest. The Department of Agriculture had had its observers and workers outside Washington busily instructing farmers in the Extension way. Yet, it took the arrival of a vast cloud of Great Plains soil over the Capitol dome to carry Hugh Bennett's point in Congress. What should have been understood through efforts of departmental workers in interpreting the creeping disaster to the nation, came by the force of revelation through this dark portent.

In 1935 the Soil Erosion Service was taken from its birthplace and put inside the Department of Agriculture as the Soil Conservation Service. Immediately, its chief was faced with a problem of relating his work to the established Extension Service. Much lies between the lines in his statement on the problem: "It is difficult to say where our coöperative relations with the Extension Service begin, or to measure them in a quantitative way." He concluded a "Memorandum of Understanding" with the Extension Service and hoped for the best.[5]

In 1935 another rural agency in the federal government, the Rural Electrification Administration, was created. Although the dream of electric light and power on the farms of America had been shared by farm leaders, the new agency was set up outside the Department of Agriculture. If it posed any threat, however, the threat was less to the established order of agriculture than to entrenched utilities. Yet it grew to maturity outside the agricultural structure. It was brought inside the department in 1939.

In 1937 the President's Committee on Farm Tenancy reported and the Resettlement Administration was moved into the department as the Farm Security Administration. This program now seemed established, and its survival ensured. The Department of Agriculture had by these sudden accretions become the most rapidly growing branch of the government and also the largest. Correlatively, however, the administrative pattern had become confused and overlapping. The disorder came mainly from conflicting objectives, but it tended to be seen as a simple problem in the mechanical efficiency of administration.

The uneasy relationships inside the Department of Agriculture tended to become more rather than less serious. The fiction (and it seems to have been recognized for that inside the department) that the problem was one of "coördination" was useful in the various solutions that were attempted. Indeed, there was a real need for coördination. The problems of vanishing soil, ignorant and poverty-stricken farmers, submarginal land in use, all these were inter-related and no one of them could be solved without consideration of the others.

The problem of coördination came to a focus in 1938. In that year a large group of representatives from the land grant colleges and the Department of Agriculture met at a former observation station of the Weather Bureau in Virginia. There they signed a famous document, the Mount Weather Agreement, which became the basis for what seemed the beginning of land-use planning in the United States.

This sought to define once and for all the relationships between old and new among the department's programs. More than this, how-ever, it sought to stabilize the relationships of power among the old and the new in the administrative structure—the Extension services and the colleges as faced with the new agencies. Nothing in the docu-ment betrays awareness that any parties other than those who signed were involved. The first part of the document sought to explain away the conflict which had prevailed in the past: "Both the Department of Agriculture and the Land Grant Colleges and Universities wish to perpetuate and strengthen the harmonious and mutually helpful relations that have long existed between them." There was more piety than accuracy in the statement. It was inaccurate in that con-flict did exist, and that this conflict lay not between the department and the colleges but between parts of the administration and the forces behind the colleges.

The document provided for the establishment of a nation-wide system of county land-use planning committees, to be set up by each state Extension Service. Each county committee was to consist wholly of farm people, with the county agent as nonvoting secretary, but a subcommittee was to include local officials of the Agricultural Ad-justment Administration, the Soil Conservation Service, and the Farm Security Administration. The state organization was to con-sist primarily of governmental officials under the chairmanship of the state Extension director, with a representation of farmers. These committees had a twofold purpose: coördination of existing agricultural programs and planning of land use.[6]

The program which emerged from this agreement assumed a vitality that has perhaps been underestimated. Given the political realities in organized agriculture, it seems folly that such high hopes should ever have been entertained. Beyond all else, the Mount Weather Agreement was a political agreement—in the word of one observer, a truce. It was, moreover, concluded in the shadowland of administration. The active political forces were not overtly committed to the truce. Yet there were those who saw in the machinery established at Mount Weather a new "democracy" in agricultural administration.[7] These observers emphasized the participation of actual farmers in planning and the implication of decentralization of administration. This view combined two familiar American delusions about the nature of democracy: the idea of direct democracy and that of the grass roots.[8]

The land-use planning committees had aroused enthusiasm from another source as well, those who were interested primarily in planning. When the program was finally destroyed, this group looked back remorsefully for the source of the failure. The proper question was asked: Why had the program not been supported by the dirt farmers, who had been expected to operate the plan? And part of the answer was given: it had not in fact been operated by dirt farmers.[9] So the conclusion was reached that the program lacked vitality.[10] Nevertheless, the fact that the entire structure of the committees came under frontal attack is important evidence that the committees had acquired real vitality. They had acquired such vitality that they had become potential centers of power. The error of the enthusiasts lay in their own refusal to assess the realities of power. The failure of the committees lay in the fact that their power could not be developed quickly enough for their own preservation. Despite the concession of Extension Service leadership, the establishment of county land-use planning committees was a crucial step in arousing the hostility that overtook the entire Department of Agriculture in the early 'forties.

In the meantime, the reorganization of agencies of the Farm Credit Administration brought them from long-standing independent status into the Department of Agriculture, a development which seems to run contrary to the general pattern. The dominant power group had hitherto sought inclusion of independent agencies of rural interest in the department; here it opposed such inclusion. Two factors may account for this seeming paradox. First, the credit agencies had been long established and were well decentralized. This implied a stabilized relationship with the external part of the power complex, the Farm Bureau." Second, the inclusion took place in 1939, just after it had become apparent that a potential independence movement in the department was being formed.

Thus, by 1940, the various agricultural programs had been concentrated in the Department of Agriculture, and the department itself had been reorganized. With a real awareness that the hitherto existing local organization had been lacking in democratic qualities, the department was now actively intervening in the counties and local communities to make its program both effective and extensive in coverage. Increased responsibility was given to the Bureau of Agricultural Economics for program planning. To cap the structure, an Office of Land Use Coördination was created. The Department of Agriculture was on its way to emancipation. It is not to be wondered that the Farm Bureau repudiated Henry Wallace and moved toward an open break with the reorganized department.

The declaration of war came at the December, 1940, convention of the Farm Bureau, which also marked the beginning of the fight against the F.S.A. The declaration carried a full statement of objectives. Since these were consistently the objectives of many campaigns, they must be examined in detail. Viewed retrospectively, the first two points listed under the "national farm program" were first in importance:

The new programs which have been provided in the agricultural legislation enacted during recent years in the normal process of growth have resulted in too much overlapping and duplication of activity. The many agencies needed to carry on this program have been the natural result of the process of considering each subject separately. A woeful lack of coördination and planning in carrying out these programs is evident to every farmer. On too many occasions one agency recommends an activity in conflict with that of another agency. Too many instances prevail where personnel is employed to accomplish an activity already embraced within the functions of another and existing agency. Farmers do not want numerous agents consulting them on farm programs. They want coördination of these efforts, consistency in administration without duplication and overlapping, and above all, administration with the least expenditure of government funds.

We believe that the remedy for this situation lies in the unification of administration in the hands of a five-man nonpartisan Board within the Department of Agriculture. This Board should be representative of the nation's agriculture. It should be independent in its position with respect to other bureaus and agencies of government. It should cover the administration of the A.A.A. and Crop Insurance, the Soil Conservation and Domestic Allotment Act, Surplus Marketing and Disposal, including the Stamp Plan, Commodity Credit Corporation, the Soil Conservation Service, and the planning activities now in the Bureau of Agricultural Economics.

The second point came under the heading of "state administration."

In the field of administration within the states, we know of no existing agency so well qualified as the Extension Service of the Land Grant Colleges to have general supervision of all these programs. Its knowledge of rural people and rural problems and its broad and successful experience in working with farmers makes the Extension Service ideal for this function. It will be necessary, however, that it function in a different manner with respect to different types of programs.

We recommend that the Director of Extension, after consultation with statewide membership farm organizations, submit annually to the proposed Federal Board nominations of persons to compose the state committee. The state committee will be responsible for administration of the Agricultural Adjustment Act, including conservation practices and crop insurance. Insofar as state administration is practical, it will be responsible for administering the surplus marketing and disposal program and the Commodity Credit Loan program.

The functions and activities of the present county committees as they are now constituted and their relation to the county agent should be continued, with such county committees responsible to the state committee.

The Extension Service should be responsible for the administration of the Soil Conservation Service and the home and farm management phases of the Farm Security programs, and for the statewide planning program of the Bureau of Agricultural Economics.

In accordance with the foregoing administrative changes, funds should be transferred from appropriations provided by Congress, to the Extension Service and to the state A.A.A. committee for state and local administration of the laws making up the farm program.[12]

The peculiar merits of this remarkable plan require no comment. What does require comment is the fact that this plan was the actual program of the Farm Bureau. When O'Neal came before the subcommittee of the House Appropriations Committee, this was the plan he offered to that body.[13] The committee protested its incompetence as an appropriations committee to force such legislation, but the Farm Bureau men would not be gainsaid. Their research director, W. R. Ogg, embarked upon a new interpretation of the Extension Service, one that is interesting principally because neither the departmental leaders of Extension nor the leaders of the colleges themselves repudiated it.

The conception of the Extension Service, therefore, was that it should serve as the connecting link between individual farmers and the agricultural college experimental stations and the U.S.D.A. The Extension Service was to be the extension of these educational and research agencies in aiding farmers to solve their problems, both individually and collectively.

In recent years a different conception of the extension program has grown up; namely, that it is solely a teaching function in the academic sense of distributing or imparting information, so that there has grown up in some quarters a tendency to separate education from action.

The fact is education and action cannot be separated without disaster to both lines of endeavor.[14]

The Farm Bureau witnesses were too importunate. As we have seen in connection with the F.S.A. story, the undertaking was too big. There were several realists among the congressmen, and the men of the Farm Bureau Federation found themselves under fire. A copy of the reorganization plan was sent to the Department of Agriculture and an analysis of the plan was returned by Secretary Wickard.[15] The reply was terse and bitter. Wickard asked why the Farm Bureau had advanced the proposal. The first reason, he found, was the Farm Bureau's dislike of the department's land-use planning procedures. The second was that the department had attempted to stop Farm Bureau recruiting by county agents. Third, the Farm Bureau and the Extension Service had had a long and close association.[16] Thus the Farm Bureau and the department were now at war themselves. The Extension Service, moreover, was repudiated by its own superior.

Although the F.S.A. was placed high on the Farm Bureau executioner's list, originally it was preceded by the land-use planning scheme and the Bureau of Agricultural Economics. The maneuvers of the Farm Bureau, the informal telephone calls and visits with individual congressmen, the directed pressure of telegrams and letters were not visible, and one can only speculate on what was done by way of emphasizing selected aspects of the Farm Bureau program when it became apparent that the whole could not be won in a single battle. Yet the first success of the Farm Bureau can be discovered. It was at the expense of the land-use planning system. Congress forbade the use of any of the appropriation for 1942 in state and county land-use planning. The story was circulated that Howard Tolley of the Bureau of Agricultural Economics was using the land-use committees "to create a new farm organization to re-place the Farm Bureau."[17] The history of this rumor would be interesting to know. It is unbelievable in itself, and it is unlikely that anyone in the Farm Bureau leadership really believed it. However, the actual intent of the land-use planning committees was without doubt to bring about an infusion of elements other than those of the Farm Bureau into the directing of agricultural policy. In this sense, the committees and the land-use planning scheme constituted a long-range threat to Farm Bureau power.

The land-use planning committees and the system headed by the Office of Land Use Coördination were the first victims of the Farm Bureau war. It is impossible to say definitely that this position of priority in time corresponded to a similar position in the list of Farm Bureau aims. This, however, is likely. It was the belief of Secretary Wickard in 1941.[18] The reason for the inclusion of the land-use planning committees in the proscribed list, certainly, is clear. The committee system reached down to the grass roots and challenged Farm Bureau power at its very source. It was an immediate dilution of Extension Service influence. While the Farm Bureau leadership must have been aware of the limitations of the committees which restricted them in becoming nuclei of power, the violence of Farm Bureau reaction suggests that its leadership was keenly aware of the sources of its own power. As in earlier days, the bureau was alert for any indication that other groups might be following the route which it had traveled itself.

In order to prevent any survival of the land-use planning organization, the Farm Bureau fought to curb the Bureau of Agricultural Economics. The cut in the latter's appropriation and the limitation on its expenditure of 1941 was followed up by further cuts in 1945 and 1946. In 1945 the responsibility of the Bureau of Agricultural Economics for program planning was taken away and placed in the office of the Secretary. Just in case the agency retained any disposition to intervene in political actualities, Congress lopped off its regional offices. The Farm Bureau job was done as thoroughly as it could be without actual liquidation of the agency.[19]

In July, 1941, the Department of Agriculture created a system of local boards for its own administrative purposes in the defense program. The purpose of these defense boards (later war boards) was to assure a means of communication from the department down to the last farmer, and it became the boast of the department that it could reach every farmer in the nation within twenty-four hours. The boards were probably a technical necessity for the rapidly changing wartime program in agriculture. What is important here, however, is that they were geared to the machinery of the A.A.A., and the Extension Service was ignored. One Extension director cried, "We've got our backs up now; we are going to fight."[20] However, the fighting done by state Extension directors, at least before Congress, was limited to an appeal for appropriations for 1942.[21] They remained silent on the pressing questions of policy with which the congressional committee was struggling, and left the fighting to the Farm Bureau.

Since Secretary Wickard had been responsible for the decision to form the defense boards around the A.A.A. organization (Wickard had come up via the A.A.A.), his name became anathema. He paid the price by becoming a nearly impotent bystander in his own department when the main functions of the department were later placed under the War Food Administration headed by Chester Davis. This reorganization was for the duration of the war only, but it drastically curtailed the "dangerous" activities and tendencies of the department. Perhaps O'Neal had this accomplishment in mind when, speaking before a congressional committee on the possibility of the creation of a new organization of farmers, he said, "In order to prevent any such development we have cracked down on Henry Wallace, we have cracked down on Wickard, and we will crack down on any group that will do that."[22]

In December, 1941, when the Farm Bureau caught sight of the opportunity offered by the Byrd Committee investigations, Carr and other investigators were instructed to find material not only on the F.S.A. but on the Soil Conservation Service as well." That the attack before the Byrd Committee was limited to the F.S.A. was, by the Farm Bureau's own account, due solely to lack of time.

In 1943 the Farm Bureau scored another success. This time the victim was the A.A.A. For some time, the major A.A.A. resistance to the Farm Bureau had come from the agency's north central division. At last the director of that division was forced out of his job. The charge against him was that he had been engaged in political activity. The political activity involved was that of resisting the Farm Bureau."

This, then, was the general pattern of the Farm Bureau campaigns during the early 'forties. Their remarkable success was possible only because of the single-mindedness of bureau leaders at a time when most of the other people in the country were preoccupied with a quite different war.

It is apparent that the war of the Farm Bureau from 1940 on was not directed against the F.S.A. alone. The F.S.A. battle was the most important because it was the largest and most bitterly fought, and the substantial issues were the greatest. However, at times it seems as though the destruction of F.S.A. plans was only of incidental interest to the Farm Bureau.

It will have been noted that all the agencies and programs which fell under Farm Bureau displeasure and which were thereby marked for liquidation were New Deal programs. Was the Farm Bureau striking at the New Deal itself? Here it becomes necessary to look further into Farm Bureau likes and dislikes.

In the hearings that marked the opening of the Farm Bureau campaign, in which the grand scheme for dissolving the Department of Agriculture into forty-eight different parts was set forth, O'Neal expressed generous approval of the Rural Electrification Administration and the Tennessee Valley Authority for having carried out plans of extensive decentralization." The Rural Electrification Administration, it will be recalled, had been brought into the department in 1939. A reorganization followed. Its director, Harry Slattery, thereby earned the good will of O'Neal and the agency enjoyed a long trouble-free period.

The T.V.A. is peculiarly interesting since it has been one of the showpieces of the New Deal. An excellent study on this point is Philip Selznick's *TVA and the Grass Roots.*[26] According to Selznick, a decision was made very early in the life of the agency to trade control of its large agricultural program in return for political support for the electric power program. The parties to this bargain were Dr. Harcourt Morgan of the local land grant college on behalf of the Farm Bureau–Extension forces and David Lilienthal on behalf of the power program. The whole bargain was overlaid with a philosophy of grass-roots democracy which became the joint property of Morgan and Lilienthal. This philosophy has attracted much attention and has been regarded as something new in political thinking. Anyone, however, who has followed addresses of Extension leaders since the early part of the century will find it familiar.

The agricultural program of the T.V.A. has paralleled the general contours sketched here for every activity in which the Extension Service has had a part. The T.V.A. farm program has been dominated by concern for the welfare of the more prosperous farmers. It has had a few new features simply because the resources of the agency are greater than those normally available to the Extension Service. The T.V.A. fertilizer program is an illustration. The electrical power generated at the agency's dams can produce either nitrates or phosphates. The former, to reduce the alternatives to their simplest terms, is in the Tennessee Valley typically a poor farmer's fertilizer; the latter is a prosperous farmer's fertilizer. On the advice of the land grant colleges, the decision was made in favor of phosphates. While this decision was justified in terms, presumably good, of building soil and a more stable agriculture, it was plainly an instance in which the human values of the equation were ignored.[27]

In terms of political power, the T.V.A. is built upon a broad concession to the Farm Bureau. This power was ensured by the long presence of Dr. Harcourt Morgan on the governing board of the agency. He had a free hand with the agricultural program. As the former president of a land grant college, he made the greatest possible use of the Extension services and enforced the fullest possible decentralization. These conditions all result in heavy Farm Bureau influence.[28]

It is now possible to return to some of the questions posed earlier in this chapter. The attack on the F.S.A. was but one step in a large plan to remake the Department of Agriculture. In this particular attack the Farm Bureau mobilized all its natural auxiliaries of an interested and class character: the Cotton Council, the Irrigated Cotton Growers, the Associated Farmers, parts of the Chamber of Commerce, the large grain interests of Minneapolis, the political opportunists in Congress who stood to gain from the defeat of New Deal programs, and so on. A case can be made that F.S.A. programs constituted a real and present threat to established systems of large-scale farming. According to this, the key to the situation is in a cheap and docile labor supply. So far as the F.S.A. rehabilitation program succeeded, farmers were rooted to their own land and did not take to the migration road. So far as F.S.A. labor programs succeeded in improving the conditions of life among migrants, it reduced the in-security on which the agricultural labor market of, say, California, has been based. So far as the F.S.A. sought to make the labor market efficient, it sabotaged the consistent efforts of corporation farmers to maintain an oversupply of labor.

To this argument might be added several others: that the F.S.A. was actually undermining the plantation system of the South, again an issue of a cheap labor market; that the F.S.A. was a threat to Twin City commercial domination of the Dakotas. Each had an element of truth. Yet, even when all these are added up, it seems unrealistic to say that the F.S.A. constituted a serious economic threat to estab-lished interests. The whole remains inadequate, considered purely as direct economic motivation for what occurred.

When we consider the large war of which the F.S.A. was but a part, the role of the Farm Bureau becomes central. The common element in the entire story has been told here. What was the basic policy of the Farm Bureau itself? The answer is plain: the Farm Bureau sought at every point to maintain its own power, which, in turn, was based upon its influence over the Extension Service. Farm Bureau power was expanded by using the Extension Service to con-trol other more vital parts of the departmental program. Where such control could not be extended, what remained uncontrolled had to be destroyed. In all this, perhaps the most striking feature is Farm Bureau consistency. This may be traced not only through the organi-zation's faithfulness to its 1940 program but through the sameness of this program to that enunciated by O'Neal in his letter of dissent to the Report of the President's Committee on Farm Tenancy of 1937. This letter was cited in 1944 by a Farm Bureau spokesman and was again spread upon the public record.[20]

Farm Bureau policy was the same in 1944 as it had been in 1940, and this in turn was the same as it had been in 1937. The goal was power.

II

POLITICS, ADMINISTRATION, and EDUCATION

Agricultural politics since the end of the Second World War presents a picture of almost unparalleled confusion. The amount of time spent in congressional committees and on the floor of Congress discussing farm policy has been prodigious. Although nearly everyone has agreed that the early development of a permanent or long-range policy was necessary, it has so far been impossible to reach a decision on the character of that policy. A great number of bills have been introduced; the hearings on them have been interminable. Again and again, argument on the substantial merit of this policy or that has been diverted to questions of administrative organization. Indeed, most of the bills have included important sections on this topic; some have been directed exclusively to it. Nearly every measure has been highly complicated.

Though it might be assumed that details of administrative structure are of minor importance, this is belied by the heat and rancor with which the argument has been conducted. Increasingly, the realization has spread that the organization of the agricultural programs has an importance at least equal to that of their substance. It was observed, in the last days of the Eightieth Congress, that, while it was possible to compromise on the character of the agricultural program, it was impossible to do so on the distribution of functions between the various agencies.[1]

The meaning of the bitter struggle which has been going on in

127

Congress, the Department of Agriculture, and outside of government has been obscured by several factors. The first of these is the intrinsic complexity of the argument. The farm program is involved, its methods are varied, and the agencies which carry it out are many. The second factor is that since the death of the Farm Security Administration there has been no clear-cut issue on which the conflict could be focused. From time to time, in momentary flashes, the character of the conflict has been sharply delineated, but these have subsided and the battleground has again become a darkling plain.

And yet this struggle is not new. It is the same conflict which pervaded agricultural politics in the 'thirties and which resulted in the destruction of the F.S.A. It is the same conflict that once raged over land-use planning and the activities of the Bureau of Agricultural Economics. However, there are differences that distinguish the present period from those which are past. The most striking is the difference in the antagonists. The American Farm Bureau Federation is numerically far greater than at any time in its history. It emerged from the war years with a membership swollen well beyond the million mark.[2] Moreover, it is stronger for the victories of the earlier years. On the other hand, its structure of power is beginning to show cracks which may prove serious. The opposition to the Farm Bureau is somewhat different in character, also, and now includes not only enlarged rival farm organizations and parts of the department but spokesmen for the administration as well. This last change may well prove critically important.

After the successes of the early war years, the Farm Bureau Federation dropped its insistence upon the general plan to reorganize the department which had held first place in its program for several years. Convention resolutions made little mention of administrative reorganization and public statements gave it little emphasis. The 1944 resolutions placed democracy and balance and the substantial parts of a national farm program ahead of reorganization.[3] The 1945 resolutions, for the most part, omitted references to administration.[4]

This, however, represented no change in the determination of the Farm Bureau. By the time the 1946 convention met, the drive to complete the bureau's unfinished task had been resumed. The immediate object of attack now became the Soil Conservation Service

(S.C.S.). This agency, still under the direction of Hugh S. Bennett, had achieved a position of prestige, but, more important, it had managed to erect an administrative system by which its agents were able to deal directly with farmers. Like other New Deal "action" agencies in agriculture, it operated with the assistance of local associations, in this case the Soil Conservation districts. Soil Conservation engineers and technicians were working with only a small fraction of the total number of farmers, but more and more farmers were being reached, and Soil Conservation districts were increasing in number. This was the condition which, in Farm Bureau eyes, required correction.

Here the Farm Bureau had an excellent rationale to develop for a program of reorganization. The Agricultural Adjustment Act of 1938, which had been the long-term replacement of the act invalidated by the Supreme Court, included provisions for payments to farmers in return for their practice of soil conservation. In itself, this was a highly praiseworthy attempt to reform long-established destructive practices. In large degree, however, the inclusion of these provisions had been dictated by the strategy of lawyers concerned for the survival of the act in a court test. Criticisms have not been lacking that the provisions became additional pretexts for payments designed to secure parity for farmers. Whatever the merit of these criticisms, the local organization under the 1938 act concentrated on soil conservation. Federal expenditures for this purpose appeared against the names of two agencies, the Soil Conservation Service and the Production and Marketing Administration (formerly the A.A.A.).[5] Expenditures by the latter were much the larger. Thus, duplication existed.

The Farm Bureau now demanded a reform of this confusing situation. The plan of reorganization, however, went far beyond anything necessary to solution of the problem. It called for "decentralization," a term whose specialized meaning in Farm Bureau circles is now familiar. Authority and responsibility for the combined program were to be placed in the hands of local, district, and state farmer committees. The whole, moreover, was to be operated on the basis of grants-in-aid to the states.[6] It became abundantly clear that the agency which the Farm Bureau regarded as competent to take over administration of soil conservation was the Extension

Service. It was also clear that such a reorganization would involve liquidation of the S.C.S.[7]

Even if the history of previous campaigns of the Farm Bureau were unknown, the tendency of its postwar administrative program should have been apparent in 1945. In the spring of that year, O'Neal appeared before the appropriation committees and insisted upon "economy, simplification, better coördination, and a greater measure of decentralization."[8] The substance of this appeal appeared in his opposition to a proposed cut in Extension Service funds and to a proposed increase in S.C.S. appropriations.[9] Just after the 1945 convention, the board of directors of the Farm Bureau passed a resolution making concrete the somewhat indefinite resolutions of the convention. This specifically included recommendations that the Extension Service should take over the functions of the S.C.S. (albeit with the latter's personnel as well), the educational and informational work for all programs, and the giving of assistance to individual farmers. It further included the proposal that the whole agricultural conservation program be put on a grant-in-aid basis to the states.[10] There was thus no ambiguity: the S.C.S. was to lose its identity completely.

This became the issue on which the battle of farm politics was fought until 1949. Stated very narrowly, should the S.C.S. be permitted to survive? Such a question, obviously, was one to stir few men's souls. Some of the participants in the struggle may, perhaps, have been deceived into believing that the issue was as narrow as just stated. Technically, the problem was neither vast nor complex. It is even likely that a simple device such as the often-proposed housing of all local public agricultural agencies in one building (a pleasant modern architectural plan for county agricultural buildings was drawn) would have solved it, *if* it were simply a matter of "administrative coördination."

In all probability, however, the actual principals in the fight were not in the least deceived. Certainly, the Farm Bureau Federation was not to blame if anyone considered this the whole of the problem. For the same resolution passed by the federation board of directors early in 1946 carried a clear statement of the general plan. Besides the points already mentioned, the following demands were included: "coördinate" the A.A.A. with the Extension Service; enlarge the state A.A.A. committees to include directors of experiment stations and state Extension services and additional farmer members appointed on nominations submitted by Extension directors in consultation with state-wide farm organizations; give the Extension Service responsibility for helping farmers with farm forestry and for assisting F.S.A. clients; and move the Grazing Service from the Department of the Interior into the Forest Service.[11]

Although the simple justification which O'Neal offered for this plan was that it would save one-third to one-fourth of the cost of administration, mere statement of the plan should have been enough to suggest its far-reaching purpose. It was, in fact, the postwar counterpart of the federation plan of 1940.

Far more than the fate of the S.C.S. was at issue, then. This agency actually was less important than the array of administrative organizations gathered loosely in the Production and Marketing Administration.[12] The latter was clearly within the compass of the federation's postwar plan of reorganization. Moreover, the new version of the plan extended beyond the precincts of the Department of Agriculture. The Grazing Service of the Department of the Interior was specifically mentioned in the 1946 resolution. Subsequently, activities within the normal purview of other departments came to be included. The first of these was the agricultural labor program. Although this had been in the hands of the Extension Service since 1943, there was an expectation that it would be placed elsewhere at the end of the war emergency. The proposal to transfer the labor program, however, was strongly opposed by the Farm Bureau.[13] Somewhat less definitely, the federation stated a claim on behalf of the Extension Service for exercise of jurisdiction over the agricultural activities of the Bureau of Reclamation.[14] It is likely that this agency will receive increasing attention from the federation.

Lastly, it is worth repeating that the Farm Bureau was not satisfied with its accomplishment in bringing about the end of the F.S.A. The fact that the ghost of the F.S.A. was still present in the mild Farmers' Home Administration called for action. The program here was, as before, that loaning functions should be placed together under an "independent national bipartisan board," and supervisory functions should be given to the Extension Service.[15]

This comprehensive plan touched nearly every aspect of agricultural administration except those which had been in continuous operation since before the New Deal. O'Neal gave as his premise that the year 1933 had inaugurated a completely new approach in agricultural administration. He certainly did not deplore the main tendency of agricultural policy—the Farm Bureau continued to take credit for this. He insisted, however, that the administrative structure set up in the depression emergency had been a distortion of the historic and proper system. In his view, the essential fact was that a special field organization under federal control had been created. This was the evil, rather than any duplication or unnecessary expenditure.[16]

The choice of the S.C.S. as the immediate opponent in the battle that ensued was made for several reasons. It will be recalled that the agency had been scheduled for attack at the time of the F.S.A. campaign. The S.C.S. was thus the next objective in the strategic design. The S.C.S. was a relatively minor agency and apparently weaker than the structure of the Production and Marketing Administration. It could be destroyed without danger to the substance of the price-support system in which the Farm Bureau remained interested. Moreover, the S.C.S. was proceeding steadily with its organization of farmers (i.e., at the grass roots) in Soil Conservation districts, which were now organized into an independent national association.[17] It may be guessed that this was the most important factor. Here was the return of a specter which had been seen before: a private farm association organized about a governmentally subsidized service over which the Farm Bureau could expect to exert little influence. As in the earlier instance of the A.A.A. committees, the Farm Bureau leadership could envision an imitation of the Farm Bureau's own formation.[18]

The struggle over the S.C.S., which continued with intensity throughout 1947 and 1948, was reminiscent of the F.S.A. battle in some respects.[19] The technique of the fighting was similar in character, although the preparation was less elaborate. General charges were supported by a scattering of letters making specific complaints on local situations. Hugh Bennett, head of the S.C.S., was subjected to a hostile and highly personal questioning in committee.[20] The refrain was repeated endlessly that farmers were becoming "increasingly concerned over duplication, overlapping and conflict in the administration of the agricultural conservation program."[21] The picture was painted of farmers in a state of hopeless confusion throughout the nation, being told one thing by this agency and another by that, of farmers having to go from one office to another and never learning what their government really meant.

In 1947 the Farm Bureau adopted a somewhat new line of attack. The recommendation was made for a reduction in the expenditures of the Department of Agriculture.[22] The proposed reduction was general, that is, it was to apply to the administrative spending of agencies other than the Extension Service. As for the latter, the Farm Bureau had already been instrumental in the passage of the Bankhead-Flannagan Act of 1945, which authorized a progressive increase in Extension funds in three yearly steps. Since the third increment of $4,000,000 failed of favorable action in the appropriations acts, the Farm Bureau campaigned steadily for its inclusion.[23] This demand on behalf of the Extension Service has in no way diminished the insistence of the Farm Bureau on the general reduction.

The main difference from earlier Farm Bureau campaigns lies in the opposition which it developed. Friends of the S.C.S. appeared in force and struck back effectively. The first stage of this counterattack was the introduction of a bill for a National Land Policy Act.[24] This measure would have increased the power of the Secretary of Agriculture for the purpose of building up the functions and size of the S.C.S. It was framed in such a way that narrow problems of land management would have been given priority over problems of people living on the land. It had poor prospects in Congress, but it did serve as a counterweight to the Extension-oriented proposals.

The direct conflict between the two administrative approaches resulted in a stalemate. Congress was unable to decide on a measure to end the struggle, and so extended the life of the existing system year by year. It was not open to doubt that the conflict between the two agencies had become serious. There remained—and remains— a genuine need for reorganization. The difficulty, however, has been widely misinterpreted. From too many sides it has been regarded as merely a problem of administrative efficiency. This mistaken approach has operated to the advantage of the Farm Bureau. Considering the lesser scale of the S.C.S., there would appear to be arguments of expediency in sacrificing it to achieve the goal of harmony. However, warnings have been heard increasingly in recent years that a more serious problem is involved. Thus Gould Beech, editor of the *Southern Farmer*, cautioned a congressional committee:

When I was an employee of the Alabama Agricultural Extension Service ten years ago I heard a lot of talk about farmers being confused by too many agricultural agencies. It has been my observation that some of the leaders of the Extension Service have been so busy trying to get a monopoly on all farm services for the last ten years that it has had little time to do its job ... [speaking of one of the proposals] Of course the power of the Extension Service to force farmers to join the Farm Bureau will be increased. Likewise, its power over the politics of the Farm Bureau will be increased. Any farmer who does not go along with the idea of the Extension Service can have any Government service cut off. The farmer will live in the insecurity of not knowing what will happen to his quota, whether he will be able to get the services of Soil Conservation technicians and so on. Finally, the education function of the Extension Service will be endangered ... If Congress will settle once and for all whether it is to remain an educational service and will insist that it stop trying to grasp control of other agencies, we can have a pattern of coöperation among farm agencies. The suspicion and distrust which has been created will be ended.[25]

One of the nation's leading agricultural economists, Theodore W. Schultz, made an even more forceful statement:

Underneath all this is a concealed issue that burns all of our minds, which is not brought to the surface and analyzed and treated, which seems to me a larger issue than getting the tasks done. In our day we are more concerned with who has power and what we have done to power relationships and the whole political aspect than with the thing that is accomplished. What we are worried about most is what we have done to ourselves in the political structure and relationships.[26]

In the meantime, a different, quieter, and yet perhaps more exciting drama was being played. The story here properly begins with the convention of the land grant colleges in 1944. At this meeting a report was made by the association's Committee on Post-War Agricultural Policy. This report was distinguished by its orientation to the problems of human beings. Previously, the colleges and their association had been concerned primarily with problems of production. The report advocated, among other things, high-level production, acceptance of a farm-to-city movement as normal, retention of price control, improvement in the conditions of tenancy, extension of social security, and conservation of range and water resources.[27] It recommended the formation of a permanent committee, representing the colleges, the department, and the farm organizations, which could propose legislation; it advocated state committees (of vague definition) and county councils consisting of members drawn from all farm organizations, agencies, and groups. This part of the recommendation was less significant than the indication that the colleges were prepared to consider the bitter social and economic facts of agriculture.

In 1945 the colleges' association showed the change of attitude even more dramatically. The Committee on Post-War Agricultural Policy questioned the tendency to "modernize" the parity formula, and pointed to the fact that the 6,000,000 farm families reported by the census are not a homogeneous segment of the population. Here were challenges to two of the central tenets of "organized agriculture," that parity is an expanding concept and that agriculture is a coherent entity.[28] In discussions in succeeding conventions there was no lack of self-criticism.[29] Among the points made was the importance of restoring the Extension Service to its proper function, education.[30] In line with this, the meeting advocated that the farm labor program be taken away from the Extension Service.[31]

All this was truly impressive when set against the previous history of the colleges' association. In 1947, however, alarm was expressed over the agricultural activities of the Bureau of Reclamation. A resolution was passed calling for curtailment by Congress of that bureau's activities.[32] In 1949 the association insisted that the colleges be recognized as the focal points of coördinating agricultural reclamation programs.[33]

Representatives of the land grant colleges took part in a general assessment of the Extension Service made by a committee on which appointees of the department and outsiders also served. The report of this committee in 1948 was something of a landmark.[34] At the very outset, the committee emphasized that the primary function of the Extension Service is education.[35] It recognized criticisms that the service had given preferential treatment to certain groups, and insisted that the benefits of Extension should be available to "the

people of the United States" (the language of the Smith-Lever Act).
Moreover, the conviction was stated that "it would be in the public
interest for any formal operating relationships between the Extension Service and any general farm organization such as the Farm
Bureau to be discontinued at the earliest possible moment."[36]
Finally, the committee recommended that Extension should not be
allowed to become an emergency or administrative agency.[37]

In January, 1949, one more study of agricultural administration
bearing the stamp of the old land grant college point of view appeared. This was the Task Force report on agricultural activities of
the Hoover Commission.[38] Superficially this report appears to share
the preoccupation of the commission with economy in expenditure.
However, the effect of the recommendations is to parallel in important respects the milder plans of the Farm Bureau. Indeed, economy
has been a favored slogan of the Farm Bureau in recent years. This
report recommended that the S.C.S. be dismantled and its components distributed between the Extension Service and various other
offices,[39] and that the Farmers' Home Administration should be
brought into a general Agricultural Credit Administration.[40] On the
critical question of the power of local farmer committees, however,
the Task Force clearly indicated that the function was to be purely
advisory.[41] Thus, although the report showed the unmistakable mark
of the Farm Bureau point of view, the whole recommendation was
distinctly temperate in quality.[42]

The movement of the land grant colleges and their leaders has not
been altogether certain or assured; backward steps have alternated
with those taken forward. Too often, the position of the colleges'
association has been ambiguous; to cast off the role of ruler but to
retain the perquisites thereof. Yet the whole tendency is now toward
the goals of education and research. After an interlude of three
decades the realization is dawning that the functions of education and
government, while related, are distinct.

In 1950 this dawning was signalized by a victory-in-defeat that
is perhaps the most important of the current period. A bill was introduced in Congress to bring about a formal separation of the Extension Service from the Farm Bureau. This was the bill introduced by
Representative Walter Granger of Utah.[43] It provided that no payment should be made to any land grant college or any state unless

the state's share was derived from public sources or from private donations to land grant colleges the terms of which bestow on the donor no direct personal benefits from or control over the Extension Service. The Granger bill would also have prohibited payments to any state which permits employes of the Extension Service to perform nongovernmental functions or requires or permits political or quasi-political farm organizations to function as official coöperating or sponsoring agencies for the Extension Service, or permits preferential treatment among farmers or farm organizations. It would have applied the terms of the Hatch Act (forbidding political activities of federal employees) to Extension workers.

The Granger bill was strenuously opposed by the Farm Bureau. Twenty state Farm Bureau presidents were assembled to testify against it. In addition, two representatives of one land grant college argued the Farm Bureau case. On the other side, in favor of the bill, an impressive number of witnesses appeared, including representatives of the Farmers' Union, the National Grange, the National Livestock Exchange, and the National Association of Mutual Insurance Agents. In this group also were M. L. Wilson, director of the Extension Service, and—representatives of the Association of Land Grant Colleges and Universities. The Granger bill was shelved by the House committee[44] and the measure was lost. However, the issue had at last been brought into the open.

Not surprisingly, other effects have begun to appear. In November, 1950, a Kansas judge ruled that a county Farm Bureau had no authority to pay dues to the state Farm Bureau, and ordered a separation of the county and state organizations.[45] Lastly, the Farm Bureau of the State of Maine, one of three farm bureaus which had never affiliated with the American Farm Bureau Federation, voted to change its name.[46]

The tenure of power is never completely secure.

12

PARITY
and PARTY

In the spring of 1949 a new substance was cast into the cauldron of agricultural politics. Secretary Brannan announced his now famous plan for reconstructing agricultural policy. Since 1947 there had been extensive review of the course of policy and much discussion about the turning it should take. Now the time limit on the life of the existing measures was drawing near. Congress had labored for several years to develop a new basis for governmental intervention in behalf of "agriculture," but without success. Until this time the dispute centered on administrative structure. In 1949, however, the whole mass of agricultural policy became involved in controversy.

In order to see what emerged from the controversy precipitated by the Brannan Plan it is necessary to glance briefly over the course of agricultural policy since 1938. The Agricultural Adjustment Act of that year had replaced the temporary system of parity supports created by the 1936 act. The political impetus behind the passage of both of these acts came from several sources. The first was the Farm Bureau in uneasy alliance with other farm organizations. The second was the Democratic administration in power. The first A.A.A. had been, in a very real sense, the policy of the Democratic party. This fact was more or less generally accepted in the early 'thirties, both by the administration and by its opponents. It derived in large part from the sharp contrast between the A.A.A. and the not-forgotten Farm Board policy of the Hoover era. Moreover, the entire issue was dramatized by the Butler decision and the subsequent "court-packing" struggle, with the result that the prestige of the Democratic party became heavily involved. And, indeed, the A.A.A. plan (and its successors) seems to have paid off in electoral votes.

The Farm Bureau gave little sign of uneasiness over the fact that its policy on parity was shared with the Democratic party. Until 1940, in fact, the Farm Bureau was content to share credit for the system of payments to farmers with the Democrats. The conflict over the structure of administration which began in that year, however, marked a significant change in attitude toward the idea of parity and the means of its achievement. During this period, much soul-searching went on inside the department regarding the direction of agricultural policy. The term "economy of scarcity" was often heard in departmental discussions and there was uneasiness over the failure of the A.A.A. to reach down to the lower third of the farmers. Yet the Farm Security Administration was still alive and it could be said that the department's programs included something for all the nation's farmers, large and small. This ferment was an important element in the causes which led the Farm Bureau to launch its protracted assault upon the administrative system of the newer agricultural agencies.

In 1941, mainly because of Farm Bureau urgings, the Bankhead Commodity Loan Act was passed, requiring mandatory loans for "basic" commodities at 85 per cent of parity.[1] Soon thereafter the requirement was extended to cover nonbasic commodities. In 1942 the support level required was raised by legislation to 90 per cent of parity. This series of acts became the basis for the system of price supports which endured into the postwar period.

The formulation of agricultural policy now became a disputed function. No longer was the Farm Bureau willing that the administration should have a share in it. Farm Bureau influence, moreover, was now at one of its highest peaks. Much was heard of the "farm bloc" in Congress and, in fact, the measures of 1941 and 1942 were passed by means that were highly reminiscent of the days of the first agricultural bloc of the early 'twenties.[2]

These price-support measures were passed, however, not so much over opposition from the administration as independently of any aid from it. What crystallized the latent opposition was the Emergency Price Control Act of 1942. Here the Farm Bureau and the

Administration came into head-on collision over the level at which price ceilings on agricultural commodities should be placed. President Roosevelt and the administration asked that these be put at 100 per cent of parity; the Farm Bureau insisted that they be put at 110 per cent of parity.[3] Additional issues arising from wartime price control were consumer subsidies and the control of price administration; the Farm Bureau wished to keep the latter from the much-feared Office of Price Administration.

Throughout the postwar period the fundamental propositions of agricultural policy have been reëxamined in every group concerned with farm problems. The Farm Bureau has restated its program; the land grant colleges have formulated a new approach; the department has traveled far in its own reformulation. And yet the policy in force has continued to be that drawn in the early 'forties. In 1947 and 1948 Congress held extended hearings on a long-range agricultural policy. Many shades of opinion in different parts of the country were heard, but no firm conclusion emerged.

In 1948 it seemed as though a resolution of the problem had been achieved. The compromise Hope-Aiken Act of that year was regarded by some participants (including the Farm Bureau) in the long controversy as the awaited settlement on the direction of agricultural policy. The crucial issue in this act was that price supports should be flexible, that on occasion they should be permitted to sink as low as 60 per cent of parity. The part of the Farm Bureau's leadership in securing passage of this act opened a serious rift in the organization.

The outstanding achievement of the Farm Bureau during the presidency of O'Neal had been to weld the dominant economic interests of the Middle West and the South. With O'Neal working alongside Earl Smith of Illinois, the Farm Bureau had been made to appear a unity. Smith had retired in 1945, however, and at the end of 1947 O'Neal announced his own resignation. Allan Kline of Iowa became president and Romeo Short of Arkansas vice-president. The fundamental pattern of regional alliance was thus perpetuated, but the exchange in the top position actually reflected the official policy of the organization.

The issue splitting the organization was that of flexible price supports versus rigid supports at 90 per cent of parity. Kline and the

Middle Western group favored the flexible provisions of the 1948 act. The Southern—cotton—group favored the prevailing high supports, whatever the costs in regimentation. The matter reached an impasse in the 1948 convention. Although the Farm Bureau–supported act of 1948 was already on the books, the new flexible-support device was 'not yet in operation; so the matter was in one sense still pending. Moreover, the results of the national presidential election had cast a serious doubt on Farm Bureau control of its own membership. Whatever controversies may have been carried on in private rooms at the Farm Bureau convention, it is clear that no agreement was reached on this issue. As a result, the delegates were called upon to pass a remarkable resolution authorizing the board of directors to seek such amendments to the 1948 act "as may be deemed to be in the interest of farm people and the national welfare."[4] This was a striking demonstration of faith in the board's judgment. More than this, however, it was a confession of inability to resolve the conflict.[5] When the board met, the problem was discussed, but no decision was made to change the policy on flexible supports.[6]

This was the situation into which the Brannan Plan was injected. The system of price supports had grown in gradual fashion out of New Deal measures, but had been removed in recent years from the aegis of the Democratic party. The presumed stabilization of the system as a "permanent" plan had come about under the auspices of the Farm Bureau. However, the bureau itself was by no means unified behind the program contained in the act of 1948. Moreover, the administration was now in a position of strength as a result of the recent election. Thus the presentation of the Brannan Plan came at a psychological moment as an alternative to the Farm Bureau program.

The Brannan Plan came substantially as an administration measure. It was opposed not so much to anything offered by the Republicans as to the existing "farm-bloc" measures. That it was a conflict between party and pressure groups became clear when the Farm Bureau denounced the plan as an assault on the "bipartisan" farm policy.[7] On its face, the term "bipartisan" was a misnomer. The structure of price supports owed more historically to the Democratic party than to any collaboration between the two parties. Yet this was true: farm policy had been wrested out of the hands of both parties. To a considerable degree, the Farm Bureau had made good its claim of being the source of agricultural policy. Politically, this was precisely what Secretary Brannan challenged.[8]

The bitter struggle for the control of government in agriculture now shifted from the forms of administration back to policy. Even in this, however, the character of the struggle remained unchanged. The decision on policy, presumably made in passage of the 1948 act, was brought back for reconsideration. Immediately, it was evident that there were not two conflicting proposals but three: the flexible support system, the rigid support system, and the Brannan Plan. The Farm Bureau had taken its stand in favor of the first; flexible supports were the policy of the organization. With the intrusion of a different measure, presented from an external source, the whole question of organizational power was raised. What ensued was reported by the Washington correspondent of *Wallaces' Farmer and Iowa Homestead.*

The Farm Bureau is given credit for helping to line up enough Republican and Southern Democratic votes to put over the Gore bill [this would postpone the job of writing a farm law by extending the supports at 90 per cent of parity]. But why did the Bureau do it? The Gore bill asks for 90 per cent of parity. The Bureau has advocated flexible supports. By practical politicians, the Bureau is credited with some sharp maneuvering. First job Allan Kline and his folks had to do was to repair the breaches in their own ranks. Southern Bureau men did not like flexible supports.

So the Bureau came out for 90 per cent fixed supports for cotton and tobacco. That got the southern Farm Bureau men back in line.

Next job was to beat the Pace version of the Brannan plan. The Hope-Aiken law favored by the Bureau had no chance of approval in the House. But the Gore bill, extending Steagall 90 per cent supports for one year, did have a chance.

The Bureau therefore backed the Gore bill in order to beat the Pace-Brannan bill.

Then, in the Senate, the Bureau helped to beat production payments on hogs, and is working for Senate modification of the Hope-Aiken law. In conference, the Senate's preference for the Hope-Aiken bill may outweigh the House's preference for the Gore bill.

And, if the whole thing is deadlocked, that leaves the Hope-Aiken law on the books. And the Bureau favors the present act.[9]

In the outcome, a temporary compromise measure replaced the act of 1948. The Brannan Plan, however, was thus decisively beaten.

A number of things emerge from this story. The first is the great complexity of agricultural politics. This is not a game played by simple dirt farmers. Second is the continued existence of "commodityism" as an organizational problem inside the Farm Bureau. Third is the willingness of the Farm Bureau to change its own policy in order to retain control of public policy.

The question of control was crucial. The Farm Bureau had fairly clear reasons for opposing the Brannan Plan. The plan would permit fluctuations of market prices with little restriction, and thus discard the concept of parity prices. Moreover, the plan would have placed limits on the substitute payments to farmers; it was equalitarian in orientation.[10] Both reasons, however, were less important than the fact that agricultural policy had been made a party concern. Probably the Brannan Plan's immediate defect in Farm Bureau eyes was that the Farm Bureau had not been consulted in its formulation.

Thus the Farm Bureau came into open warfare with the Democratic administration. After the defeat of the Brannan Plan, Farm Bureau officials and the Secretary of Agriculture exchanged recriminations in numerous speeches.[11] The charge heard before in earlier phases of the developing hostility between the bureau and the administration was repeated, that the administration was using the administrative mechanism to influence farmers in favor of administration policy.[12] The controversy was complicated by the fact that the Farmers' Union had come to support the Brannan Plan.[13] The Farmers' Union, however, stood virtually alone. Both the National Grange and the National Council of Farmer Coöperatives followed Farm Bureau leadership.[14]

The conflict precipitated by the Brannan Plan was actually the culmination of the hostility of many years. The open break had been foreshadowed since 1942, or, indeed, since 1940, when the Farm Bureau began its campaign to reorganize the Department of Agriculture. Only the statement that agricultural policy had become a "bipartisan" matter was new. In one sense it may be said that the Farm Bureau has now traveled full circle, back to the position it occupied in the early 'twenties, when the first "agricultural bloc" was organized in the Washington office of the Farm Bureau. At that time the Farm Bureau had fashioned a political organization that cut straight across party lines and, in so doing, had come into open warfare with the dominant party, then the Republican party. The successes of the 'thirties and 'forties, however, had been achieved, as indeed had much of the Farm Bureau's organizational strength, by working with the Democratic administration on important parts of the latter's program.

Now, however, there is a difference in the situation, and an important one. The Farm Bureau of the 'fifties has become vastly more powerful than the fledgling organization of the 'twenties. Its strength and influence are not to be measured even by the great increase in membership since its first decade of existence. The Farm Bureau is now more nearly able to make good its claim of being "The Farmer's Voice" in the sense that it can nearly drown out rival farmer voices.[15] If the Farm Bureau can solve its perennial problems of "commodityism" and regionalism, there is a strong likelihood it can succeed in withholding the issues of agricultural policy from party consideration.

Granting, then, that we may well have a "bipartisan" policy in agriculture, what is its significance? First, a "bipartisan" policy is a no-party policy. That is to say, it is superior to *either* party. A Republican administration might be as unable to influence it as a Democratic administration. Second, in the existing context of political reality a "bipartisan" agricultural policy will be a Farm Bureau policy.

If a policy is "bipartisan" it is plainly elevated above partisan argument. The presumption must exist that at its base lies a fundamental consensus that is not to be questioned. Does this consensus in fact exist in regard to parity, the core of the matter? Is the concept of parity in its present highly complex form beyond criticism except by scattered discussion groups and the board of directors of the American Farm Bureau Federation?[16] This would be a simple question to answer even if parity concerned only farmers. Parity, however, is clearly a concern of every citizen in the land.[17]

13

ORGANIZATION
and MEMBERSHIP

The present is an era of organization; this is one of the clichés of our time. In almost any field, we find not one organization but many. It often appears more accurate to say that the present era is characterized by a chaos of organizations. So it seems of agriculture. To list the organizations concerned with farming and rural life today would be a formidable undertaking.[1] Even if one attempted to name only those which have a political character, uncertainty would cloud the undertaking. Few have remained wholly aloof from politics. Whether by seeking control of a state legislature or a congressional district, or merely by sending letters to Congress to ask for increased appropriations for country roads, most farm organizations have acted politically. However, farm organizations vary greatly in the degree of their political aggressiveness and effectiveness. Those which are actually influential on a large scale are few.

If the task of singling out the most powerful farm organization were presented, it would be necessary to consider each in the light of its own objectives. Granting that the real goals of each organization could be discovered, it would be necessary to construct a device for measuring the achievement of goals that differ in character. The most powerful group might well turn out to be one of the smaller organizations, such as the National Cotton Council or the National Coöperative Milk Producers' Federation. It might also develop that there are highly powerful farm organizations that we do not ordinarily recognize as such, the Bank of America, for example.

145

Here, however, the task is somewhat simpler. It is to consider the power of farm organizations whose influence is based at least in part upon membership and which exercise influence upon national policy. The three national, so-called "general" farm organizations, in terms of size, are the American Farm Bureau Federation with 1,452,210 members, the National Grange with 850,000 members, and the National Farmers' Union with 500,000.' All three operate on a national basis, although none has strength in every state. All three are heavily involved in attempting to influence the course of national policy. Since they are by profession "general" farm organizations, they are all forced to make some kind of reconciliation among the different subgroups of agriculture, both commodity and regional. Here it is clear that different policies have prevailed—or at least that different successes have been achieved—among the three. The Farm Bureau has built an alliance between the Middle West and the South. The Farmers' Union has made a similar alliance between the Great Plains and the South. The Grange pattern is less clear, but its strength is greatest in the Northeast.

In one respect this comparison is distorting. The Farm Bureau is the only one of the three that has consistently pursued this party-like strategy of regional combination. The Farmers' Union has to some degree followed a policy of building on a class basis. Its literature is filled with reference to the family farmer (as against the corporation farmer or the planter) and in a lesser degree to tenants and farm workers. Its attacks upon the Farm Bureau follow this line, as have some of its political actions, as, for example, its support of the Farm Security Administration and the Brannan Plan.

The Grange, as the inheritor of both an organization and a tradition of considerable age, is far less consciously directed toward these practical considerations of power. In fact, its preoccupation with governmental policy has only fairly recently been revived. It is not unlikely that the Grange's revival of interest in policy is due in great part to the pressure of the other groups upon the Grange. That is to say, political activity became necessary to the Grange for the welfare of the organization itself. This is true of the other two, but they reached the point of entering the political conflict earlier than the Grange made its reluctant reëntry. On this score, the Grange had a cushion of organizational security, for much of its appeal lay in ritual and lodgelike activities. For this reason and because of the sheer inertia of long life, the Grange has not been so politically aggressive, or so apt, as either of the other two.

The Grange has often placed its strength at the disposal of the Farm Bureau leadership. Frequently this has been done unwittingly, to all appearances. At times the Grange has been merely passive in situations manipulated by the Farm Bureau. Ideologically, the difference between the two has often seemed slight. Again, we may take the issues of the Farm Security Administration and the Brannan Plan as examples. It is not implied that the Grange is dominated by the Farm Bureau or that it is the latter's appendage. At times, as in the argument over the recent Granger bill (for divorce of the Extension Service from the Farm Bureau), the Grange has openly opposed the Farm Bureau. Locally, moreover, the Grange has offered effective opposition to Farm Bureau campaigns. Yet, on the whole, the Grange has been susceptible to manipulation by the Farm Bureau leadership for the latter's purposes.

For three reasons, then, it is apparent that the Farm Bureau is by far the most politically powerful of the three general farm organizations. Its membership is greatest; its pattern of regional alliance is strongest; it has been able to add Grange influence to its own. Moreover, Farm Bureau leadership has been the most skillful during the greater part of the period in which the three organizations have existed together.

In recent years a fourth organization has sometimes been presented as a "general" farm organization. This is the National Council of Farmer Coöperatives. In 1945 it claimed to represent two and a half million farmers (through the coöperatives which are pyramided into the council).³ Although this figure would seemingly overshadow the membership of other organizations, it is actually of little importance except on measures relating to coöperatives. This is not to say that the council itself is unimportant, but rather that its importance does not rest on its membership total.⁴ The council "membership" has frequently been used as a sounding board in Farm Bureau campaigns.

The commodity and other specialized farm organizations belong in a marginal area in which it is difficult to say whether or not we are dealing with farmer organizations. The National Coöperative

Milk Producers' Federation and the National Cotton Council seem at times to resemble businessmen's associations rather than farmer organizations. Yet this distinction is not entirely meaningful. Increasingly, farm organizations show business traits and business sympathies.[5]

This is evident when questions on agricultural labor arise. It was observed during the sharply ideological conflict over the Farm Security Administration. Although that campaign was directed by the Farm Bureau, auxiliary forces were contributed by the specialized groups having an interest in a cheap labor supply. The most conspicuous example was the Irrigated Cotton Growers. The entire problem of agricultural labor has increasingly placed the mark of the class struggle upon the alignments of farm organizations. Most of the issues of recent years have centered about the use and treatment of migratory labor. These conflicts have characteristically been veiled in argument over forms of administration. The pattern of alignment has been one of combinations among the Farm Bureau, commodity groups (with sugar groups being particularly conspicuous), and employer groups.[6]

It should be emphasized that there is no serious problem of rivalry between the Farm Bureau and the specialized groups. The latter tend to take a more sharply defined position than does the Farm Bureau. This is as true in matters of labor as in questions of price. This does not mean disagreement, however. The difference is in degree only, and lies in the fact that the Farm Bureau must reconcile the different claims of various producing groups within its own ranks; this necessarily results in compromise and a greater degree of temperateness in its own demands. Fundamentally, however, this compromise is not difficult, since demand for high prices can readily be generalized to accommodate most groups, as can demands for cheap labor. Since there is agreement on these, coöperation occurs naturally. The Farm Bureau, as the possessor of the experience and the pretensions in the area of general farm legislation, assumes the position of leadership.

Thus the influence of the specialized farm groups tends to line up behind that of the Farm Bureau and reinforce it. Conflict does occur at times. The opposition of Charles Holman and the milk producers to Farm Bureau policy was apparent in 1937, for example. Yet it may be hazarded that this sort of conflict will be avoided by the Farm Bureau wherever possible. Farm Bureau policy will be made to adjust to the demands of the narrower groups up to the point where these demands conflict among themselves. The Farm Bureau as an organization has little to gain and much to lose by opposing any one of the narrowly focused and powerful groups. It is not that these organizations are all part of one great super-organization; it is that on almost all large questions they agree.

	None	Farm Bureau	Grange	Special*	Farmers' Union	Other	Total†
	per cent	*per cent*	*per cent*	*per cent*	*per cent*	*per cent*	*per cent*
National total.....	70.5	17.7	3.4	4.7	2.2	4.3	102.8

BY ECONOMIC STATUS

	None	Farm Bureau	Grange	Special*	Farmers' Union	Other	Total†
High..............	49.8	30.2	4.6	9.2	5.8	7.2	106.8
Medium..........	70.9	17.9	4.2	4.3	0.9	4.0	102.2
Low..............	86.7	6.3	2.1	1.8	0.9	2.7	100.5

SOURCE: *Public Opinion 1935–1946*, edited by Hadley Cantril and prepared by Mildred Strunk (Princeton University Press), p. 5.
   * This category was "For special farmers: Dairymen's League, Poultry Association, etc."
   † The percentages total more than 100 because some respondents gave more than one answer.

It is apparent, then, that despite the multiplicity of farm organizations, the American Farm Bureau Federation holds the crucial position in farm politics. We have seen its rise to power and have traced the manner of its arrival. It remains to analyze the nature and the sources of this power. Before this can be undertaken, it is necessary to look more closely at the Farm Bureau and its organization.

The Farm Bureau is frequently referred to as an organization of "big" farmers. Usually, little evidence is given in support of the statement, other than that Farm Bureau policy in this instance or that appears to favor "big" farmers. What evidence is there to support or disprove this charge? In 1942 the Elmo Roper organization asked this question of a national cross section of farmers: "Do you belong to any farm agricultural organization?" The answers appear in the accompanying tabulation.[7] One of the first points to be observed from the table is that the membership of *any* farm organization is drawn most heavily from groups of high economic status.[8]

This is a fact worth recalling in discussions of farm organizations. The interesting point here, however, is the degree to which Farm Bureau membership is weighted by farmers of high economic status.[*]

An older set of data is from a study made by the national Farm Bureau of its own membership. This was based on a questionnaire sent out in 1936 to 5,000 members, of whom 1,844 replied. The material is open to some question, but, since it shows no great disagreement with what is otherwise known, it is worth considering. As reported in the pages of *Nation's Agriculture*, the findings included the following: (1) 83.9 per cent of the respondents were owner-operators, and only 57.2 per cent of all farmers were owner-operators; (2) the average respondent owned 299.8 acres while the average farmer owner owned only 121.8 acres; (3) the average respondent operated 367 acres as against a national average of 154.8 acres; (4) the respondents' average land value was $17,716 compared with the national average of $4,823; (5) the value of the respondents' livestock averaged $2,639, whereas the average value nationally per farm was less than a third of this figure; (6) the value of farm equipment on respondents' farms averaged $1,618, while that of all farms was $515; (7) for every 100 farms reported in the survey, there were 120 automobiles, 68 tractors, and .39 trucks; for every 100 of all farms there were 66 automobiles, 15 tractors, and 14 trucks; (8) the average gross income of Farm Bureau farms reported on was $4,510; the average income in the entire country was $1,195; (9) the average Farm Bureau family had lived on the same farm for 22.7 years and had five members.

The official magazine commented on these findings as follows: "The information thus obtained confirms our previous idea that Farm Bureau members as a class are much above the average on almost any basis of comparison that you wish to suggest . . ."; and "The returns prove what we have felt certain of for a long time, and that is that the Farm Bureau group is truly a group of superior farmers. They are the leaders in thousands of rural communities."[10]

The figures are averages, which is not the most satisfactory method of presenting data. The questionnaire, moreover, was made when the organization was less than a fourth of its present size. Yet they do support the general conclusion drawn from the *Fortune* survey. They also give the Farm Bureau's own picture of itself—a picture which has sometimes been presented quite differently, though in far less detail.

It may be concluded that, so far as the character of membership is the test, the Farm Bureau is the organization if not of the "big" farmers, at least of the more prosperous farmers. This is not to say that small farmers do not belong to it. There have been reports of tenants being "herded" into the Farm Bureau.[11] Moreover, the "big farmer" is a nebulous figure. Yet it is clear that the Farm Bureau member is indeed well favored by Providence.

The geographical distribution of Farm Bureau membership is a factor of primary importance. The national organization, in fact, is framed on a regional pattern. The territory of the Farm Bureau is divided into four regions: the Middle West, with a total of 719,725 members in twelve states; the South, with 474,362 members in thirteen states (and Puerto Rico); the Northeast, with 143,065 in nine states; and the West, with 115,058 in ten states.[12] Thus it is abundantly evident that Farm Bureau leadership has succeeded in building an alliance of Middle Western and Southern elements. However, the farm bureaus in New York and California are two important outlying strongholds. In terms of sheer size of membership, the New York organization ranks third after Illinois and Iowa.[13] Some state farm bureaus are conspicuously weak: in the Middle West, South Dakota and Nebraska; in the West, Montana, Oregon, and Washington; in the South, Virginia. In the Northeast, Rhode Island has no affiliate of the national federation.[14]

Since 1939, membership has increased impressively, but the gain in the South has been the most striking. The Western region, too, has grown at a rapid rate, but obviously it cannot hope to rival either the Middle West or the South in size.[15]

Membership, however, is only one of the indices of an organization. We are increasingly aware that an organization is something other than the totality of its members. Not only may members join for different purposes but the interplay of their aims may result in an organizational objective that differs from that of the majority of the members. Moreover, as the organization is formalized, the leadership develops interests and objectives of its own. There is no assurance that the interests and goals of the leaders will coincide with those of the members. Indeed, it is not difficult to find examples of conflict.[16] It is necessary, then, to turn to the organization itself.

The basic unit of Farm Bureau organization is the county Farm Bureau. In 1946 there were 2,111 organized counties.[17] A well-organized county Farm Bureau is likely to have subordinate local units. Only nine states in 1946 did not have such subunits. The local organizations vary in character, but many of them are rather informal, consisting of discussion groups which meet in homes. In twenty-eight states they have been increasing in number. Ohio has 1,500, Kansas and Minnesota each have more than 1,200, and four other states each have more than 500 of these groups. Despite the increasing size of the federation, the center of gravity in the local organization is likely to remain in the county bureau. The reason is that the county is the smallest unit of rural government in most parts of the country, and the Farm Bureau has consciously made its organization parallel to that of the formal government.

Although there is a great deal of variation from county to county and more from state to state, the county is generally the vital unit for the Farm Bureau. In some states the county farm bureaus own their own buildings. Some are quite impressive, providing housing for governmental officers as well as for officials of the organizations. Elsewhere, the county Farm Bureau may be little more than an activity carried on by the county agent. The well-organized county Farm Bureau, however, is likely to employ full-time personnel. Thus, 293 out of 386 Middle Western county organizations had full-time paid staffs,[18] whose work was supplemented by the efforts of volunteers.

Business activities—coöperatives of various kinds—are conducted through the county farm bureaus in some states. According to the 1946 survey, only twenty-three states reported no business activities in their county organizations. For the rest, the county bureaus are preoccupied with organization work and matters of quasi-public concern. Their primary objectives are to attract and hold the interest of members and to secure new members. The county bureau arranges social events and meetings, and may publish a paper.[19] Its quasi-public activities include assisting in formation of a rural electrification coöperative, influencing the county government to provide roads, arranging for the housing and policing of (and sometimes the procuring of) migrant farm labor, and coöperating with the county agent in his educational efforts.

Activities of county bureaus vary not only in character but in scale. This is clear from the differences in the amount of money available. Dues paid by the individual family range from $2 to $20. Of these amounts, $1 is sent to the national organization. The remainder is divided between state and county in different ways. In Illinois, the largest Farm Bureau state, $10 remained in the county Farm Bureau and $4.50 went to the state organization in 1946.[20] It is a matter of policy that the county bureau should retain the largest share of the dues. Even when, as at present, the national federation recommends large dues, it apparently does not seek great increase in the amount sent to the national headquarters. The relative share of the state organizations does not rise with the increase in dues. This restraint on the part of the higher levels of the organization results from the fact that the greater part of the organization work is conducted through the county bodies. This is a fact of no slight importance.

Repeated reference has been made to the use of the time and efforts of county agents in organizing county farm bureaus. This has been of vital importance to the organization, and even in recent years the practice has not ceased,[21] although Farm Bureau spokesmen have minimized it in recent testimony.[22] Considering the present size and resources of the organization as a whole, there would seem to be some justification for such minimization. It is highly probable that the Farm Bureau has in most places passed the point where the services of county agents are essential. However, great local differences exist. Thus the county agents are more important to county farm bureaus in parts of the South than they are in efficient and well-established organizations in the Middle Western states.

This raises a point which has been touched before, that the county agent "runs" the county Farm Bureau. This remark has been associated almost wholly with the South. It appears also to have been associated with poor communities. It is certainly not true in the states in which the Farm Bureau is strongest, as, for example, in Illinois and California. In neither of these states is the Farm Bureau dependent on county agents for organizers, and it never has been. A certain contempt is reserved in Farm Bureau circles for organizations "run" by county agents of the Extension Service.[23] Situations probably do exist in which the county agent and the county Farm Bureau are virtually synonymous, but their number may be expected to decline.[24]

At the next level, moving upward, we find forty-seven state Farm Bureau federations (and one in Puerto Rico). The pattern is roughly similar to that traced in the county organizations. A few of the state federations have directly owned businesses; most do not.[25] Some organization work is carried out at this level, though far less than in the counties. The most consistent activity, however, is frankly legislative. All but three of the state federations reported this as a purpose.[26] Other functions include education, the improvement of farm-labor relations, sponsoring of coöperatives for marketing, auditing of coöperatives, coöperative purchasing of farm supplies, and the operation of insurance, canning, and retail machinery companies.[27]

The state federations frequently own their own buildings, which are centers for substantial paid staffs. The Illinois Agricultural Association employed ninety-four and the California Farm Bureau Federation sixty-four in 1946.[28] Regionally, the Middle Western state federations have the largest staffs.[29]

At the national level, the American Farm Bureau Federation takes on some of the character of a holding company. Structurally, it is a federation of federations, and thus is far removed from the grass roots which it frequently invokes. Its staff is not impressively large, considering the size and influence of the organization. It included in 1946 fourteen professional workers and fourteen clerical workers at Chicago, the headquarters; eight professional and technical workers and two clerical workers in Washington, D.C.; and eight workers at Mount Morris, Illinois, where *Nation's Agriculture* is published. In addition, there were two employees of the Farm Bureau auxiliary, the Associated Women.[30] This total of forty-eight paid workers of the national federation is not a large number compared to the nine hundred eighteen full-time workers employed by all components of the organization.[31]

The activities of the national organization, although on a grander scale than the local and state organizations, are comparable. There is the same heavy concern with maintenance and promotion of membership. In 1946 five of the fourteen professional workers at Chicago were organizers. In fact, the estimate was made that 45 per cent of all time available to the Farm Bureau went into membership and organization work.[32] The national organization has eight departments: legislative, publicity and information, organization, research, legal, international affairs, rural youth, and commodity. This last department has attached to it committees on livestock, fruit and vegetables, poultry, dairy, and field crops.[33] The relative importance of the two offices of the federation may be judged from the fact that the Chicago establishment is relegated to the direction of the secretary-treasurer. The major focus of Farm Bureau activities is in Washington. This results necessarily from the legislative (and administrative) preoccupation of the organization.

There is no way of measuring the extent of Farm Bureau intervention in public affairs. The Washington office formerly kept a record of its legislative activities: in 1937 it had twenty-seven legislative projects; in 1939, forty-two such projects.[34] A project may be a planned campaign, with research material gathered from the Department of Agriculture and from Farm Bureau investigations in the field, and with elaborately organized testimony reiterated by as many as twenty state Farm Bureau heads. Alternatively, it may be no more than a letter from the national Farm Bureau president to a congressional committee. Quite as important may be a casual word dropped to a friendly congressman by telephone. Even less discernible are the calls and quiet pressures on administrative officers which sometimes achieve results comparable to those from appearances before congressional committees.[35]

The customary spokesman for the federation is its president. His skill in testifying before a committee is an important element in the successes which are achieved. O'Neal was probably as competent in his use of the combination of flattery and veiled threats that is common in committee rooms as any witness who has regularly appeared in recent decades. The president is assisted by the legislative representative of the organization. These two may be joined by the vice-president, the federation counsel, the secretary-treasurer, and the board of directors. These may be reinforced on special occasions by state Farm Bureau presidents who are not members of the national board. All these officers are politically influential in their own right and are so recognized in Congress.

Although the president of the national federation is the most conspicuous figure in the Farm Bureau organization, he is subject to control by the board of directors, an elective body chosen in the convention on a basis of regional representation. At present it has twenty-one members. The board meets four times a year. Its most important meeting is that which follows the annual convention; here the resolutions which have been passed by the convention are elaborated in specific terms. As in the flexible-supports issue at the 1948 convention, the board may make the actual decision at this time. When the board is not in session, an executive committee, consisting of four or five board members, has authority. It seems not unlikely that this executive committee is the actual controlling body of the entire organization.

Since the federation has nearly a million and a half members, most of whom may be presumed to be contributing $1.00 each (formerly 50 cents) to the national organization through their local bodies, a comfortable fund is available for national operations. Dues, in fact, seem to be nearly the only source of money on which reliance is placed.[36]

The national convention is, in theory, the body which determines policy for the forthcoming year. However, the convention of the federation is in no way different from large conventions held by other organizations: it is a mass meeting to generate enthusiasm, not a deliberative body. A small number of voting delegates are present to pass the official resolutions and to elect officers, but these are generally lost among the thousands who come for the excitement of the convention atmosphere.[37] Speeches are delivered by well-known national figures, usually chosen for their friendliness to the organization. Community singing ("old-time religion"), a "parade of the states," memorial services, presentation of awards, all provide the show which is expected of a large convention.

This is not to say, however, that nothing of importance happens during a convention. The regions caucus at an early stage and elect their own directors; the commodity groups get together and reach decisions on their own problems. Most important, the leaders of the various regions and interests meet in hotel rooms and decide the vital questions before the organization.[38] The comparison with party conventions has some merit. The principal difference seems to be that an American Farm Bureau Federation convention is more sedate and less susceptible to stampeding by dissident groups on the floor. It is likely to be a very well-run affair, with decisions prepared away from the public eye. Officers tend to be elected—and, in recent years, reëlected—unanimously.[39]

Obviously, the convention offers little opportunity for enforcing any concept of democratic responsibility, whatever the terms in which it is praised as an exemplification of grass-roots democracy. The fact of indirect election practiced through the convention together with the absence of any party organization should dissipate this illusion. However, it should be recalled that decision making is, after all, not the function of a convention.[40]

Somewhat the same process goes on in the state organizations, although their number makes generalization dangerous. The studied, formal decentralization of the national organization has resulted in opposition of several state farm bureaus to the position of the national federation. Thus, the Georgia federation opposed the national organization on the issue of flexible supports. The Vermont and Ohio federations came to the support of the Farm Security Administration. The latter two state organizations, in fact, have frequently been thorns in national federation flesh. Yet it is significant that this sort of difficulty is not serious. State federations do not take recalcitrant positions often, and the Vermont and Ohio groups are readily isolated. The American Farm Bureau Federation has achieved remarkable success in building a unified organization which gives little embarrassment to its leaders on a pattern of geographical decentralization.

14

The RATIONALE of ORGANIZATION

At this point it is necessary to seek meanings, to ask, in the words of Theodore Schultz, what "we have done to ourselves in the political structure." The complex questions that arise are important, not only for the intrinsic importance of agricultural policy and organization, but, perhaps, for the windows that their correct answers may open on the nature of our society.

The area in which these questions lie may be approached by considering several explanations of developments which have been traced in earlier chapters. The first interpretation is that one agency of the federal government, the Agricultural Extension Service, has created a pressure group which serves to extract appropriations from Congress for that agency and to cripple or destroy its rivals. The Farm Bureau Federation has, indeed, been partly the creation of the Extension Service. It has sought increased Extension appropriations; it has fought consistently to enhance the functions of Extension at the expense of its rivals. Repeated charges have been made in some localities that the county agents dominate and "run" the county farm bureaus. Instances of such domination are relatively few, however, and probably transitory. Many more voices, both within and outside the Extension organization, have been raised to say that the function of the county agents is merely to perform chores for the Farm Bureau. The charge of domination, therefore, cannot be taken seriously. It fails, moreover, to provide any adequate explanation for the great strength and influence prevailing at the topmost level of the federation. At this level, the Farm Bureau

158

is not paralleled by any influential Extension Service direction. While the federation is powerful in Washington, the Extension Service there tends to be merely a service branch of the whole agency. "Decentralization" has operated to opposite effects in the two organizations.

In an even more serious way, the view that the county agent "runs" the Farm Bureau results in a distortion of the entire picture. It is true that the American Farm Bureau Federation is a pressure group, but this is only one aspect of its significance. The federation is considerably more than the groups of officers who appear before congressional committees. It is not simply a million and a half farmers in search of federal aid.

The second interpretation of the Farm Bureau is that of a weapon in the hands of a few mercenary officers. Thus it is implied that by building an organization of farmers in politically important localities the national federation officers have acquired an irresponsible power which they offer to use for a price. The somewhat lurid charge of "influence for sale" has on occasion been leveled at the Farm Bureau.¹ Again, it is possible to cite instances in which this has occurred. In 1933, two high officials of the national organization were exposed as having sought to peddle the influence of the federation to business interests in return for fees to be pocketed by the officials. They were removed from office, although somewhat tardily for the good of the organization's name.² Doubts have also been cast upon Farm Bureau activities in connection with projects for developing Muscle Shoals.³ Nevertheless, it would be a mistake to place great emphasis on these episodes in Farm Bureau history. There is no evidence that the board of directors was not genuinely disturbed by the apparent derelictions of the officials involved. If the organization seriously engaged in mercenary activity of this character, the Farm Bureau would be unlikely to have had the success and the consistency in policy which in fact it has had. Moreover, it is unnecessary for pressure groups of a business character to buy Farm Bureau support with money. This support is obtainable either because of ideological sympathy or, more importantly, because pressure groups operate on a logrolling basis. The price exacted by the Farm Bureau is far more likely to be support from business groups in Farm Bureau legislative campaigns than money for the officers' pockets.

The third interpretation of the Farm Bureau to be considered here is much the most important. It is that the Farm Bureau is essentially the tool of large business and industrial interests. The Farm Bureau, according to this view, is simply one of many disguises in which the dominant nonagricultural interests of the country appear for the furtherance of their own purposes. Many points can be made in support of this theory.' The widespread participation of business groups in the founding of the Farm Bureau movement has been traced in these pages. Farm Bureau action in legislative affairs not strictly related to farm matters has frequently coincided with the desires of business groups, particularly in connection with questions involving labor.' Thus, the Farm Bureau has taken part of the credit for passage of the Taft-Hartley Act.' And, from time to time, Farm Bureau leaders have made speeches hostile to organized labor.' There is, with little doubt, a strong affinity between the standpoint of the Farm Bureau and of such groups as the National Association of Manufacturers and the Chamber of Commerce. However, is this affinity and the frequent concurrence of policy sufficient evidence for the view that the Farm Bureau is a political device of large industrial and commercial interests?

It seems doubtful. In the first place, this view underestimates the character and degree of power which the Farm Bureau has developed independent of industrial and commercial sources, and, indeed, is partially contradicted by that just previously considered (that the Farm Bureau power is mercenary), with which it is sometimes linked. Second, this view vaguely implies some superorganization of business heads which gives subtle direction to many spokesmen, of which the Farm Bureau would be one. The difficulties of forming and of maintaining such a superorganization would be huge. Third, the Farm Bureau sometimes appears in actual conflict even with business organizations with which it is assumed to be meshed. In 1935, when certain Agricultural Adjustment Act amendments favored by the Farm Bureau were being considered in Congress, not only the Chamber of Commerce and the National Association of Manufacturers but representatives of organizations supposedly close to the Farm Bureau—General Mills, Swift and Company, and the National Canners' Association—were in direct conflict with the Farm Bureau.'

These interpretations, then, are inadequate to explain the course of events which has been traced here. The last view examined, however, does raise, in however crude a fashion, a fundamental issue of interpretation. The observation has recently been made that there are two different interpretations of social stratification and political power: one emphasizing the political media of power and the other emphasizing the economic bases of organization. Although these emphases rest on different aspects of society and give rise to different types of theory, the feeling persists that they relate to many of the same phenomena and are in some sense rivals. In fact, much of the controversy about social questions in Europe during the past one hundred years has been pitched in the key of just this conflict. Nevertheless, the sense also remains that the two do not necessarily conflict, that to accept the insights from the one need not preclude acceptance of the insights from the other. The problem is to relate the two.

We have seen that there are good grounds for believing that the American Farm Federation is founded upon one stratum (or perhaps a group of strata) of farmers. Our initial problem, then, is to seek to understand why this is so and how it came to be.

In general terms, it may be said that there is a rationale of organization.[9] Whatever the purpose of the organization, or, more correctly, the presumedly shared objectives of those belonging to it, the primary problem is to maintain the existence and well-being of the organization itself. For example, an organization which wins its objective of the moment but fails to collect a sufficient amount in dues to pay its officers and staff may endanger its own life. It is reasonable that the welfare of the organization should come first, before any attempt is made to fight external battles. Otherwise, the battles fought for external objectives may be lost. However, this may lead to compromise and change of the presumed objectives. It may also lead to apparently irrelevant preoccupations. The current "business" activities of the state farm bureaus are examples of the former; the "social" affairs conducted among the Farm Bureau's Associated Women are examples of the latter. Both types of activity tend to strengthen the organization and to cause adherence of members, although they have little to do with the legislative objectives with which the leadership is primarily concerned.

In the simplest terms, an organization unifies—organizes—a group of individuals. In a voluntary association, however, this unification or organization must be preceded by a process of selection according to some principle. The principle may be vague; indeed, in some associations it is merely good fellowship. Typically, it will be most vague in the early life of the organization when members are being greedily sought. The process of selection should not be thought of as consisting only of a set of exclusive rules. The external policies of the organization at any given point will serve to winnow the prospective membership. Thus, a "patriotic" society whose actions are characterized by racial intolerance will hardly attract Negro applicants.

What has been the Farm Bureau's principle of selection? What is its potential constituency, the body of individuals that, completely organized, would make it complete? Superficially, the answer is that the Farm Bureau is a general farm organization. It seeks farmers as members. However, there is reason to believe that the principle of selection is narrower than this. If this were the actual selective principle, some kind of settlement of two types of conflict would be implied: the conflict between different commodity and regional groups, and the conflict between large and small farmers. As we have seen, the Farm Bureau has worked for reconciliation among commodity groups and among regional groups, particularly between Middle Western and Southern regional groups. On the second score, however, it has not sought to reconcile the needs of large and small farmers, commercial and subsistence farmers, rich and poor. Quite the contrary, the conflict between large and small farmers is in no slight degree the product of the Farm Bureau's rise to power.

How has the principle come to be drawn in just this way? An organization has need of internal agreement—not merely the appearance but its reality. Certainly this is a characteristic of any organization that engages in struggles with external forces. Accordingly, an effective organization can be built upon a narrow base more readily than upon a wide one. A political party, whose task it is to secure a majority of all those voting, is the most difficult kind of an organization to frame. An organization in which the conflicts may be resolved by suppression is (where the means for this are available) the simplest. There is strong temptation to solve the problem of building unity in just this way. However, such actions in a voluntary organization result in the departure of those who inevitably have suffered from this suppression. Quite as important is the effect of decisions arrived at, even by majority vote. As time goes on, an increasing number of decisions are taken which alienate increasing numbers. The effect here is felt not so much in terms of lost members as in the loss of potential members, in the reduction of the original constituency. The organization may well grow, but its potential size is reduced. In other words, the tendency of organization is that its principle of selection becomes narrower. Since this process of narrowing necessarily takes place from some starting point, that starting point has peculiar importance.

The formation of the Farm Bureau was largely the work of county Extension agents emerging from the pioneer efforts of Seaman A. Knapp. His demonstration method concentrated on the most competent farmers. There were seemingly good reasons for this. By convincing the leading, that is to say, the most prosperous, farmers of each community, he hoped that the lessons would be taken to heart not only by the men on whose farms the demonstrations were made but also by the other farmers. The "principle of leadership" remains one of the central tenets of Extension Service teaching methods. This, indeed, may be an economical use of teaching experts, but it has resulted in giving special attention to those already favored in education, intelligence, and, perhaps, good fortune. Thus, so far as the lessons of the county agents have been successful, they have widened the existing gap between the successful and the unsuccessful.

Another characteristic of the Knapp methods has become more apparent in results as time has passed. The technical farming problems to which they were applied were principally production problems. Gradually, these were extended to include the more general problems of commercial producers, the purchase of proper fertilizers under favorable conditions, the formation of coöperatives for marketing, and so on. The tendency has been to cast the partially commercial producers in the same group with subsistence farmers. In the most dramatic instance, this grouping appears today as a contest between corporation farms and family farms, although this is but one phase of the difference.

In one sense, the organizations that were nurtured for the excellent purpose of widespread improvement of farming methods were an aspect of a movement that was sharpening the class distinctions within agriculture. The county farm bureaus were organized originally for the purpose of guaranteeing bands of disciples through whom the county agents could disseminate their gospel. The efforts of the county agents in their first decade were concentrated upon building these local organizations. The agents' success—or at least their hope of extensive success—seemed to depend on the degree to which organizations were created to make their words resound. As the work advanced, the motive of acquiring financial support through such local organizations was added. It is a matter of record that the federal government gave not only informal support to this, but, after passage of the Smith-Lever Act, formal support as well.[10]

It should be clear that all this was done with the greatest good will and with no intention that the rather faint lines of social stratification in agriculture should be made more distinct. This is true even of the substantial support given by business firms and industries which had felt the attack of a true agrarian mass movement, the Populist revolt. Yet it was but natural that, because of fears surviving from that twilight episode of the nineteenth century, business groups should lend assistance to the elements of the farm population which seemed to offer the least hostility to business. These elements, again, were the most prosperous and the most successful. Perhaps some half-instinctive motivation was at work here—a desire to educate the erstwhile menacing agrarians in the ways of success, and in return to escape the heedless wrath of embattled farmers. It is very doubtful whether the long-term effects were foreseen. Yet business groups supported both the Extension Service and the Farm Bureau at their very beginning.

The part played by educators was important at the beginning of the current era, before the farm bureaus began to federate; but, until very recently, college leaders seem not to have appreciated the significance of their political involvement. The Farm Bureau federations quickly reduced education to an incidental feature of their own programs, but most of the colleges have been satisfied to continue the association, apparently for the gains, real or illusory, in appropriations derived from a powerful pressure group ally. The costs are incalculable; they are to be measured in terms of blindness within the colleges and suspicion of their integrity from without. When even so friendly an observer as Russell Lord, himself a former county agent, can say, "It surpasses understanding how completely insensitive most Land Grant College graduates were to the wide-spread spectacle of a grinding rural poverty and the degradation of rural labor,"[11] the suspicion seems not wholly unjustified. It is rather strange that an organization fed in part by education, with its presumed idealism, should develop on the principle of selection we have seen in the American Farm Bureau Federation.

Another problem appears in the conflict between large and small farmers. Since the gap between them is not wide, it is difficult to discover much reason for the conflict. One might rather expect that the two groups would be indifferent to each other. Yet, as with the Farm Security Administration, the Farm Bureau has acted as the poor farmer's antagonist.

One of the elements of an organization's effectiveness is size of constituency. Even the Communist parties, which restrict the inner core of membership, seek a mass base. They try to establish them-selves as the parties of the working class. Their actions are made in the name of the human race. Similarly, the Farm Bureau Federation, although it has excluded, or has failed to act for, many farmer groups, yet claims to be the voice of the farmer and seeks a monopoly of organization in agriculture. Other farm organizations, even those which organize groups in effect rejected by the Farm Bureau, seem to be its rivals. Thus, while its actual constituency has been narrowed by an understandable process, the Farm Bureau still has a need to prevent that narrowing from proceeding to extremes (witness the recent efforts to reconcile regional differences on flexible supports).

The result is that the Farm Bureau has been antagonistic to the Farmers' Union. It has, on the whole, been tolerant toward the Grange, since the latter has frequently served its purposes, although doubtless many Farm Bureau leaders would prefer that there be only one farm organization. The Farm Bureau has been particularly alert to any budding organization of farmers built around the func-tions of governmental services, as with A.A.A. committeemen and Soil Conservation districts. The Farm Bureau's own manner of development has not been forgotten.

Thus the Farm Bureau, like most organizations, is jealous. It seeks to destroy the basis of its rivals' power and to maintain its own.

15

DECENTRALIZATION

One of the ideas most frequently encountered in agricultural politics is decentralization. This too infrequently analyzed idea is commonly used in a manner which implies that it has an intimate and self-evident relation to democracy. In one form or another, it is used as a touchstone in almost every controversy over farm organization, the administration of public policy, or the structure of power in agricultural affairs. It is important not merely because it is in high favor among farm leaders, but because it is in fact one of the keys to understanding the system of power which has been built.

Decentralization has a variety of meanings. At the most general level, it is one form of the concept of devolution. Geographical devolution, that is, decentralization, is most familiar here, but the other major form, functional devolution, has gained wide acceptance among farm spokesmen. This appears in the unstated but implicit belief that agricultural legislation and administration are the concerns of farmers only. Stated thus bluntly, the idea is absurd; anything that affects the price or supply of food and clothing is certainly a matter of general concern. In fact, however, the idea is rarely stated thus bluntly and the insistence that farmers should make decisions on farm affairs enjoys much respect. A different but related belief is that only farmers are competent to decide on agricultural matters. Congressional committees insist on hearing from real "dirt farmers" on involved economic questions, and the Department of Agriculture has a definite preference for employing people with farming backgrounds, even where the tasks require technical competence in law or statistics.

166

The attempt to isolate segments of public policy for decision by those most directly affected is common in American politics and is a general problem. Geographical decentralization, however, is peculiarly associated with agricultural affairs. The strength of its hold today can be explained in part historically. Many of those who give decentralization first importance as a political concept look back to the time when the nation was predominantly agricultural and most farming was of the subsistence variety. In the time of John Taylor, local problems were often the important political problems, and it was possible to envisage a society of loosely federated local communities having little need for common action. To imply today that local problems are the only important problems, however, would be absurd. Yet the idea of decentralization frequently seems to carry this implication.

The idea has a deceptively simple air. Organization of farmers and administration of government should be taken down to the grass roots, to "the real people." Perhaps there is a suggestion here of that assumption of moral superiority which Jefferson expressed: "Those who labor in the earth are the chosen people of God." Yet it is fairly evident that this is not the core of the concept. Its essential meaning seems to lie closer to the concept of direct democracy. If direct democracy in which the many make the actual decisions of government is the goal, decentralization has a certain relevance. Discussion and debate are possible only in small groups. The merits and defects of a political officer or candidate can be known better if he is a neighbor than if he is a stranger. These arguments have some value, but they are hardly central.

Several other elements are suggested in current discussions of decentralization. The most common is that administrative officers who make decisions in far-off Washington tend to lose sight of the actual conditions in which their decisions are applied. This argument probably rests on the fact that to many people national problems appear unreal. Moreover, it is true that some administrators seem to forget that they are dealing with human beings.

Closely related to this idea is the belief that anyone who exercises authority from a distance of many miles is somehow irresponsible. This is a serious charge. What is its merit? At the very outset it is necessary to ask, responsibility to whom? If it is responsibility to a particular locality, there can be little doubt that administration or governing from a distance is likely to mean a decrease in responsibility, since the distant officer will have a responsibility to other localities as well. Yet beyond this question lies another which is more important. What is the proper unit to which responsibility is to be related? The extreme position on this question would be that responsibility is exclusively to the individual. This may reach an ultimate position of anarchism. Certainly, it is not without interest that some of the outstanding statements of anarchism have had an agrarian origin. Yet if this rejection of government is ignored, what basis is there for choosing the neighborhood, the locality, the county, the state, or the nation? All are in some sense abstractions, and it becomes necessary to seek elsewhere for the basis of choice.

A geographical basis is only one of many possible bases of establishing units to which governmental responsibility is owed. Occupational, racial, and religious bases are equally conceivable. Any one of these would to some extent cut across geographical lines. Thus the problem is capable of being made almost infinitely complex. However, it happens to be true that all these possible dimensions of social difference are not equally important. It may be doubted whether the geographical dimension is intrinsically the most important. The test that seems important here is this: What are the probable effects, in terms of these other dimensions, of defining the units to which responsibility is paid on different geographical lines, local, state, regional, or national?

The classical American discussion of the problem appears in Number 10 of *The Federalist*. While this relates in its context to the large society of the nation, the principal stated applies equally here.

The smaller the society, the fewer probably will be the distinct parties and interests composing it: the fewer the distinct parties and interests, the more frequently will a majority be found of the same party; and the smaller the number of individuals composing a majority, and the smaller the compass within which they are placed, the more easily will they concert and execute their plans of oppression. Extend the sphere, and you take in a greater variety of parties and interests; you make it less probable that a majority of the whole will have a common motive to invade the rights of other citizens; or if such a common motive exists, it will be more difficult for all who feel it to discover their own strength, and to act in unison with each other.

Thus, on whatever dimension we may choose, a process of decentralization is likely to result in a narrowing of the basis of control. The particular basis may, indeed, vary from locality to locality, but within any particular unit the "distinct parties and interests" which vie for supremacy will be fewer than if decentralization had not taken place.

This, however, is not the end of the story. Decentralization does not mean renunciation of larger organization. It tends to become, rather, the basis for a federal form of large-scale organization. As the leaders or representatives of local units are brought together in a larger organization, a process similar to that noted by *The Federalist* is intensified to the degree that intermediate stages of federalization are inserted. This has been made particularly clear in discussions of corporation finance. Through the phenomenon of "pyramiding," a modest investment can be made to control a large empire of small operating companies through intermediary holding companies. A similar process can be applied in the political sphere. This process in theory is one of building on majority control. As in the corporate sphere, however, it is in practice rarely necessary at any one stage to have an absolute majority in order to dominate at that level.

Thus, decentralization under contemporary conditions is likely to lead to a pattern of domination based upon a narrow constituency. It should be clear that decentralization would not have this effect if there were no "distinct parties and interests" in a given locality.[1] This condition was implied by John Taylor in the early part of the nineteenth century, and, in fact, during his time it was just conceivable that it could be realized. The nation would have become a thoroughly decentralized congeries of self-sufficient communities each consisting of equal and independent farmers. Such a condition and such a development are unthinkable today. Decentralization today is apt to mean just the opposite of what some enthusiasts hope from it, domination in the interests of a small group.

In actual farm politics, one organization, the American Farm Bureau Federation, has succeeded in establishing itself in a position of great power. Some of the elements of its strength have little to do with its own internal organization. Its competence in securing the acquiescence and even complicity of other farm organizations is an example. Yet it is significant that the Farm Bureau has formed an independently influential organization that is somewhat narrowly based and which is, in outline, a federation of federations of small local units. In this instance, federalism has meant decentralization, and the Farm Bureau claim that its primary organization lies at the grass roots is true. The charge sometimes made that the Farm Bureau does not speak for the farmer is not wholly meaningful. "The farmer" is an abstraction. However, the question, for *what farmers* does the Farm Bureau speak, is highly meaningful. The Farm Bureau, in the words of its own publication, is an "organization of superior farmers." Moreover, the record of its actions shows that it has served as the spokesman of these "superior farmers." Thus, the narrowed basis of Farm Bureau organization approaches one of *class* within agriculture.[2]

It should be evident that the key to Farm Bureau policy is its own organizational power. This has determined not only the policy followed in its external affairs but the form of its internal organization as well. Decentralization—building on a basis of small localized groups—has permitted a minimizing of the number of "distinct parties and interests" in its ranks. In itself, decentralization has permitted the formation of small majorities which may be pyramided into an apparently unified power easily exercised by a small group of national leaders who have arrived at their positions through the stages of state and national federations. So far as leader selection is concerned, moreover, there is even a regional stage.

Since the basis of narrowing the constituency of the Farm Bureau is one of class rather than of producer groups, it is clear that local bureaus will show considerable diversity on the latter score. A cotton group will appear as the dominant group in a cotton area, a dairy group in a dairy area, a livestock group in a livestock area. The Farm Bureau leadership has accepted the costs of this diversity. However, these costs have not been great. State farm bureaus have seldom opposed the national organization, and the conflict of interests between commodity groups has been minor and transitory. It is a type of controversy readily adapted to settlement by bargaining and logrolling among a few leaders. Thus, support for a labor policy desired by Southern or California interests can quite easily be exchanged for support of a price policy desired by Middle Western groups. The two policies do not conflict and, while the one side to the bargain may gain nothing from the other's policy which it agrees to support, neither does it suffer any loss. The result is that the national organization adopts both policies. This would appear to be the solution to the seeming paradox that, although the great center of Farm Bureau organization is in the Middle West, the Farm Bureau consistently follows a policy on matters of farm labor that benefits plantations and corporation farms in other parts of the country. Any opposition to this policy would have to come on a class basis, and the Farm Bureau organization has been formed in a way which makes this impossible.

So far as the organization of the Farm Bureau itself is concerned, then, decentralization has been the actual policy followed, and it has provided the means by which groups of farmers, diverse among themselves in some respects but similar in the important respect of class, have been unified in a national organization. Selection of the class basis of organization was somewhat of a historical accident, but, once chosen, the class basis was inevitably intensified. The effect of decentralization has been to reinforce that intensification.

Decentralization as a Farm Bureau slogan, however, has had an additional meaning, distinct from that which applies to its own organization. This is decentralization of the agencies of the federal government. From 1940 onward the Farm Bureau has sought to dismantle all "action" agencies possessing administrative structures in which there is a hierarchical flow of responsibility to the Secretary of Agriculture. This campaign culminated in a demand that the work of these agencies be placed in the hands of the state Extension services, which would be supported by a system of grants-in-aid. This is the meaning of decentralization as it is most frequently used by Farm Bureau spokesmen.

This form of decentralization is quite different from that applied by the Farm Bureau in its own organization. While the scheme of decentralization existing in the Farm Bureau permits a strong leadership at the top, the plan advocated for the governmental agencies would effectively block the national administrative direction of the agencies. The function of the Washington office would become one of passing out appropriated funds for the state organizations to spend. This function would, moreover, be substantially divorced from control of the spending. Not only would it result in forty-eight different programs, as Secretary Wickard observed, but it would introduce a system of administrative responsibility entirely different from that which now prevails in most of the "action" programs. Administrative responsibility under such a plan of decentralization would be owed to some authority in the states and would not flow upward to Washington, except in a highly attenuated fashion.

What power, under such a plan, could be expected to exercise authority in any given state? It would be that power which is dominant in the state. We are brought back to the same set of considerations which applied to the organization of the Farm Bureau. The effect of decentralization would be to permit wide diversity among the states. It would reduce the constituency to which the political head of the programs would be answerable. Moreover, it would give additional resources to the locally dominant groups. It would be rash to assume that these groups would not use the newly delivered resources to increase their existing power. The end result would be to sharpen the lines of class differentiation within agriculture.

As long as administrative programs involve the regulation or the distribution of benefits, that is to say, the functions of government, we do not gain by drawing a rigid distinction between politics and administration. This applies to the distinction between political and administrative decentralization.[8] The effects of administrative decentralization may arrive by a more roundabout way than those of political decentralization; they will, however, be the same.

Decentralization of political organization and government in agriculture today has two effects of great importance. The first is the narrowing of the political base. In theory this narrowing might have taken place on any of a number of different lines, but in fact it has occurred on a basis of class. The already existent lines of class have been sharpened. The second effect is the building of a structure of political power. Decentralization has been an essential condition to this structure. In effect, the Farm Bureau has become an association of already existing élites in agriculture joined on a basis of class. The political power of the whole organization has, in turn, served to elevate the position of these élites, even while respecting their mutual differences.

16

The STRUCTURE of POWER

The structure of power whose rise has been the outstanding feature of agricultural politics in the first half of the twentieth century now extends from a base of social organization in a multitude of localities to a peak of direct influence over the exercise of governmental authority in the entire nation. To say that it is a pressure group, a grass-roots association of farmers, or an alliance of special interests is to ignore the whole of which these are but parts. Neither the size of the American Farm Bureau Federation, nor the position of the county agents, nor the character of the Department of Agriculture, nor the personnel of the committees of Congress explains the quality or the extent of this power. It is a vertical structure that rises through every level of political organization in America. Little that it has touched has been left unchanged.

It is not often possible to see the means by which social dominance is converted into political power. In isolated cases, indeed, bribes have been given and benefits returned. Yet these are pathological. The extension of social influence into the political sphere is far more general, even though it is most often sensed without any discovery of tangible interconnections. In agricultural affairs, however, the interconnections are visible. They have the form of organizations, both public and private.

One interesting aspect of this relationship is that the flow of influence is not in a single direction. We are familiar with the phenomenon of social structure determining the character of political organization, but it is less common to find that political organization affects social structure. Yet so it seems in agriculture. Another aspect relates to the nature of governmental power. Although governmental power tends to be confused with legitimacy and authority, it may be compared to the power exercised by a private association. Very frequently it is apparent that the power in the hands of governmental officials is actually wielded by forces external to the government. At times, however, government officials seem to have an actual choice in political matters, that is to say, where they wield power. In general this happens when there is a balance among the external forces. In agricultural politics, public officials have seemingly wielded power in a way contrary to the aims of the power complex discussed here. This conceivably could mean either that the power complex is less strong than is suggested here or that governmental officials are actual holders of power. The meaning, however, is quite different: this power complex, built vertically from local organizations of farmers up to the Washington apex, has been counterbalanced by its ultimate natural opponent, a political party.

Here, in fact, are alternative and rival forms of political power. The one is a power structure narrowly based on a class of minimum inclusiveness extending through all levels of formal government. The other is a political party broadly based on a loose and shifting alliance of diverse elements. The former may enter into the framework of the latter up to the point at which it is able to challenge the power of the latter. At that point the two engage in a struggle for which the formal government is the ground of battle. This is the point which the vertical structure of power in agriculture has reached.

It would be a serious error to focus exclusively either on the peak or on the base of this structure. Viewing the topmost feature, power over national politics, we have seen that the effects of national political action have extended throughout the structure, down to the very grass roots. The periods of greatest membership gain in the Farm Bureau have coincided with the periods of the greatest intervention of government in agricultural affairs. These began with the appointment of county agents. The earliest period of rapid growth, however, was during the First World War, when the government deliberately fostered farm bureaus on a large scale. In the 'twenties, the Farm Bureau Federation coasted briefly on the lingering influence of governmental intervention, but then steadily declined. During the depression of the 'thirties, after the New Deal had been born, a vast new intervention of government in agriculture occurred. The Farm Bureau took a new lease on life. It grew steadily from 1934 onward. The Second World War provided the impetus for an expansion which continued for several years after the war. In the last few years the rate of growth has again become slower. To a very important degree, Farm Bureau growth or decline is dependent on national political action.

The leadership of the Farm Bureau is able to direct the force of the organization with ease. The mechanics of decentralization make this possible. The only problem is that the leaders shall agree among themselves. Such agreement need not involve a large number of leaders. Nothing is more revealing about the operation than the action of the national convention in delegating the making of the decision on flexible price supports to the board of directors in 1948. This was open confession that resolution of major conflicts within the organization can be achieved by a process of bargaining among a few leaders.

Nothing is more illusory, however, than the impression that the Farm Bureau is not an organization of actual farmers. It is a great deal more than a group of farm leaders. The national influence of the leadership would be trifling without the firm foundation of a large membership and the presumption that beyond this membership lies an even larger constituency of potential members. The Farm Bureau has sedulously cultivated the belief that it speaks for agriculture. Where it has failed to absorb within itself all farmers who might be organized in its framework, it has succeeded in drawing overlapping farm organizations in its wake by highly adroit management. The Farmers' Union is the single point of complete failure. The important fact, however, is that the Farm Bureau has actually organized farmers. The successes of national political influence are just as dependent on this as the other way around.

The fundamental unit of power is the county Farm Bureau. Subunits do exist and will, as the total membership grows, become more numerous. Yet they will not displace the county organization because the county is (for most parts of the country) the smallest unit of rural government. Since the Farm Bureau achieves the preponderance of its effects through the medium of government, it has followed a policy of paralleling the governmental structure. Most of the counties, however, are small enough to permit the development of organization on clear lines of class.

The historical reason for the development of strong organization at the county level, of course, has been that this was the level of the county agent. Observers of agricultural politics agree that the Farm Bureau would not have become what it has, if the peculiar invention of the county agent's job had not been made.[1] Historically, the county agent has served as organizer and general functionary of the Farm Bureau. A segment of the public bureaucracy has been captured and made to serve as the bureaucracy of a private association. The Extension Service has been made a "chosen instrument." At a rudimentary stage of development this has resulted in occasional domination of the private association by the county agent. Yet it is in the nature of the situation that this power does not remain in the hands of the agent. His position becomes one of dependence as soon as the organization is formed and articulated.

Much attention has been paid to the anomaly of Farm Bureau contribution to the salaries of county agents.[2] However, the amount of this contribution is now usually small. It in no way accounts for the degree of influence over the agent exercised by the Farm Bureau. The fact that appropriations, hiring of personnel, supervision, and so on are subject to political influence by the Farm Bureau is far more important. That the most successful and prosperous farmers are given special attention by the local Extension Service is another highly important factor tending to enhance the sense of responsibility of the individual agent to the local association. Some of the strongest state farm bureaus have been able to dispense with the formal tie of financial contributions. Nevertheless, it is difficult to justify continuation of the formal anomaly. Some measure similar to the 1950 Granger bill is likely to pass in the future. This, however, will not destroy the Farm Bureau or even measurably weaken it.

Perhaps the greatest usefulness of the county agents to the Farm Bureau is that they represent a bureaucratic organization-in-being with established ties to the Farm Bureau. In a period of emergency, or any period of new extension of governmental activity in agriculture, the county agents are presented as the appropriate repositories of the new responsibility. This happened during the First World War, the early period of the Agricultural Adjustment Administration, and the Second World War. The county agents are seemingly expert in any problem affecting agriculture, whether in organizing the distribution of production cutbacks or in allocating the supply of labor. Even where local committees have been appointed to share in the administration of national programs, county agents have been put in key positions as secretaries of committees or as individuals capable of influencing selection of committeemen.

Influence over the county agents thus is highly important. There is nothing for which the Farm Bureau will fight with more determination than to secure for county agents a monopoly of local administration in agriculture. Not only does this maintain Farm Bureau influence over the county agents, but, more significantly, it ensures that the agents will be able to make a maximum return to the Farm Bureau. Any rival local administrative organization of the Department of Agriculture, or other department for that matter, is, therefore, a threat to the structure of power, and its destruction must be sought. This, more than a direct threat to the agricultural labor supply, white supremacy in the South, or anything else, was the cause of the downfall of the Farm Security Administration. It is the key to the confused battle over administrative form in the years just after the Second World War. The goal of the Farm Bureau has been the same since 1940: to reduce all federal agricultural programs to a system of grants to be administered with the aid of locally drawn committees of farmers through the offices of county agents. The generally valid assumption is that the committees can be controlled with little difficulty.

At the state level there is an interesting peculiarity of structure. While decentralization of agricultural programs to the states is an essential means of control, it is to a particular state agency that decentralization is sought. The Farm Bureau has strongly opposed any decentralization to state departments or commissioners of agriculture. It is true that this decentralization would be effective, but the Farm Bureau seeks something even more effective. This is found in the Extension services of the land grant colleges.

Entirely aside from the fact that the Extension services are the historic centers of formal supervision over the agents, they offer a number of practical advantages. First, the existing Extension services are decentralized more fully than any state agricultural department is likely to become. The existing organization, with the center of gravity at the county level, is ideal for Farm Bureau purposes.

Second, the head of a state department of agriculture will probably owe his position in part to a political party. This, in turn, will mean responsibility to a large constituency. The state Extension Service, on the other hand, is a branch of the local college, and the college board of trustees or regents enjoys a large measure of autonomy and independence from political control. The justification is, of course, that the issues of education are beyond politics. The great breach in the justification is that the Extension services have been led, with the willing compliance of college heads, into the work of government. As organs of government, the state Extension services then come under a mantle of political immunity. Since this provides an effective barrier to the one real rival structure of political control, the party system, the Farm Bureau is able to enforce its own system of responsibility.

Decentralization to the state Extension services has a third advantage. Since each land grant college jealously guards its individuality, the flow of administrative responsibility is effectively cut off at the state level. It is true that the Extension Service has a national administrative organization, but its central staff is small and its powers of control are limited. The device of using educational institutions for administrative centers thus provides an effective barrier to any form of political control except that of the Farm Bureau. The fact that the colleges' own educational aims can be drawn into discussion is simply an incidental propagandistic advantage.

The organization of regional offices for administrative purposes has been distasteful to the Farm Bureau. This was one of the specific complaints it directed against the Farm Security Administration and the Bureau of Agricultural Economics. Since regional organizations imply a degree of centralization, it is not difficult to understand why the Farm Bureau should oppose them. In its own structure, the Farm Bureau has been concerned to parallel the formal structure of government. Its regional organization tends to be somewhat informal and to exist for the purposes of selecting national leaders and resolving issues of "commodityism." Yet it is significant that some regional organization has grown up in the Farm Bureau.

At the national level, a number of natural advantages of our political system accrue to this vertical power structure. For one thing, other similar structures exist, although none is so well developed on such a large scale. Coöperation is more frequent than competition among them. Their influence is not sold but bartered. Moreover, the federal government is an agglomeration of fragments. Not only is it characterized by the separation of powers, but the legislative branch is bicameral and given to government by committees. The executive branch is divided into a multitude of agencies; the Department of Agriculture is a constellation in itself. This condition is highly conducive to the operation of "the invisible government," as pressure groups have been termed. Most of the achievements of the Farm Bureau in Washington are won in congressional committees. These are many and only a few get headlines. Other results are won in private conversations between Farm Bureau leaders and well-situated administrators.

In Congress, agriculture is overrepresented and becomes steadily more so, since it involves a steadily declining number of persons. In the Senate the reason is obvious: the states are equally represented, but unequally populated. In the House of Representatives there is a long lag in reapportionment. And, since the Farm Bureau speaks for "agriculture," it gains by this situation.

Farm Bureau influence is stronger now in the Senate, now in the House. The House has probably tended to be the greater stronghold. The principal reason for this would seem to be that the means of selecting congressmen are decentralized. Thus a rural congressman is more likely to be indebted to the Farm Bureau for assistance than is a senator.

In the administrative structure, Farm Bureau influence is founded on the fact that each agency must secure an annual appropriation. Power to influence this appropriation is power over the agency that receives the appropriation. Not the least element of the structure of power traced here is the unusual competence in the art of lobbying possessed by the Washington office of the Farm Bureau. Nevertheless, the greatest weakness of the structure of power is at this point. Much of the administrative structure is drawn on a hierarchical pattern with responsibility flowing to political heads, ultimately to the President. This means centralization and responsibility to a broad constituency and subjection to the check of the party system. And, as we have seen, this is the point over which the greatest battles have been fought.

This structure of power is not omnipotent. It has a rival in the party system. It contains divisions within itself. Neither is it unique. There are others, though none that have the degree of its strength or the peculiar advantages which it enjoys. Nevertheless, it is already formidable. And the drive for still greater power goes on.

The years that have passed since the end of Populism have witnessed more and greater changes than we like to acknowledge. The language and the cries of the old agrarianism are still to be heard and they continue to be given respect. Yet the sources from which they now come are vastly different from those out of which they emerged in the nineteenth century. Few changes have been more drastic than the transformation of American agrarianism.

Perhaps the central political belief of nineteenth-century agrarianism was that power must be circumscribed and limited. The belief was not peculiar to the agrarians; others shared this characteristically American view of democracy. To a great degree, however, farm movements and farm leaders made themselves its particular guardians. From the time of Thomas Jefferson and John Taylor down to the era of the Populists, farm movements were preoccupied with the problem of the system of power emerging from capitalist organization. In our time not only has this historic cause been abandoned, but an entirely new structure of power has been built within agriculture itself. This is the greatest change of all.

Whatever the immediate economic demands of the old agrarianism, its fundamental political doctrine was constant: power is suspect; the channels of political expression must be kept open to all. It was the political program of the common man. Recently we have come to regard mass movements with deep uneasiness. The historic agrarian movements were mass movements. However, it is clear that their programs were based less upon the knowledge that farmers were a majority than upon the conviction that no one, however mean his status, should be shut off from effective influence upon his government. The decline of this conviction has come about not through mass organization but through class organization.

The great paradox of modern farm organization in America is that an intensified social stratification has occurred within agriculture, the source of much of our equalitarian tradition. This has come about in part through the medium of political organization. It is not the working out of any devious political design. It is not the deliberate fabrication of any mesh by men of ambitious purpose. Nevertheless, the political result of the process has been the development of a structure of power. The result in economic terms is an apparently senseless rivalry of large and small farmers set against each other. It remains senseless only so long as we ignore the strange rationale of organization.

The objectives of the dominant agricultural power of the era seem often to conflict with the varied goals we sometimes refer to as "the public interest," but this fact gives less cause for alarm than does the fact that the conditions of power exclude so large a part of the farm population from the benefits of the political process. We could view the rise of this structure of power in agriculture with equanimity if there were alternative structures open to those for whom it has no part nor place. The pluralism of American society is one of its greatest political virtues. Yet for this to continue as virtue presupposes that the means of power shall not be made the property of the few. This presupposition has failed in agriculture.

Herein lies the condition which the agrarian program of limiting power was designed to prevent. Its existence today is the measure of the change that has come about. Agrarian democracy is gone from our scene. The loss is agriculture's—and the nation's.

Appendix

TABLE 1
American Farm Bureau Federation Membership

Year	Number	Year	Number
1921.................	466,421	1936.................	* 356,564
1922.................	363,481	1937.................	409,766
1923.................	392,580		
1924.................	301,747	1939.................	398,197
1925.................	314,473	1940.................	443,850
1926.................	278,759	1941.................	518,031
1927.................	272,049	1942.................	591,230
1928.................	301,699	1943.................	687,499
1929.................	301,932	1944.................	828,486
1930.................	321,195	1945.................	986,136
1931.................	276,052	1946.................	1,128,259
1932.................	205,347	1947.................	1,275,180
1933.................	163,246	1948.................	1,323,826
1934.................	222,178	1949.................	1,409,798
1935.................	280,917	1950.................	1,449,715
		1951.................	1,452,210

Sources: Figures for 1921 to 1937 inclusive are from Gladys Baker, *The County Agent* (University of Chicago Press, 1939), p. 23. These were obtained by Miss Baker from the main office of the American Farm Bureau Federation. Figures for 1939 through 1951 are from annual reports of the federation, which did not carry such data before 1939.

TABLE 2
American Farm Bureau Federation Membership, by Regions

Year	Midwest	Southern	Northeast	Western	Total
1939.............	208,739	97,141	65,312	27,005	398,197
1940.............	229,953	113,031	71,244	29,622	443,850
1941.............	248,544	168,474	70,658	30,355	518,031
1942.............	293,211	182,351	80,351	35,375	591,230
1943.............	342,036	207,587	97,542	40,334	687,499
1944.............	408,478	252,626	119,703	47,679	828,486
1945.............	480,756	313,215	140,460	51,705	986,136
1946.............	557,446	366,544	141,616	62,653	1,128,259
1947.............	640,386	405,549	154,615	74,630	1,275,180
1948.............	652,842	432,636	151,936	88,412	1,325,826
1949.............	672,576	483,515	152,901	100,806	1,409,798
1950.............	710,416	479,753	152,950	106,596	1,449,715
1951.............	719,725	474,362	143,065	115,058	1,452,210

Source: American Farm Bureau Federation, *Annual Reports*.

TABLE 3

AMERICAN FARM BUREAU FEDERATION MEMBERSHIP in 1951, BY STATES

Midwest region		Northeast region*	
Illinois	183,590	Connecticut	8,648
Indiana	96,354	Delaware	760
Iowa	125,022	Maryland	10,217
Kansas	58,008	Massachusetts	5,287
Michigan	47,768	New Hampshire	4,869
Minnesota	61,954	New Jersey	8,819
Missouri	38,989	New York	82,902
Nebraska	7,956	Pennsylvania	521
North Dakota	8,752	Vermont	9,422
Ohio	58,978	West Virginia	11,620
South Dakota	2,776		
Wisconsin	29,578		

Southern region		Western region	
Alabama	61,193	Arizona	3,362
Arkansas	49,019	California	61,279
Florida	11,000	Colorado	7,626
Georgia	50,253	Idaho	11,637
Kentucky	64,188	Montana	1,242
Louisiana	10,033	Nevada	1,406
Mississippi	23,084	New Mexico	6,503
North Carolina	58,025	Oregon	4,953
Oklahoma	30,852	Utah	6,425
South Carolina	14,693	Washington	4,681
Tennessee	40,001	Wyoming	5,944
Texas	50,000		
Virginia	8,762		
Puerto Rico	3,259		

SOURCE: American Farm Bureau Federation, *Annual Report*, 1951.
* A Farm Bureau in Maine has since affiliated with the A.F.B.F.

Notes

[1] Fred E. Haynes, *Third Party Movements since the Civil War* (Iowa City, State Historical Society of Iowa, 1916), p. 268.

[2] Elizabeth N. Barr, quoted in John D. Hicks, *The Populist Revolt* (Minneapolis, University of Minnesota Press, 1931), p. 159.

[3] N. A. Dunning (ed.), *The Farmers' Alliance History and Agricultural Digest* (Washington, D.C., Alliance Publishing Co., 1891), p. 102.

[4] "Rural population" included people living in communities of less than 2,500. Although this definition obscures the size of farm population, it does include many non-farmers whose ideological affinities were agrarian. Urban population did not exceed rural population until the decade 1910–1920. Data from U. S. Bureau of the Census, *Historical Statistics of the United States, 1789–1945* (Washington, D.C., 1949), p. 29.

[5] Henry Adams, *The Education of Henry Adams* (Boston, Houghton Mifflin Co., 1918), p. 344.

[6] Cf. Hicks, *op. cit.*, p. 406; also "Demands on Congress by the Farmers' Alliance," in Dunning, *op. cit.*, p. 76.

[7] National Grange of the Patrons of Husbandry, Seventh Session, *Proceedings*, February 4, 1874, in John R. Commons and associates, *Documentary History of American Industrial Society* (Cleveland, Arthur H. Clark Co., 1911), vol. 10, p. 104.

[8] Thomas Jefferson, *Notes on Virginia*, Query XIX.

[9] It is true that Jefferson seemed to believe that only agriculture was productive. He repudiated this belief explicitly, however, somewhat late in his career. Cf. letter to Benjamin Austin, January 9, 1816, in *Writings of Thomas Jefferson*, Ford ed. (New York, Knickerbocker Press, 1899), vol. 10, pp. 7–11. Joseph Dorfman has gone so far as to tag Jefferson as a "commercial agrarian democrat." Joseph Dorfman, *The Economic Mind in American Civilization* (3 vols.; New York, Viking Press, 1946–1949), vol. 1, pp. 433 ff.

[10] "At the awful day of judgment, the discrimination of the good from the wicked, is not made by the criterion of sects or of dogmas, but by one which constitutes the daily employment and the great end of agriculture. The judge, upon this occasion has by anticipation pronounced, that to feed the hungry, clothe the naked, and give drink to the thirsty are the passports to future happiness; and the divine intelligence which selected an agrarian state as a paradise for its first favorites, has here again prescribed the agricultural virtues as the means for the admission of their posterity into heaven." John Taylor, *Arator: Being a Series of Agricultural Essays, Practical and Political*, 6th ed. (Petersburg, Virginia; printed by Whitworth and Yancy for John M. Carter, 1818), p. 189.

[11] The campaign picture of Thomas E. Dewey standing before his barnyard is perhaps sufficient reminder of the persistence with which tribute must still be paid to this belief.

[12] In the past two decades Taylor's thought has been seriously misrepresented by those who see only this aspect of his position. For discussion of Taylor's political theory see Grant McConnell, "John Taylor and the Democratic Tradition," *Western Political Quarterly*, vol. 4 (March, 1951), pp. 17–31, and literature cited therein.

[13] A. Whitney Griswold, *Farming and Democracy* (New York, Harcourt, Brace and Co., 1948), p. 180.

NOTES TO CHAPTER 2

[1] Data from U. S. Bureau of the Census, *Historical Statistics of the United States, 1789–1945* (1949), pp. 105, 108.

[2] The percentage of gainfully occupied or employed in agriculture, from Simon Kuznets, *National Income: A Summary of Findings* (New York, National Bureau of Economic Research, Inc., 1946), p. 41, is as follows:

1870	51.6	1910	30.7
1880	48.8	1920	26.7
1890	42.5	1930	21.3
1900	37.7	1940	16.9

[3] Frederick Jackson Turner, *The Frontier in American History* (New York, Henry Holt and Co., 1920), p. 3.

[4] This estimate is based on numerous assumptions which are necessarily open to question. See U. S. President's Water Resources Policy Commission, Report of the Committee, *A Water Policy for the American People* (1950), vol. 1, pp. 154–159. An estimate of a needed 53,000,000 more acres by 1975, made in Martin R. Cooper, Glen T. Barton, and Albert P. Brodell, *Progress of Farm Mechanization*, U. S. Department of Agriculture, Misc. Publ. no. 630 (1947), p. 75, is based on a smaller estimate of population growth.

[5] For an extended list of technological changes of recent and future importance, see U. S. Department of Agriculture, Special Report by an Interbureau Committee and the Bureau of Agricultural Economics, *Technology on the Farm* (1940), pp. 6, 7.

[6] *Ibid.*, p. 12. For data on numbers of farm tractors see Cooper, Barton, and Brodell, *op. cit.*, p. 85.

[7] Theodore W. Schultz, *Agriculture in an Unstable Economy* (New York, McGraw-Hill Book Co., 1945), p. 76.

[8] Cooper, Barton, and Brodell, *op. cit.*, table 4, p. 7.

[9] *Ibid.*, table 3, p. 5. In 1870, one farmer supported 5.6 persons; in 1900, 8; in 1920, 9.9; in 1945, 14.5.

[10] Kuznets gives these estimates for the percentage of national income originating in agriculture: 1869–1879, 20.5 per cent; 1919–1929, 12.2 per cent (or 10.5 per cent by different estimate). Kuznets, *op. cit.*, p. 40. For 1949 the figure of 7.9 per cent and for 1950 the figure of 7.4 per cent are given in U. S. Department of Commerce, *National Income and Product of the United States, 1929–1950* (1951), p. 17.

[11] The prices of cotton, corn, and wheat (yearly averages) were as follows:

Year	Cotton (cents per lb.)	Corn (per bushel)	Wheat (per bushel)
1918	28.8	$1.52	$2.05
1919	35.3	1.51	2.16
1920	15.8	0.65	1.82
1921	17.0	0.51	1.03
1922	22.8	0.73	0.96
1923	28.6	0.81	0.92
1924	22.9	1.06	1.24
1925	19.6	0.70	1.43
1926	12.4	0.74	1.21
1927	20.1	0.84	1.19
1928	17.9	0.84	0.99
1929	16.7	0.79	1.03
1930	9.4	0.59	0.67
1931	5.6	0.32	0.39
1932	6.5	0.31	0.38

SOURCE: U. S. Bureau of the Census, *Historical Statistics of the United States, 1789–1945* (1949), pp. 106, 108.

[12] Tenancy has been widely taken as a symbol of all the recent ills of farming. It is worth recalling that tenancy in 1890 was somewhat higher (28.4 per cent) than it is now (26.8 per cent). The most alarming stage, of course, was in the early 'thirties, when tenancy reached a level of more than 42 per cent. See U. S. Bureau of the Census, *Historical Statistics ...*, p. 96; and for 1950 data, U. S. Bureau of the Census, *Farms, Farm Characteristics, Farm Products*, Series AC50-1 (1952).

[13] The figures are presented by O. E. Baker, *A Graphic Summary of the Number, Size*

and Value of Products, U. S. Department of Agriculture, Misc. Publ. no. 266 (1937), pp. 5, 68. This pamphlet has been widely quoted.

¹⁴ *Ibid.,* p. 5.

¹⁵ Forty-eight per cent of the farms produced eleven per cent of the product. Farms of this same group produced less than $600 each, in gross value. U. S. Bureau of the Census, *Census of Agriculture, 1945, General Report* (1947), vol. 2, p. 567.

¹⁶ Part-time, residential, and abnormal (e.g., institutional) farms are tabulated together in preliminary reports from the *Census of Agriculture, 1950.* This group approximates a third of all farms. U. S. Bureau of the Census, *Farms, Farm Characteristics, Farm Products* (1952). See also Kenneth L. Bachman and Ronald W. Jones, *Size of Farms in the United States,* U. S. Department of Agriculture, Tech. Bull. no. 1019 (1950), p. 8.

¹⁷ The problem of discovering the extent of low incomes among farmers is not simple. During the 'thirties the simple figures for farm incomes were probably better indications than they are today. The opportunities for supplemental off-farm income are better now than then. The nonfarm elements of incomes of farmers have been emphasized recently. See Nathan M. Koffsky and Jeanne M. Lear, "Size, Distribution of Farm Operators' Incomes in 1946," *Studies in Income and Wealth* (New York, National Bureau of Economic Research, Inc., 1951), vol. 13, pp. 220–265. However, there is a suggestion that poverty among farmers has not been eradicated in the fact that almost a fifth of the strictly defined commercial farms had gross cash incomes of less than $1,200 in 1949. See U. S. Bureau of the Census, *Farms, Farm Characteristics, Farm Products* (1952).

¹⁸ This is the term used by Bachman and Jones, *op. cit.,* p. 2.

¹⁹ See Koffsky and Lear, *op. cit.,* chart 5, p. 246.

NOTES TO CHAPTER 3

¹ Similar reactions against organizations with any but the most tangible goals may be seen in the following: "Each 'ism' has stood but as an evanescent and iridescent dream of poor humanity groping blindly in the dark for its idea; and it has caused many a heart-wrench to relegate some idealism of movements which do not move, to the dead ashes of blasted hopes and promises." Samuel Gompers, *Labor and the Common Welfare* (New York, E. P. Dutton and Co., 1919), p. 7. "The farmers' natural love for liberty and individuality of expression accounts largely for the vast number of rival organizations that sprang up. This so divided and confused the farmers' strength and unity of action that it was only on the great central thought of governmental relief and reform of one kind or another that the farmers of the period could unite." O. M. Kile, *The Farm Bureau Movement* (New York, The Macmillan Co., 1921), pp. 43–44.

² It is true that a new farm organization was formed in the first decade of the twentieth century on the old mass plan, the Farmers' Union, but its growth was slow and its significance remained regional for nearly a generation. For its origin, see Edward Wiest, *Agricultural Organization in the United States* (Lexington, University of Kentucky Press, 1923), pp. 475–476.

³ "The justification of a democratic form of government lies in the fact that it is a means of education." Liberty Hyde Bailey, *The Holy Earth* (New York, Charles Scribner's Sons, 1917), p. 146. A similar point of view is set forth in his *What Is Democracy?* (Ithaca, N.Y., Comstock Publishing Co., 1918). Dr. Bailey may be regarded as the philosopher of American agriculture, particularly in the early part of the century. He has been, among other things, chairman of President Theodore Roosevelt's Commission on Country Life. His personality looms large in the agricultural history of the first two decades of the twentieth century.

⁴ The Morrill Act had an important precedent in the Land Ordinance of 1785, by which the township system of surveying was established and section 16 of each township was reserved for the support of schools.

⁵ Dr. True's judgment is perhaps open to question, but his volume is the most useful on the history of the land grant colleges. A. C. True, *A History of Agricultural Education*

in the United States, 1785–1925, U. S. Department of Agriculture, Misc. Publ. no. 36 (1929), pp. 109–110. An account of the passage of the Morrill Act is given in Earle D. Ross, *Democracy's College, The Land Grant Movement in the Formative Stage* (Ames, The Iowa State College Press, 1942), pp. 46–47. See also U. S. Office of Education, *Survey of Land Grant Colleges and Universities*, directed by Arthur J. Klein, Bulletin 1930, no. 9 (1930), pp. 1–33; and George A. Work and Barton Morgan, *The Land Grant Colleges*, U. S. Advisory Committee on Education, Staff Study no. 10 (1939), pp. 8–17.

[6] W. H. Shepardson, *Agricultural Education in the United States* (New York, The Macmillan Co., 1929), p. 29.

[7] For an account of these stations see A. C. True, *A History of Agricultural Experimentation and Research in the United States, 1607–1925*, U. S. Department of Agriculture, Misc. Publ. no. 251 (1937).

[8] Regarding the institutes and related activities, see A. C. True, *A History of Agricultural Extension Work in the United States, 1785–1923*, U. S. Department of Agriculture, Misc. Publ. no. 15 (1928), pp. 14–41.

[9] "Civilization oscillates between two poles. At the one extreme is the so-called laboring class, and at the other are the syndicated and corporate and monopolized interests. Both these elements or phases tend to go to extremes. Many efforts are being made to weld them into some sort of share-earning or commonness of interests, but without very great results. Between these two poles is the great agricultural class, which is the natural balance-force or the middle-wheel of society. These people are steady, conservative, abiding by the law, and are to a greater extent than we recognize a controlling element in our social structure." Liberty Hyde Bailey, *The Country Life Movement* (New York, The Macmillan Co., 1911), p. 16. Dr. Bailey made his position more explicit a few years later: "I must point out the dangers in those kinds of organized effort that seek to gain their ends by force of numbers, by compulsion and strategy. I trust that we shall avoid class legislation by farmers." *What Is Democracy?* pp. 102–103.

[10] The best volume on Knapp is by J. C. Bailey, *Seaman A. Knapp, Schoolmaster of American Agriculture* (New York, Columbia University Press, 1945). See also O. B. Martin, *The Demonstration Work, Dr. Seaman A. Knapp's Contribution to Civilization* (Boston, The Stratford Co., 1921). A useful short account appears in True, *A History of Agricultural Extension Work . . .*, pp. 58 ff.

[11] Cf. J. C. Bailey, *op. cit.*, pp. 152–160.

[12] The term is that of Bailey, *ibid.*, p. xi.

[13] Bailey suggests that there was outright opposition. *Ibid.*, pp. 193–197.

[14] A good illustration is workers' education, which combines the concept of adult education with that of the labor movement. Supporters of workers' education come from both sides, education and organized labor. The former emphasize economics and English; the latter stress union organization and parliamentary law. The mutual antagonism is at times rather thinly disguised, though seldom explicit.

[15] Letter dated August 10, 1908, reprinted in Commission on Country Life, *Report* (Chapel Hill, University of North Carolina Press, 1944), p. 41. The *Report* was originally published as Senate Document 705, 60th Cong., 2d sess., 1909. It was also reprinted by the Spokane Chamber of Commerce in 1911.

[16] Commission on Country Life, *Report*, pp. 30–31. John Taylor said it better.

[17] Liberty Hyde Bailey's position on this was probably shared by the commission generally: "The real problem before the American people is how to make the country population most effective, not how to increase the population; the increase will be governed by the operation of economic law." *The Country Life Movement*, p. 34.

[18] Commission on Country Life, *Report*, pp. 39–40. The other two problems were the townward movement and the special drain of rural youth. The ugly word "disadvantaged," which seems to have been the coinage of Liberty Hyde Bailey, became the possession of the Department of Agriculture in the 'thirties.

[19] *Ibid.*, p. 144.

[20] *Ibid.*, p. 30.

[21] The members of the commission were Liberty Hyde Bailey (chairman), Henry Wallace, Kenyon L. Butterfield, Walter Hines Page, Gifford Pinchot, C. S. Barrett, and W. A. Beard. Bailey and Butterfield were from the colleges, though Butterfield had also been with the General Education Board and was close to the Department of Agriculture and a friend of Knapp. Pinchot took an active interest in the appointment of the commission. His part is touched on in his autobiography, *Breaking New Ground* (New York, Harcourt, Brace and Co., 1947), pp. 340–344. These three were the most active members, with Bailey probably responsible for most of the writing. Just to consider these three is to cover a fair range of social opinion.

[22] Commission on Country Life, *Report*, p. 19.

[23] J. C. Bailey gives credit to the Commission on Country Life for passage of the Smith-Lever Act. *Seaman A. Knapp*, p. 250. Although the commission was influential, such a claim underestimates the far more important organized campaign which developed in later years.

[24] True, *A History of Agricultural Education . . .*, p. 205.

[25] John M. Gaus and Leon O. Wolcott, *Public Administration and the United States Department of Agriculture*, Public Administration Service (Chicago, 1940), p. 15.

[26] Carleton R. Ball has divided the history of the department into four periods. The second period, from 1888 to 1912, is characterized in his scheme by protection and regulation. His third period is characterized by education and extension. The years which he gives for this period are 1912 to 1932. It would seem that he might have dated this third period rather earlier. See Gaus and Wolcott, *op. cit.*, p. 9 n.

[27] An entertaining sidelight is that W. J. Spillman of the Bureau of Plant Industry, who helped form the Broome County (New York) Farm Bureau, drafted a resolution introduced by Senator Kenyon calling for removal of the Rockefeller money from the department's administration in 1914. Russell Lord says that Spillman had just read Ida Tarbell's *History of the Standard Oil Company*. Cf. Russell Lord, *The Agrarian Revival* (New York, American Association for Adult Education, 1939), p. 82.

[28] The writings of A. C. True are official publications of the department. They are, on the whole, good examples of government scholarship, but show the signs of the "clearance" with interested parties that is a not infrequent prerequisite of such sponsorship. However, Dr. True's estimate of the work of the colleges does emerge. It is not flattering to the colleges. See, for example, his *History of Agricultural Education . . .*, p. 128.

[29] The term is Knapp's. It appears in U. S. Department of Agriculture, *Yearbook of Agriculture, 1909*, pp. 153–160.

[30] J. C. Bailey, *Seaman A. Knapp*, p. 178.

[31] Cf. unsigned article, "The Lever Bill," *The Banker-Farmer*, March, 1914, p. 13.

[32] American Bankers' Association, *Proceedings*, 1911 Convention, p. 387.

[33] *The Banker-Farmer*, published by the Agricultural Commission of the American Bankers' Association in Champaign, Illinois. It took no advertising and was a nonprofit venture. After 1928 it was replaced by a much more modest bulletin.

[34] American Bankers' Association, *Proceedings*, 1913 Convention, p. 60.

[35] Speech by George Allen of New York, American Bankers' Association, *Proceedings*, 1912 Convention, p. 222.

[36] *Ibid.*, p. 218.

[37] B. F. Harris, chairman of the Agricultural Commission, pointed out that 90 per cent of the banks were small country banks. "These percentages, the comparatively small size of the average bank and the interdependence of these bankers and farmers, proves how little basis there is for 'buncombe' talk of the political agitator and demagogic statesman, who would have you believe that bankers are all of great wealth with interests and motives diametrically opposed to those of their communities." Report of the Agricultural Commission, American Bankers' Association, *Proceedings*, 1913 Convention, p. 180.

[38] Agricultural Extension Committee of the National Implement and Vehicle Association, *Agricultural Extension as Related to Business Interests* (Memphis, 1916).

[39] W. E. Taylor and P. G. Holden, respectively.

[40] This partial list is from a variety of sources. True, *A History of Agricultural Extension Work* ..., gives repeated references of this sort. See, for example, p. 74. Such references are also frequent in the pages of *The Banker-Farmer*.

[41] In a speech before the Association of American Agricultural Colleges and Experiment Stations (A.A.A.C. and E.S.), *Proceedings*, 1911 Convention, p. 123.

[42] J. C. Bailey, *op. cit.*, p. 259.

[43] Speech before the A.A.A.C. and E.S., *Proceedings*, 1912 Convention, pp. 102–104.

[44] One of the reasons given for expanding the Extension program of the association was that this would bring within the organization "the active managers of Extension work, who have already formed an organization of their own." A.A.A.C. and E.S., *Proceedings*, 1909 Convention, p. 35.

[45] The Farmers' Union and the Grange gave some support to the Page bill, but this support was not very effective. Cf. True, *A History of Agricultural Extension Work* ..., p. 105.

[46] Cf. A.A.A.C. and E.S., *Proceedings*, 1910 Convention, pp. 93–106.

[47] This is the interpretation of, among others, J. C. Bailey, *op. cit.*, pp. 250 ff.

[48] A.A.A.C. and E.S., *Proceedings*, 1909 Convention, p. 81.

[49] A.A.A.C. and E.S., *Proceedings*, 1911 Convention, p. 42.

[50] The argument of H. L. Russell of Wisconsin, A.A.A.C. and E.S., *Proceedings*, 1909 Convention, p. 74.

[51] A.A.A.C. and E.S., *Proceedings*, 1913 Convention, p. 131.

[52] It is not the least of many ironies that the proceedings of the association were printed under its own auspices for the first time in 1911. Previously, they had been printed by the department.

NOTES TO CHAPTER 4

[1] The quoted phrase is that of Edward Wiest, *Agricultural Organizations in the United States* (Lexington, University of Kentucky Press, 1923), p. 475.

[2] C. S. Barrett, *The Mission, History and Times of the Farmers' Union* (Nashville, Marshall and Bruce Co., 1909), p. 12. Barrett was one of the first presidents of the Farmers' Union.

[3] *Ibid.*

[4] *Ibid.*, p. 108.

[5] *Ibid.*, p. 25.

[6] Wiest gives the average membership for 1908–1910 as 121,826, and for 1917–1919 as 140,066. *Op. cit.*, p. 476. His figure for the year 1930 is 91,109. See his article, "Farmers' Union," *Encyclopedia of the Social Sciences*, vol. 3 (1937), pp. 132–133.

[7] National Grange, *Annual Proceedings*, November 11, 1908, p. 20.

[8] A vague stand on the last was taken in 1913.

[9] See Alice M. Christensen, "Agricultural Pressure and Government Response in the United States, 1919–1929" (unpublished doctoral thesis, University of California, 1937), p. 13 n.

[10] Cf. table in Wiest, *Agricultural Organizations in the United States*, p. 395; also the chart on p. 396. It is notable that the period 1896 to 1920 was one of great growth—from 131,942 to 541,158. The figures include women and children over fourteen years as well as men.

[11] Jennie Buell, *The Grange Master and the Grange Lecturer* (New York, Harcourt, Brace and Co., 1921), editor's preface, p. v.

[12] The intensity of feeling about the League can readily be sampled from a few of the books and pamphlets that came out at its time of conquest in North Dakota. Herbert E. Gaston, *The Non-Partisan League* (New York, Harcourt, Brace and Co., 1920), and C. E. Russell, *The Story of the Nonpartisan League* (New York, Harper and Bros., 1920) should be set alongside Andrew A. Bruce, *The Non-Partisan League* (New York, The Macmillan Co., 1921), to get the range of feeling. The myriad schisms which plagued the organization may be sampled in William Langer, *The Non-Partisan League* (Man-

dan, N.D., Norton County Farmers Press, 1920). Apparently, no one touched by the League in any manner could remain neutral.

[13] See J. A. Everitt, *The Third Power* (Indianapolis, The Hollenbeck Press, 1903), pp. 239–243. The best account of the American Society of Equity is by Theodore Saloutos and John D. Hicks, *Agricultural Discontent in the Middle West, 1900–1939* (Madison, University of Wisconsin Press, 1951), pp. 111–148.

[14] Everitt, *op. cit.*, p. 89.

[15] Cf. Christensen, thesis as cited, p. 17; see also Barrett, *op. cit.*, p. 186.

NOTES TO CHAPTER 5

[1] Hearings on Farm Organizations, House Committee on Banking and Currency, 66th Cong., 3d sess., 1922.

[2] The entire question of responsibility is well dealt with by Gladys Baker in *The County Agent* (University of Chicago Press, 1939), chaps. v, vi. This excellent study is the most valuable in the field. See also M. C. Burritt, *The County Agent and the Farm Bureau* (New York, Harcourt, Brace and Co., 1922).

[3] C. B. Smith, *Coöperative Extension Work, 1924, with Ten-Year Review*, U. S. Department of Agriculture, Office of Coöperative Extension Work (1926), pp. 4, 5.

[4] *Ibid.*, pp. 4–6. In money terms the increase was much greater. In 1924 the amount spent in the program totaled $19,394,639. This included that spent on the auxiliaries of the county agents, home demonstration agents, county club agents, and Extension specialists. The latter, combined with the regular agents, give a total of 4,764 workers in the whole program. These auxiliaries undoubtedly played a part in the political movement that emerged from Extension, but the county agent was far more important.

[5] See chap. 3.

[6] M. C. Burritt, "What Organization Should Precede Food Emergency Agents in a County?" Association of American Agricultural Colleges and Experiment Stations (A.A.A.C. and E.S.), *Proceedings*, 1917 Convention, p. 275.

[7] Cf. C. W. Thompson, "How the Department of Agriculture Promotes Organization in Rural Life," U. S. Department of Agriculture, *Yearbook of Agriculture, 1915*, pp. 272A–272P.

[8] L. R. Simons, *Organization of a County for Extension Work—The Farm Bureau Plan*, U. S. Department of Agriculture, Circular no. 30 (1919), p. 4.

[9] "Why didn't they [the federal and state governments] coöperate in extension work directly with the Grange in counties where the Grange is strong, or with the Farmers' Union in counties where the Union is strong, or with the Equity, where the Equity is strong? The reason is simple enough. Practically all of these are secret organizations, or commercial organizations. In a considerable degree they are exclusive organizations, and since the work of the Federal and State governments is financed by all the people and in the interest of all the people, these institutions felt the necessity of developing a nonclass, nonsecret, noncommercial, and permanent institution open to all the farmers in the county, and through which all could find expression and could deal directly and in an organized way with the State Colleges and Federal Department of Agriculture." Speech by C. B. Smith, chief of Extension Work, North and West, 1920, reprinted in Hearings on Farm Organizations, House Committee on Banking and Currency, 1922, p. 94.

[10] This Farm Bureau (Broome County) is generally taken as the first in the country. See, for example, O. M. Kile, *The Farm Bureau Movement* (New York, The Macmillan Co., 1921), pp. 94–99. However, it is fairly obvious that this organization was intrinsically similar to the earlier group which Seaman Knapp assembled in Terrell, Texas, and quite different from the farm bureaus of later decades, which after all do have farmer members. For Dr. Spillman's part in the formation of this "first" Farm Bureau, see letter to George A. Cullen, printed in a pamphlet, *The Cradle of the Farm Bureau Idea and Marketing Possibilities of the Bureau*, address by Cullen to Broome County Farm Bureau, Binghamton, New York, August 21, 1920. Cullen was Lackawanna traffic manager in 1911.

[11] This was decided at a meeting of county agent leaders in 1916. Cf. W. A. Lloyd, *County Agricultural Agent Work under the Smith-Lever Act, 1914 to 1924,* U. S. Department of Agriculture, Miscellaneous Circular no. 59 (1926), p. 14.

[12] A rather good indication of the changing point of view of the department is given by the use of small letters in the words "farm bureau." The initial letters were later capitalized.

[13] Speech reprinted in Hearings on Farm Organizations, House Committee on Banking and Currency, 1922, p. 93. Cf. also the statement by Dr. True that the farm bureaus "were organized originally on the suggestion of the Extension forces." *Ibid.* p. 130. Also, speech by L. A. Clinton, of the Department of Agriculture, before the A.A.A.C. and E.S., *Proceedings,* 1915 Convention, p. 225. Such statements are not hard to find.

[14] "These [local county farm bureaus] are expected to take the initiative in securing local financial support for the agent, to join in his selection and appointment, and to stand behind him in his efforts to advance agricultural interests." Report of the Secretary of Agriculture for 1915, p. 40.

[15] See Hearings on Farm Organizations, House Committee on Banking and Currency, 1922, p. 124.

[16] See statement by Dr. True, *ibid.,* p. 132.

[17] Simons, *op. cit.,* p. 22.

[18] The depth of this particular well of illusion was sounded in 1915 by an unnamed delegate: "It seems to me that it is rather an imposition on the local bureau to lead it to think it is directing when really it is not." A.A.A.C. and E.S., *Proceedings,* 1915 Convention, p. 225.

[19] *Ibid.,* p. 128.

[20] See paper by M. C. Burritt with this title, A.A.A.C. and E.S., *Proceedings,* 1919 Convention. See also paper by R. K. Bliss, director of the Iowa Extension Service, "Relation of Extension Work to the New Farm Bureau Movement," and that of T. R. Bryant, assistant director of the Extension Service in Kentucky, "Should Extension Workers Aid in Organization of Farm Bureaus?" Association of Land Grant Colleges and Universities (new name of A.A.A.C. and E.S.), *Proceedings,* 1920 Convention.

[21] A.A.A.C and E.S., *Proceedings,* 1915 Convention, p. 226. A reply to Dr. Ousley was made by a high official of the department a few years later: "The County Farm Bureau is the best agency thus far devised for insuring the interest and coöperation of a rural people in the great work of food production and conservation. Through this organization the College and Department not only may extend their help, but it affords a ready opportunity for the expression by farmers of what help is needed to make the farm business more prosperous and rural life more enjoyable." Clarence Ousley, Assistant Secretary of Agriculture, in L. R. Simons, *op. cit.,* p. 1.

[22] Cf. Lloyd, *op. cit.,* p. 15.

[23] These state laws have persisted on the books, with superficial amendment, in Arizona, Kansas, Kentucky, Maine, Michigan, Minnesota, New Mexico, New York, Rhode Island, West Virginia, Connecticut, Delaware, Illinois, Iowa, Missouri, and Nebraska. The last six do not include the words "farm bureaus" in their laws. This distinction is not of great importance, however; the effect of the laws is the same. A model law was presented at the 1917 convention of the A.A.A.C. and E.S. and such laws were enacted in Maine and Rhode Island. The Farm Bureau in Rhode Island is not affiliated with the federation. For collected excerpts of these laws see H. W. Gilbertson, *Extension–Farm Bureau Relationships, 1948,* U. S. Department of Agriculture, Extension Service (1949; mimeographed), Exhibit A.

[24] For a discussion of the effects of the war on the Extension system, see W. A. Lloyd, *Status and Results of County Agent Work, Northern and Western States, 1918,* U. S. Department of Agriculture, Circular no. 37 (1919).

[25] See Report of the Secretary of Agriculture for 1917. The point is specifically made there that the increase was the work of the agents.

[26] Regarding this controversy see M. C. Burritt, *The County Agent and the Farm Bureau,* pp. 93–110.

[27] Localities differ, of course, in the degree to which this change has taken place. The agent even today is more of a leader in some areas than in others. There is also the factor of personality differences among agents.

[28] M. C. Burritt, "What Should Be the Relation of the County Agent to the Farm Bureau?" A.A.A.C. and E.S., *Proceedings*, 1919 Convention.

[29] Cf. Lloyd, *County Agricultural Agent Work . . .* , p. 9.

[30] *Ibid.*, p. 15.

[31] See Kile, *op. cit.*, pp. 113 ff.

[32] *Ibid.*, p. 113.

[33] *Ibid.*, pp. 128–132.

[34] Hearings on Farm Organizations, House Committee on Banking and Currency, 1922.

[35] *Ibid.*, p. 26.

[36] *Ibid.*, p. 94.

[37] The evidence ranged from a Georgia agent's use of Department of Agriculture stationery while signing as both agent and Farm Bureau secretary, to the statement of Dr. True that "it [forming a Farm Bureau without an agent] *might* be done" (italics mine). *Ibid.*, pp. 103, 133.

[38] *Ibid.*, p. 158.

[39] Howard was able to make one hostile committee member repudiate a threat to cut off Smith-Lever funds from the county agents for organizing purposes. Perhaps his peroration on the federation's accomplishment in stemming the tide of bolshevism had something to do with his success: "At this time, in this Nation, the farmers are sorely pressed. They are about ready for bolshevistic Movement. There is an outcropping of socialism here and there and everywhere over this country.

"Last week I was with a distinguished party of people on the St. Lawrence trips, including two governors of States, whom I do not care to mention, but who came to me on that trip and said that the man who writes the history of this period 50 years from now 'will give you and your organization credit which you do not now have because you have kept down in a large measure that unrest among farmers.'

"Why have we kept down that unrest? Because we have had a serious group of men who have been students of agricultural colleges in many cases, who have had connection with government work, as our advisors and assistants, and the rank and file of the farmers have confidence in these men." *Ibid.*, p. 227.

[40] The theory was apparently the invention of C. B. Smith. See speech reprinted in *ibid.*, p. 96. That it is still official doctrine is to be seen in the 1949 work of Gilbertson, *op. cit.* Cf. also C. B. Smith and M. C. Wilson, *The Agricultural Extension System of the United States* (New York, John Wiley and Sons, 1930), p. 152.

[41] Dr. True at this time was ex officio a nonvoting member of the executive committee of the federation. On one occasion he carried the official greetings of the federation to the colleges' association, of which he was also an officer.

[42] "Memorandum of Understanding," *The Farm Bureau and the Extension Service*, April 22, 1921, signed by A. C. True, director of the States Relations Service, Department of Agriculture, and J. R. Howard, president of the American Farm Bureau Federation. This is commonly called the True-Howard Agreement.

[43] Statement by Henry C. Wallace, Secretary of Agriculture, August 25, 1922, "Relation of Federal Coöperative Extension Employees to Agricultural Organizations," Association of Land Grant Colleges and Universities (new name of old A.A.A.C. and E.S.), *Proceedings*, 1922 Convention, p. 220.

NOTES TO CHAPTER 6

[1] In sheer membership figures, we may compare the end-of-war figure of approximately 400,000 as given by W. A. Lloyd, *County Agricultural Agent Work under the Smith-Lever Act, 1914 to 1924*, U. S. Department of Agriculture, Miscellaneous Circular no. 59 (1926), p. 14, with that of 466,421 for 1921, as given by the American Farm Bureau Federation. The latter was obtained by Gladys Baker, *The County Agent* (University of

Chicago Press, 1939), p. 23. It is perhaps worth mentioning that frequently there is a discrepancy in the membership data of the Farm Bureau. Its membership is "family membership," and this sometimes allows for generous translations into numbers represented. Thus President Howard mentions "a paid membership of more than a million in the first year," in O. M. Kile, *The Farm Bureau Movement* (New York, The Macmillan Co., 1921), p. lx. The figure of a million and a half for the membership in 1921 was used in testimony at the Hearings on Farm Organizations, House Committee on Banking and Currency, 66th Cong., 3d sess., 1922, p. 219. In view of subsequent history, the data obtained by Miss Baker seem reasonable.

² See Appendix, table 1.

³ On this score, we may compare the disfranchising effect of a poll tax of one dollar.

⁴ Kile, *op. cit.*, p. 118.

⁵ An interesting comparison may be made with the course of labor organizations during the 'twenties. Unlike farm organization, labor organization tends to grow in time of prosperity. However, in the 'twenties for the first time in American history this tendency did not operate; labor organization declined. Most discussions of this phenomenon give a large place, in the reasons assigned, to the concerted open-shop drive of employers. E.g., H. A. Millis and R. A. Montgomery, *Organized Labor* (New York, McGraw-Hill Book Co., 1945), pp. 155 ff., and Norman J. Ware, "Trade Unions—United States and Canada," *Encyclopedia of the Social Sciences*, vol. 15, pp. 40–45. It is likely that the business community was as politically astute in its dealing with agriculture as it was with labor.

⁶ The concept of organizational purpose must be used with caution. Here it refers both to stated purposes and to general lines of action taken.

⁷ The first dispute was resolved by the allowance of one director for each state plus one additional director for each 20,000 members; the second dispute was left to state determination, subject only to the requirement of payment of 50 cents per member to the national federation. See Kile, *op. cit.*, pp. 114–123.

⁸ Again a familiar pattern may be observed in that three representatives of the Department of Agriculture and an agricultural college dean were present also. Alice M. Christensen, "Agricultural Pressure and Government Response in the United States, 1919–1929" (unpublished doctoral thesis, University of California, 1937), pp. 59–61. Miss Christensen had access to the minutes of this meeting contained in files of the Washington office of the federation.

⁹ By 1922 the farm bloc was so strong that it was called "the most effective political force in the United States." John K. Barnes, "The Man Who Runs the Farm Bloc," *World's Work*, vol. 55 (November, 1922), p. 52. "The Man" referred to was Gray Silver. For a discussion of the bloc by one of the senatorial leaders see Arthur Capper, *The Agricultural Bloc* (New York, Harcourt, Brace and Co., 1922). See also two articles, "The Agricultural Bloc—Its Merits," by Arthur Capper, and "The Agricultural Bloc—Its Perils," by George H. Moses, in *Forum*, vol. 61 (December, 1921), pp. 461–475.

¹⁰ Cf. Christensen, thesis as cited, p. 67. Cf. also Barnes, *op. cit.*

¹¹ Christensen, thesis as cited, pp. 102–103.

¹² Gray Silver was by no means a novice in legislative methods. He had served for twelve years in the West Virginia legislature and had been president of its Senate.

¹³ Christensen, thesis as cited, p. 65. This was drawn from the minutes of the meeting.

¹⁴ John Barnes reported that Silver stated this apprehension at a meeting of the executive committee of the federation. Barnes, *op. cit.*, p. 59.

¹⁵ Cf. article by J. R. Howard, "Coöperative Marketing," *The Banker-Farmer*, vol. 8 (January, 1921), p. 4. This was the substance of a speech he gave at the 1920 convention of the American Bankers' Association.

¹⁶ The board was held to be a creature of the Farmers' Union. See O. M. Kile, *The Farm Bureau through Three Decades* (Baltimore, Waverly Press, 1948), pp. 83–84. Kile was assistant to Silver in the Washington office in the early 'twenties and has remained close to the organization. This is the best available book on the Farm Bureau.

It contains a highly favorable preface by Alan Kline, current president of the federation, and was printed for the Farm Bureau. It is sold by the national office of the federation. While the book is avowedly not an official history, it is a close approximation. Considering the author's access to official and informal sources of information, it constitutes one of the illuminating volumes on American politics.

[17] The department's point of view was peculiarly well represented by Secretary Henry C. Wallace, who had a definite preoccupation with prices. Cf. his posthumously published book, *Our Debt and Duty to the Farmer* (New York, The Century Co., 1925).

[18] See Wesley McCune, *The Farm Bloc* (Garden City, N.Y., Doubleday, Doran and Co., 1943), chaps. 6, 8, 12. As McCune shows, the various groups coöperate on legislative programs, but without the national federation their collaboration would not be so effective.

[19] Sapiro at this time was a young and spectacular coöperative organizer from San Francisco. He seemed to have the knack of being on the spot wherever more than two people were gathered to discuss coöperatives. Among the many accomplishments of his career was the successful conduct of well-publicized litigation with Henry Ford.

[20] See the frank discussion of this in Kile, *The Farm Bureau through Three Decades*, pp. 117–19.

[21] Ohio has long been a special case in the Farm Bureau. The secretary of the Ohio federation, Murray D. Lincoln, came to the Farm Bureau as one of the early "banker-farmers"; he had been agricultural agent of the Cleveland Society of Savings. From an early date, he emphasized education and coöperatives in the hierarchy of Farm Bureau purposes. See "The Farmers' Plans," *The Banker-Farmer*, vol. 8 (August, 1921), p. 2. He has been accounted the leading liberal in the ranks of the bureau.

[22] The movement hostile to coöperative emphasis in Iowa was strongly reinforced by the highly influential *Wallaces' Farmer and Iowa Homestead* (hereafter cited as *Wallaces' Farmer*). Henry A. Wallace was editorial writer at this time, and his columns contained much criticism of federation temporizing with matters other than coöperation. Henry C. Wallace, his father, was Secretary of Agriculture until 1924.

[23] *Wallaces' Farmer*, vol. 50 (January 23, 1925), p. 103.

[24] Kile, *The Farm Bureau through Three Decades*, pp. 120–121.

[25] The committee formerly had three members for each section. The change gave an additional member for each 100,000 paid-up members. Cf. American Farm Bureau Federation, *Weekly News Letter*, December 11, 1924.

[26] The comment of Henry A. Wallace is interesting for the light it sheds on convention methods: "There was practically no discussion by delegates in open meeting as to what should be the policy of the American Farm Bureau in 1926. As usual, the real work of the convention appeared to be going on in committee and caucus rooms. In this work it was reported that Gray Silver and John Coverdale, of the deceased Grain Marketing Company, were very active. They, together with Jim Howard, seemed to be continually trying to throw discord into the ranks of those favoring the plan of an export corporation for handling the agricultural surplus. Howard publicly condemned the policy of doing nothing for the farmer . . . The plotters did their best to maintain the ancient feud between the Iowa and Illinois farm bureaus." *Wallaces' Farmer*, vol. 50 (December 18, 1925), p. 1665. The immediate context here was the fight over the first form of the McNary-Haugen bill. Wallace approved of the outcome within the organization.

[27] This would seem to be particularly true of O'Neal. The South was hardly yet committed or won over to McNary-Haugenism. Moreover, O'Neal probably had a tighter control over his constituency than did others.

[28] Cf. Kile, *The Farm Bureau through Three Decades*, p. 106. A familiar pattern of business elements in alliance with commercial agriculture is to be seen here.

[29] Henry A. Wallace said that his father, while secretary, directed a subordinate to draw up the bill which McNary and Haugen first introduced. *Wallaces' Farmer*, vol. 52 (September 2, 1927), p. 1115.

[30] Cf. Christensen, thesis as cited, pp. 218–220. Neither the merits nor the complex maneuverings of the McNary-Haugen drive can be considered here. There is a very large literature on the problem. John D. Black, *Agricultural Reform in the United States* (New York, McGraw-Hill Book Co., 1929), Part III, may be taken as an able contemporary account. For detailed discussion of the legislative campaign, see Christensen.

[31] Henry A. Wallace in 1926 called for "an alliance of West and South." *Wallaces' Farmer*, vol. 51 (January 15, 1926), p. 67.

[32] There is no suggestion here that this problem was either unreal or inadequately understood, only that it was highly selective. For a sampling of the literature see National Industrial Conference Board, *The Agricultural Problem in the United States* (New York, 1926); Chamber of Commerce of the United States, Businessmen's Commission on Agriculture, *The Condition of Agriculture in the United States and Measures for Its Improvement* (Washington, D.C., 1927); E. R. A. Seligman, *The Economics of Farm Relief* (New York, Columbia University Press, 1929); and Black, *op. cit.*

[33] Its membership was 301,932 in 1929. See Appendix, table 1.

NOTES TO CHAPTER 7

[1] This slogan appeared monthly in *Bureau Farmer* (later renamed *Nation's Agriculture*), the principal publication of the national federation.

[2] Cf. collection figures, American Farm Bureau Federation, *Annual Report*, 1930, 1931, 1932.

[3] Cf. O. M. Kile, *The Farm Bureau through Three Decades* (Baltimore, Waverly Press, 1948), p. 182.

[4] The element of "strategy" involved is suggested by the fact that neither O'Neal nor Hearst were opposed in the election. All other incumbent directors were returned. *Colorado Farm Bureau News*, January, 1932.

[5] For details see Appendix, table 1.

[6] Cf. remarks in Report to Congress, quoted in Russell Lord, *The Wallaces of Iowa* (Boston, Houghton Mifflin Co., 1941), p. 313.

[7] It consisted mainly of the export debenture device.

[8] From an interview with L. J. Taber, Master of the National Grange, in DeWitt C. Wing, "Trends in National Farm Organizations," U. S. Department of Agriculture, *Yearbook of Agriculture, 1940*, p. 950. Although this interview was apparently given at a later date, the point of view applies for the early 'thirties as well.

[9] The position of Iowa in the Farm Bureau has usually been second to Illinois. The 1930 data are drawn from figures on state collections by the national organization. Cf. American Farm Bureau Federation, *Annual Report, 1930*.

[10] For a description of such activities see Donald R. Murphy, "The Farmers Go on Strike," *New Republic*, vol. 72 (August 31, 1932), pp. 66–68.

[11] Cf. "Who and Why? The Opposition to the Farm Bureau," *Iowa Farm Bureau Messenger*, March, 1933, p. 9. See also Gladys Baker, *The County Agent* (University of Chicago Press, 1939), pp. 58, 59.

[12] John A. Simpson, national president of the Farmers' Union, announced himself as also representing the Farmers' National Holiday Association in 1933. Cf. Hearings on the Agricultural Emergency Act to Increase Farm Purchasing Power, Senate Committee on Agriculture and Forestry, 73d Cong., 1st sess., 1933, p. 104.

[13] For the full flavor of this, sample the collection of speeches by John A. Simpson, *The Militant Voice of Agriculture* (Oklahoma City, 1934). See also William P. Tucker, "Populism Up-to-Date: The Story of the Farmers' Union," *Agricultural History*, vol. 21 (October, 1947), pp. 198–207.

[14] This charge was echoed by, among others, the editors of *Fortune*. Cf. "Bounty," *Fortune*, vol. 7 (February, 1933), p. 118.

[15] *Bureau Farmer*, vol. 6 (October, 1931), p. 15.

[16] Unsigned article, "United We Stand," *Bureau Farmer*, vol. 7 (March, 1932), p. 4.

[17] American Farm Bureau Federation, *Annual Report, 1932*, p. 6.

[18] American Farm Bureau Federation, Farmers' Union, Grange, National Coöperative Milk Producers' Federation, American Cotton Association, Agricultural Press, National Live Stock Marketing Association, National Fruit and Vegetable Exchange, Mid-South Cotton Growers' Association, National Committee of Farm Organizations, Dairy and Poultry Coöperatives, Inc., Farmers' National Grain Corporation, National Wool Marketing Corporation, Pure Milk Association. *Ibid.*

[19] Simpson, *op. cit.*, p. 52.

[20] American Farm Bureau Federation, *Annual Report, 1934*.

[21] *Bureau Farmer*, vol. 9 (April, 1934), p. 27.

[22] Kile, *op. cit.*, p. 194.

[23] *Wallaces' Farmer*, vol. 57 (May 28, 1932), p. 299.

[24] The elder Wallace had at one time been critical of the coöperative phase of Farm Bureau policy.

[25] *Bureau Farmer*, vol. 8 (April, 1933), p. 5.

[26] American Farm Bureau Federation, Resolutions, 1932 Convention.

[27] *Wallaces' Farmer*, vol. 58 (October 1, 1932), p. 513. Russell Lord comments, "The Farm Bureau was fronting for the domestic allotment measure, but many of its leaders hated control of production quite as ardently and confusedly as George Peek did." Lord, *op. cit.*, p. 330.

[28] Lord, *op. cit.*, pp. 305–324.

[29] Henry A. Wallace, *New Frontiers* (New York, Reynal and Hitchcock, 1934), p. 148.

[30] Hearings on the Agricultural Adjustment Relief Plan, Senate Committee on Agriculture and Forestry, 72d Cong., 2d sess., 1933, p. 14.

[31] The program of the Farmers' Union was based upon assurance to producers of cost of production, and was quite as much oriented to the commercial farmer as was the program of the Farm Bureau. The testimony reveals that the alliance strategy of the Farmers' Union was based upon cotton and wheat as against the Farm Bureau's cotton and corn. Cf. Hearings on the Agricultural Emergency Act . . . , Senate Committee on Agriculture and Forestry, 1933, pp. 104–108, 339.

[32] The close working relationship between the administration and the Farm Bureau is illustrated by the fact that the bill was drafted by the counsel of the Farm Bureau at the request of the Department of Agriculture. Cf. D. C. Blaisdell, *Government and Agriculture* (New York, Farrar and Rinehart, 1940), p. 42; American Farm Bureau Federation, *Annual Report, 1935*.

[33] G. N. Peek (with S. Crowther), *Why Quit Our Own?* (New York, D. Van Nostrand Co., 1936), p. 93.

[34] The tags "liberal" and "agrarian" are used by Russell Lord, *The Agrarian Revival* (New York, American Association for Adult Education, 1939), p. 158. The ideological diversity of the "liberal" group is indicated by the fact that it included points of view ranging from that of Victor Christgau to that of Lee Pressman.

[35] Russell Lord has told the story in some detail in *The Wallaces of Iowa*, pp. 393–409.

[36] *Bureau Farmer*, vol. 6 (September, 1931), p. 10.

[37] Cf. unsigned article, "No!" *Bureau Farmer*, vol. 8 (December, 1932), pp. 3–6.

[38] Cf. O'Neal speech reported in *Wyoming Farm Journal*, November 31, 1932, p. 9.

[39] Editorial note by Wallace in *Wallaces' Farmer*, vol. 57 (April 16, 1932), p. 221.

[40] *Bureau Farmer*, vol. 7 (January, 1932), p. 12; vol. 8 (January, 1933), p. 6.

[41] "The farm organizations sought to remove the administration of this bill [A.A.A.] as far as possible from the hands of Congress, endowing instead with dictatorial powers the incoming and then unknown Secretary of Agriculture." Lord, *The Wallaces of Iowa*, p. 312.

[42] O'Neal speech to convention, Association of Land Grant Colleges and Universities, *Proceedings*, 1933 Convention, p. 87.

[43] H. R. Tolley, assistant administrator, A.A.A., "Agricultural Planning in a Democracy," Association of Land Grant Colleges and Universities, *Proceedings*, 1934 Convention, p. 64.

[44] George E. Farrell, "The County Production Control Association," *Extension Service Review*, vol. 5 (February, 1934), p. 23.

[45] "Agricultural Adjustment in 1934," U. S. Department of Agriculture, *Report of AAA* (1934), p. 219.

[46] "Serving American Agriculture," U. S. Department of Agriculture, *Report of Extension Work* (1933), p. 5.

[47] At the end of 1935, the A.A.A. had 6,511 employees, of whom 5,522 were in Washington. J. S. Davis, E. G. Nourse, and J. D. Black, *Three Years of the AAA* (Washington, D.C., The Brookings Institution, 1937), p. 50.

[48] *Ibid.*, pp. 71–77. Cf. also Baker, *op. cit.*, pp. 70–77; U. S. Department of Agriculture, *Report of Extension Work* (1933), p. 6.

[49] W. H. Brokaw, "Adjustment Program Influences Extension," *Extension Service Review*, vol. 5 (December, 1934), p. 179.

[50] The number of counties having agents (male) was as follows:

1929...2,323	1933...2,307	1937...2,876
1930...2,376	1934...2,814	1938...2,989
1931...2,447	1935...2,857	1939...2,990
1932...2,369	1936...2,922	

The number of counties taken as agricultural is 3,076. Since 1939, the figure of counties having agents has been quite stable. Data from annual reports of Extension Service, various titles.

[51] It is worth observing that during this period of expansion there was a steady undercurrent of criticism of Extension Service on the grounds that it was giving assistance only to prosperous farmers. In 1941 the Extension Service published a pamphlet written by M. C. Wilson, *How and to What Extent Is the Extension Service Reaching Low-Income Farm Families?* Extension Service Circular 375 (1941). Wilson concluded that, although the Extension Service is organized to give educational service in areas which are handicapped by a high concentration of "disadvantaging" conditions in comparison with other areas, in practice "Extension is reaching a somewhat larger proportion of those of higher socio-economic status." This condition was caused by "the limiting factor" of personnel (p. 20).

[52] Admittedly, other farm groups grumbled. Kile, *op. cit.*, p. 205.

[53] *Iowa Farm Bureau Messenger*, April, 1934, p. 11.

[54] "Farmers have become organization-conscious. The situation appears more propitious for organizing agriculture than at any time for many years." American Farm Bureau Federation, *Annual Report, 1933*; also an unsigned article, "Signing 'Em Up," *Bureau Farmer*, vol. 9 (April, 1934), p. 5.

[55] From 163,246 in 1933 to 356,564 in 1936. See Appendix, table 1. Ralph Russell has plotted Farm Bureau membership against cash farm income. Although the comparison is interesting, income is only one element in a complex story. "Membership of the American Farm Bureau Federation, 1926–1935," *Rural Sociology*, vol. 2 (March, 1937), p. 33.

[56] The estimate is based on dues collected by the national federation. Alabama was the largest Southern federation. It was surpassed by Illinois, New York, Indiana, Iowa, California, Minnesota, and Ohio. American Farm Bureau Federation, *Annual Report, 1934*.

[57] These were the Bankhead and Kerr-Smith acts, which may be roughly described as special A.A.A.'s with compulsory features. Cf. testimony of O'Neal, Hearings on Amendments to the Agricultural Adjustment Act, House Committee on Agriculture, 74th Cong., 1st sess., 1935, p. 298.

[58] "A special procedure has been worked out for rebuilding Farm Bureau membership in the southern states and the basic outlines of this plan with appropriate adaptions have been applied successfully in Arkansas, North Carolina, Virginia, and Mississippi. A similar plan is being organized in Louisiana. Under this plan, an organization program is carefully worked out by representatives of the national organization, state

organization, and the Extension Service, definitely allocating responsibilities, mapping out the steps to be taken, assigning membership quotas all the way along the line, and providing for a method of thorough preparation, a period of mass action with district mass meetings and leaders' conferences and a period of intensive follow-up work.

"The Extension Service in the Farm Bureau states in the southern region have been outstanding in the splendid coöperation and assistance which they have rendered in this organization movement." American Farm Bureau Federation, *Annual Report, 1936*.

[59] Cf. Baker, *op. cit.*, p. 141.

[60] For accounts of the injustices of the program see Webster Powell and Addison T. Cutler, "Tightening the Cotton Belt," *Harpers*, vol. 168 (February, 1934), pp. 312–313; C. S. Johnson, E. R. Embree, and W. W. Alexander, *The Collapse of Cotton Tenancy* (Chapel Hill, University of North Carolina Press, 1935); Minority Report of W. L. Blackstone of Southern Tenant Farmers' Union, Report of the President's Committee on Farm Tenancy, prepared under the auspices of the National Resources Committee, 1937, p. 21; Arthur F. Raper, *Preface to Peasantry* (Chapel Hill, University of North Carolina Press, 1936), p. 245; Davis, Nourse, and Black, *op. cit.*, pp. 120, 338, 346–348. See also quotation from unpublished study by Gunnar Lange in Gunnar Myrdal, *An American Dilemma* (New York, Harper and Bros., 1944), pp. 1247, 1248.

[61] Johnson, Embree, and Alexander, *op. cit.*, p. 51.

[62] Tugwell is reported to have early identified the land grant college system, the state Extension directors, and the county agents "with the ruling caste of farmers, the most conservative Farm Bureau leaders, the cotton barons of the South, the emerging Associated Farmers of California, the banker-farmers of the Middle West." Lord, *The Wallaces of Iowa*, p. 381.

[63] *U.S. v. Butler*, 297 U.S. 1.

[64] Chronology is given in American Farm Bureau Federation, *Annual Report, 1936*. See also "A New Adjustment Pattern," *Nation's Agriculture*, vol. 11 (February, 1936), pp. 4, 5.

[65] Hearings on Substitute Legislation for the Invalidated Agricultural Adjustment Act, Senate Committee on Agriculture and Forestry, 74th Cong., 2d sess., 1936, pp. 2, 3, 13.

[66] U. S. Department of Agriculture, *Report of AAA* (1937), p. 60.

[67] *Ibid.*

[68] American Farm Bureau Federation, *Annual Report, 1936*.

[69] One check paid out under the new Soil Conservation and Domestic Allotment Act was for $60,388 (to the Delta Pine and Land Company of Bolivar County, Mississippi). Hearings on the Agricultural Adjustment Act of 1937, Senate Committee on Agriculture and Forestry, 75th Cong., 1st sess., 1937, pp. 105–106. In 1936 some 116 payees received, in benefits, more than $10,000 each under the program. Cf. U. S. Department of Agriculture, Production and Marketing Administration, *Agricultural Conservation Program, Statistical Summary, 1948* (1949), table 13, p. 73. This table gives the history of payments by size-of-payment groups. Unfortunately, it is less than revealing as it is drawn up.

[70] *Nation's Agriculture*, vol. 12 (March, 1937), p. 12.

[71] Hearings on the Agricultural Adjustment Act of 1937, Senate Committee on Agriculture and Forestry, 1937, p. 9.

[72] Hearings on General Farm Legislation, House Committee on Agriculture, 75th Cong., 1st sess., 1937, p. 81.

[73] A convenient summary of the act appears in Blaisdell, *op. cit.*, pp. 60–68.

[74] American Farm Bureau Federation, *Twenty Years with the American Farm Bureau Federation* (1939), pamphlet.

[75] *Ibid.*

[76] New problems came after 1938, but these were so important that they must be treated separately, in subsequent chapters.

[77] Unsigned article, "Where Agriculture Speaks," *Bureau Farmer*, vol. 8 (November, 1932), p. 2.

[78] See Davis, Nourse, and Black, *op. cit.*, pp. 32–50.

[79] Wallace, *New Frontiers*, p. 163.

[80] "The Farm Bureau at Washington looks after them all...the cotton farmer in Alabama, and the dairy farmer in Minnesota, the sugar producers in cane regions, and the best farmers in many states..." Unsigned article, "Keeping Tab on Washington," *Nation's Agriculture*, vol. 12 (April, 1937), p. 6.

[81] H. J. King, "Stockmen Need the Farm Bureau," *Nation's Agriculture*, vol. 12 (June, 1937), pp. 1–2.

[82] The phrase appeared in *Nation's Agriculture*, vol. 14 (September, 1939), p. 14, in reference to the Smith cotton bill.

[83] *Ibid.*, vol. 15 (January, 1940), p. 18.

[84] *Bureau Farmer*, vol. 9 (January, 1934), p. 15.

[85] "Officials of the A.A.A. acted quietly in numerous ways to discourage such a development" (i.e., the rise of a new farm organization). Davis, Nourse, and Black, *op. cit.*, pp. 271–273. Cf. also Lord, *The Wallaces of Iowa*, pp. 449–450.

[86] Cf. American Farm Bureau Federation, *Annual Report, 1933*.

[87] Association of Land Grant Colleges and Universities, *Proceedings*, 1933 Convention, p. 89.

[88] H. J. C. Umberger, "The Relationship of the Land Grant Colleges to the A.A.A. Programs," Association of Land Grant Colleges and Universities, *Proceedings*, 1934 Convention, p. 108.

[89] I. O. Schaub, "Can Extension Continue an Educational Program and Administer Enforcement and Regulatory Measures?" Association of Land Grant Colleges and Universities, *Proceedings*, 1934 Convention, pp. 183–185.

[90] American Farm Bureau Federation, *Annual Report, 1936*.

[91] See, for example, the resolution on coördination, passed at the 1939 convention of the federation.

[92] The President's Committee on Administrative Management. For the reaction of the federation see *Nation's Agriculture*, vol. 13 (1938), p. 7; also the American Farm Bureau Federation, Resolutions, 1937 Convention.

[93] For example, the Bailey marketing bill, which would have made appropriations to state departments of agriculture for the encouragement of coöperative marketing by farmers, was opposed on the grounds that (1) the state departments of agriculture were primarily regulatory bodies, and (2) state directors of agriculture were political appointees in whose hands additional powers would prove "extremely dangerous." *Nation's Agriculture*, vol. 15 (September, 1940), p. 2. See also vol. 16 (May, 1941), p. 14.

[94] "Government's relation to the American Farm Bureau Federation probably is a little closer than to any other farmers' organization, because of its origin and because of the fact that its county Farm Bureau units are organized primarily for the purpose of aiding the agricultural colleges and the Federal Department of Agriculture—to do the extension work assigned these two institutions in the National Agricultural Extension Act of 1914. No other farmers' organization has such a purpose. The A.F.B.F. has always backed extension legislation to the limit." C. B. Smith, director of Extension, "Farm Bureau and Extension," *Nation's Agriculture*, vol. 15, January, 1940, p. 9.

[95] B. H. Crocheron, "Re-defining the Extension Job and Field of Action," Association of Land Grant Colleges and Universities, *Proceedings*, 1941 Convention, p. 192. Crocheron was director of Agricultural Extension in California.

NOTES TO CHAPTER 8

[1] One of the groups most acutely aware of tenancy as a farm problem was the Bankers' Association. Their publications consistently carried articles discussing it during the 'twenties. Soil conservation had been mentioned in the report of the Commission on Country Life, and the energetic career of Hugh Bennett, of course, comes to mind. Also, it should not be forgotten that an important element of essentially agricultural policy was embodied in the administration of the Reclamation Act of 1902.

[2] ... "to feed the hungry, clothe the naked, and give drink to the thirsty..." (John Taylor).

[3] For a lively account see Robert E. Sherwood, *Roosevelt and Hopkins* (New York, Bantam ed., 1950), vol. 1, pp. 46–94.

[4] Among the sponsors of the movement was Henry Ford. In the main, however, it was unorganized. Even in the depression, 1932 was the only year in recent times which saw a net migration from cities, towns, and villages to farms. Cf. Report on H.R. 369, Interstate Migration, House Select Committee to Investigate the Interstate Migration of Destitute Citizens (Tolan Committee), 77th Cong., 1st sess., 1941, table, p. 287.

[5] Cf. Russell Lord, *The Wallaces of Iowa* (Boston, Houghton Mifflin Co., 1941), pp. 300–305.

[6] Section 208.

[7] See chap. 7.

[8] Before it was superseded, the Resettlement Administration assembled a staff of approximately 18,000, more than 13,000 of whom came from the old state rural rehabilitation corporations. The term "Unsettlement Administration" came to be a byword in bureaucratic circles. Cf. James G. Maddox, "The Farm Security Administration" (unpublished doctoral thesis, Harvard University, 1950), pp. 30–32. The present chapter owes much to this thesis, which was based on Maddox' years of experience as one of the key administrators of the F.S.A.

[9] The committee was appointed on November 16, 1936, and reported on February 16, 1937. Its membership included representatives of such diverse interests as Will W. Alexander of the Commission on Inter-Racial Coöperation, Louis Brownlow of the Public Administration Clearing House, Rexford Tugwell, Clarence Poe of *The Progressive Farmer*, and E. A. O'Neal. Despite the presence of the last, the committee was weighted on the liberal side. Report of the President's Committee on Farm Tenancy, prepared under the auspices of the National Resources Committee, 1937, p. 28.

[10] As an administrator, Tugwell seems to have been capable of arousing either strong hostility or extraordinary loyalty.

[11] Not to be confused with the Bankhead-Jones Act of 1935, which gave additional support to the Extension Service.

[12] Cf. Maddox, thesis as cited, pp. 45–51.

[13] By far the best discussion of this program is by Maddox. Most of his thesis is devoted to the rural rehabilitation program. The plan of the work was unfortunately not carried out; so it must stand as devoted primarily to this program and to a lesser degree to the farm ownership program. Maddox was chief of the Rural Rehabilitation Division.

[14] Of F.S.A. funds, from 1936 to 1946, 59 per cent went to rural rehabilitation. Maddox, thesis as cited, p. 88.

[15] U. S. Department of Agriculture, Farm Security Administration, *Annual Report of the Administrator, 1940*, pp. 3, 4.

[16] Total loans to the end of 1946, the year of the agency's death, were $1,047,507,373, of which $704,689,346 had been repaid, plus $97,000,000 in interest. The ratio of collections to maturities was 87 per cent. Maddox, thesis as cited, pp. 367–368. It may be argued that this high level of repayment was itself an indication that the program was not striking deep enough in the attempt to alleviate poverty.

[17] Loans were made for the drilling of wells and the building of small dams and storage facilities.

[18] A total of $272,859,919 was lent between 1938 and 1946 in 44,331 loans. The program accounted for the distribution of 13 per cent of all F.S.A. funds. Cf. Maddox, thesis as cited, pp. 88, 424. See also Paul V. Maris, *The Land Is Mine: Farm Tenancy to Family Ownership*, U. S. Department of Agriculture, Monograph no. 8 (1950). This volume relates primarily to the later Farmers' Home Administration phase of the program's history.

[19] There is no adequate study of the projects. The best general work is by Joseph W. Eaton, *Exploring Tomorrow's Agriculture* (New York, Harper and Bros., 1943), pp.

65–100; but this is far from satisfactory. An excellent study of one project (Casa Grande) is by Edward C. Banfield, *Government Project* (Glencoe, Ill., The Free Press, 1951). Source material on the other projects is scattered, and many of the questions cannot be answered because of the headlong haste with which the projects were dismantled. Much factual data is to be found in Hearings, Select Committee of House Committee on Agriculture to Investigate Activities of the Farm Security Administration (Cooley Committee Hearings), 78th Cong., 1943 and 1944, Part III.

[20] Camps were located in Idaho, Washington, Oregon, California, Arizona, Texas, and Florida.

[21] It accounted for but 2 per cent of F.S.A. funds. Maddox, thesis as cited.

[22] Cf. Rachel R. Swiger and Conrad Taeuber, *Ill Fed, Ill Clothed, Ill Housed—Five Hundred Families in Need of Help*, U. S. Department of Agriculture, Bureau of Agricultural Economics (1944); and Rachel R. Swiger and Olaf F. Larson, *Climbing toward Security*, U. S. Department of Agriculture, Bureau of Agricultural Economics (1944).

[23] Not that the F.S.A. was altogether ineffectual; it was not, as the figures on loan repayment suggest. Maddox estimates that somewhat more than 800,000 farm families received loans under the main rehabilitation program alone. Thesis as cited, p. 365.

[24] *Ibid.*, pp. 89–96.

[25] A. Whitney Griswold, *Farming and Democracy* (New York, Harcourt, Brace and Co., 1948), p. 163.

[26] Letter to the members of the Conference on Economic Conditions in the South, preceding its report. U. S. National Emergency Council, *Report on Economic Conditions of the South* (1938). This brief, incisive report, prepared for the President, was probably the most effective of a number of reports, investigations, and studies which were part of the same movement that produced the F.S.A. The personnel of the latter, in fact, contributed heavily to most of these reports.

[27] Maddox, thesis as cited, table, p. 176.

[28] Gunnar Myrdal, *An American Dilemma* (New York, Harper and Bros., 1944), pp. 274–275. Myrdal expressed surprise that this should be so, for, at the time his study was made, F.S.A. loans were subject to approval by local committees consisting of "big" farmers. Myrdal rightly assessed the general significance of the committee system, but seems to have been unaware that the committees only recently had acquired power to pass on eligibility for loans. Cf. Maddox, thesis as cited, pp. 113–114.

[29] The objection of the dairy interests was that land withdrawn from cotton production under the A.A.A. might be devoted to dairying.

[30] The long-term nature of the problem was the subject of an excellent report of the U. S. Great Plains Committee, *The Future of the Great Plains* (Washington, D.C., 1936).

[31] Maddox, thesis as cited, p. 288. Most of the hostility centered around loans to the Farmers' Union Grain Terminal Association of St. Paul.

[32] Not all the political liabilities of the F.S.A. have been mentioned. Neither is the list complete for groups of farmers who were affected by the organization. For such a listing see Carl C. Taylor, Helen W. Wheeler, and E. L. Kirkpatrick, *Disadvantaged Classes in American Agriculture*, U. S. Department of Agriculture, Farm Security Administration and Bureau of Agricultural Economics, Social Research Report no. 8 (1938).

[33] See discussion in chap. 2.

NOTES TO CHAPTER 9

[1] For example, in a pamphlet, *Accomplishments 1919–1944*, published by the federation just after the fight against the F.S.A. had been substantially won. Its validity should be judged in the light of evidence given here.

[2] Report of the President's Committee on Farm Tenancy, prepared under the auspices of the National Resources Committee, 1937, pp. 22–24.

[3] Hearings on Farm Tenancy, House Committee on Agriculture, 75th Cong., 1st sess., 1937, p. 316.

[4] O. M. Kile reported that the Farm Bureau was "not very enthusiastic" and that

passage of the bill was the work of "other forces." *The Farm Bureau through Three Decades* (Baltimore, Waverly Press, 1948), p. 255.

⁵ "The Platform of American Farmers," *Nation's Agriculture*, vol. 15 (July–August, 1940), p. 15. From this concise statement it would appear that the federation had good comprehension of the character of the F.S.A. program—much better than it had a year later.

⁶ See chap. 10.

⁷ For a very suggestive discussion of Farm Bureau thinking for this period, see Kile, *op. cit.*, pp. 255–260.

⁸ Resolutions, 1940 Convention, *Nation's Agriculture*, vol. 16 (January, 1941), pp. 18–20.

⁹ The Farm Bureau did appear on behalf of the price elements of its program before the Senate Committee on Appropriations, but relied on House action for the desired administrative reorganization. Hearings on the Agricultural Appropriation Bill for 1942, Senate Committee on Appropriations, 77th Cong., 1st sess., 1941.

¹⁰ See chap. 10.

¹¹ See statement by W. R. Ogg, Hearings on the Agriculture Department Appropriation Bill for 1942, House Committee on Appropriations, 1941, p. 502.

¹² *Ibid.*, p. 483.

¹³ "Along last summer there was sent out to the several State Farm Bureaus, the state organizations that make up the national organization, forty in number, a request that an attempt be made to get the data on the operations of the Farm Security Administration within their respective states. This did not bring back a great deal of detailed information, but there were certain generalizations that were developed in this way." Statement of Donald Kirkpatrick, legal counsel for the federation, before the Byrd Committee. Hearings, Joint Committee on Reduction of Nonessential Federal Expenditures, 77th Cong., 1st and 2d sess., 1942, p. 793. (Hereinafter cited as Byrd Committee Hearings.)

¹⁴ Cf. Resolutions, 1941 Convention, *Nation's Agriculture*, vol. 17 (January, 1942), pp. 12–14.

¹⁵ This outline of events and the statement of the investigators' mission are drawn from the committee hearings. Testimony of Kirkpatrick, Byrd Committee Hearings, 1942, pp. 793–795.

¹⁶ This was brought out inadvertently and Senator La Follette secured its inclusion in the record. One of the investigators wrote to his chief as follows: "Enclosed you will find detailed report of observations in Shelby County and evidence secured for some criticism made. Also what we were able to locate and find out in Clark County. If this is in line with what you had hoped to receive, or if there are other suggestions you might have after looking over these notes, I hope you will do so and notify me." *Ibid.*, p. 810.

¹⁷ *Ibid.*, p. 746.

¹⁸ Testimony of Judge R. K. Greene of Alabama. *Ibid.*, p. 699.

¹⁹ *Ibid.*, p. 743.

²⁰ *Ibid.*, p. 745.

²¹ "The general public of the State of Arkansas feels that the F.S.A. is accomplishing nothing but is committing acts the results of which will take a long time to rectify." *Ibid.*, p. 832.

²² Some said that Carr spent only two or three days in Arkansas. Certainly it could not have been much longer in view of the area assigned him and the time allowed. Hearings on the Agricultural Appropriation Bill for 1942, Senate Committee on Appropriations, 1941, p. 870.

²³ The report was made the basis of an article by Carr, "The Return of the Carpetbagger," *Nation's Agriculture*, vol. 17 (April, 1942), p. 7.

²⁴ George Mitchell in a speech made in Puerto Rico. Byrd Committee Hearings, 1942, pp. 872–873.

²⁵ Report of the President's Committee on Farm Tenancy, 1937, p. 6. O'Neal had not taken exception to the statement in his letter qualifying his own signature of the report.

[26] Monsignor O'Grady appeared before the following: Hearings on the Agriculture Department Appropriation Bill for 1943, House Committee on Appropriations, 77th Cong., 2d sess., 1942, Part II, pp. 583–588.

Hearings on the Agricultural Appropriation Bill for 1942, Senate Committee on Appropriations, 1941, pp. 519–535.

Hearings, Select Committee of House Committee on Agriculture to Investigate Activities of the Farm Security Administration, 78th Cong., 1943 and 1944, pp. 629 ff. (Hereafter cited as Cooley Committee Hearings.)

[27] Hearings on the Agriculture Department Appropriation Bill for 1944, House Committee on Appropriations, 78th Cong., 1st sess., 1943, p. 1488.

[28] The context, of course, was the potential contribution of small farmers to war food production. Citation of Black and Tolley, in Hearings on the Agricultural Appropriation Bill for 1943, Senate Committee on Appropriations, 1942, pp. 1030, 1031.

[29] Statement of H. S. Casey Abbott, Hearings on the Agriculture Department Appropriation Bill for 1944, House Committee on Appropriations, 1943, pp. 1389–1392. Also disturbing was F.S.A.'s management of a program for transportation of domestic workers to areas of labor shortage.

[30] *Ibid.*, p. 1619.

[31] Cooley Committee Hearings, Parts I–IV. These hearings cover 1969 pages. The report of the committee is House Report 1430, May, 1944.

[32] Patton became president in 1940. The Farmers' Union in the previous five years had been through much turmoil over the direction of its policy. At one stage it had been drawn rather closely into the movement of Father Coughlin. Cf. editorial, "Father Coughlin and the League for Social Justice," *Farmers' Union Herald*, March, 1935. In the late 'thirties, however, the organization became a strong supporter of the F.S.A., and when Patton became president the central body was reorganized.

[33] James G. Maddox, "The Farm Security Administration" (unpublished doctoral thesis, Harvard University, 1950), pp. 496, 504.

[34] Cooley Committee Hearings, pp. 760–772.

[35] The Farm Bureau presentation appears in the middle of the hearings. *Ibid.*, pp. 797–869.

[36] Much of this part of the inquiry was on a first-name basis between O'Neal and members of the committee. Cf. *ibid.*, pp. 833 ff.

[37] *Ibid.*, p. 1542.

[38] Cooley Committee, House Report 1430, May, 1944, pp. 1 and 2.

[39] Executive Order 9070.

[40] Executive Order 9280. See discussion in chap. 10.

[41] Public law no. 45, 1943. Patton called this the "Peonage Act."

[42] F.S.A. personnel by years: 1942, 19,045; 1943, 14,862; 1944, 11,176. Hancock gave his objective for 1945 as 9,514. He more than achieved this. Hearings on the Agriculture Department Appropriation Bill for 1945, House Committee on Appropriations, 78th Cong., 2d sess., 1944, p. 962.

[43] In the first year of operation of the Farmers' Home Administration, three-fifths of the loans for purchase of farms went to veterans. U. S. Department of Agriculture, Farmers' Home Administration, Report of the Administrator, *Strengthening the Family Farm* (1947). In 1950, 93 per cent of these loans went to veterans. Farmers' Home Administration, Report of the Administrator for 1950.

NOTES TO CHAPTER 10

[1] This is the inscription cut into the western side of Hilgard Hall, one of the University of California's agricultural buildings in Berkeley. Extension people are fond of quoting it.

[2] Hearings on the Agricultural Appropriation Bill for 1942, Senate Committee on Appropriations, 77th Cong., 1st sess., 1941, p. 1016.

[3] See testimony quoted in chap. 9. The Cotton Council, it should be observed, had Farm Bureau representation in its own body.

⁴ Cf. testimony of O'Neal, Hearings on the Farmers' Home Corporation Act of 1944, House Committee on Agriculture, 78th Cong., 2d sess., 1944, pp. 28–42. O'Neal still sought placement of all F.S.A. loaning activities in the Farm Credit Administration. Drastic curtailment of these activities was not enough. Patton, curiously, was pleased in general with the congressional proposals. See his testimony, pp. 17, 18.

⁵ The statement is Hugh H. Bennett's before the Association of Land Grant Colleges and Universities, *Proceedings*, 1935 Convention, p. 211. He merely mentioned the memorandum there. His attitude was one of conciliation.

⁶ For the text of the Mount Weather Agreement see John M. Gaus and Leon O. Wolcott, *Public Administration and the United States Department of Agriculture*, Public Administration Service (Chicago, 1940), Appendix B, pp. 463–465.

⁷ Examples of this point of view are: M. L. Wilson, *Democracy Has Roots* (New York, Carrick and Evans, 1939), p. 178; Dale Clark, "The Farmer as Co-Administrator," *Public Opinion Quarterly*, vol. 3 (July, 1939), pp. 472–490; and John D. Lewis, "Democratic Planning in Agriculture," *American Political Science Review*, vol. 35 (April and June, 1941), pp. 232–249, 454–469.

⁸ See discussion in chap. 15.

⁹ Cf., for example, Neal C. Gross, "A Post Mortem on County Planning," *Journal of Farm Economics*, vol. 25 (August, 1943), pp. 644–661. This article largely follows the points made by Bruce Ryan, "Democratic Telesis and County Agricultural Planning," *Journal of Farm Economics*, vol. 22 (November, 1940), pp. 691–700.

¹⁰ To this catalogue of enthusiasts for the planning scheme might be added those whose tastes centered about orderly administration. Gaus and Wolcott may be taken as characteristic of these "administrationists." Cf. their conclusion that by 1939 the Department of Agriculture had reached maturity by becoming "more than a collection of semiautonomous bureaus." *Op. cit.*, p. 79. This refers to the reorganization that followed the Mount Weather Agreement.

¹¹ Maddox has commented that the American Farm Bureau Federation was well represented on the local governing boards of the National Farm Loan Association and Production Credit Association. James G. Maddox, "The Farm Security Administration" (unpublished doctoral thesis, Harvard University, 1950), p. 496.

¹² Resolutions, 1940 Convention. Quoted from Hearings on the Agriculture Department Appropriation Bill for 1942, House Committee on Appropriations, 1941, Part II, pp. 416, 417. Appears also in *Nation's Agriculture*, vol. 16 (January, 1941), pp. 18, 19.

¹³ Hearings on the Agriculture Department Appropriation Bill for 1942, pp. 407–412.

¹⁴ *Ibid.*, p. 487.

¹⁵ The best part of Wickard's reply was an organizational chart drawn according to the plan. It is found in *ibid.*, p. 546. The summary of the reply ran thus: "The issues crystallized by the proposal then are: (*a*) Shall the unified national farm program be broken down into 48 State programs? (*b*) Shall any of the separate State programs be dominated in any State by a farm organization? (*c*) Shall a State official have sole authority to nominate the members of any Federal Board? (*d*) Shall we experiment with a discredited form of board administration now of all times in a period calling for sensitive reaction to world forces? (*e*) Shall we sacrifice the specialized zeal of the Farm Security Administration? Of the A.A.A., of the S.C.S.? (*f*) Does the Congress wish to establish a new principle in Federal-State relations under which States, though not required to match or even furnish any of the funds, are given responsibility for the execution of federally financed programs?" *Ibid.*, p. 529.

¹⁶ *Ibid.*

¹⁷ This is according to Charles M. Hardin, "The Bureau of Agricultural Economics under Fire, A Study in Valuation Conflicts," *Journal of Farm Economics*, vol. 28 (August, 1946), p. 645.

¹⁸ Cf. statement of the Department of Agriculture quoted in note 15.

¹⁹ The Hardin article (*op. cit.*) deals with the case of the B.A.E. in some detail.

²⁰ A remark to Hardin, quoted by him, *ibid.*, p. 644.

[21] Hearings on the Agricultural Appropriation Bill for 1942, Senate Committee on Appropriations, 1941, pp. 536 ff.

[22] Byrd Committee Hearings, 1942, p. 749.

[23] See chap. 9.

[24] Director Harry Schooler made this statement on his resignation: "Ed O'Neal and Earl Smith have been whittling away at the A.A.A. for the last three years. They won't be satisfied until they have placed men in charge of the national farm program who will just carry water for the Farm Bureau." *Wallaces' Farmer*, vol. 68 (April 17, 1943), p. 253. See also the general comments in O. M. Kile, *The Farm Bureau through Three Decades* (Baltimore, Waverly Press, 1948), p. 260; and Hearings on the Agriculture Department Appropriation Bill for 1944, House Committee on Appropriations, 78th Cong., 1st sess., 1943, pp. 1506–1508.

[25] Hearings on the Agriculture Department Appropriation Bill for 1942, House Committee on Appropriations, 1941, p. 484.

[26] Philip Selznick, *TVA and the Grass Roots* (Berkeley and Los Angeles, University of California Press, 1949).

[27] *Ibid.*, pp. 98 ff.

[28] This account is based on the Selznick study, which in turn was based upon interviews in the field.

[29] Hearings on the Farmers' Home Corporation Act of 1944, House Committee on Agriculture, 78th Cong., 2d sess., 1944, pp. 102–103. For discussion of this letter see chap. 9.

NOTES TO CHAPTER 11

[1] John D. Black, *Federal-State-Local Relations in Agriculture*, National Planning Association, Agriculture Committee (1949; mimeographed), p. 2.

[2] See chap. 13 for discussion of membership.

[3] *Nation's Agriculture*, vol. 20 (January, 1945), p. 19.

[4] *Ibid.*, vol. 21 (January, 1946), pp. 13, 18.

[5] The P.M.A. replaced the A.A.A. in 1945, when the Department of Agriculture was reorganized. This reorganization brought a substantial number of the bureaus of the department under one administrator. Charles M. Hardin considers that this has resulted in so great a concentration of power within the department that the administrator of the P.M.A. has become a political figure rivaling the Secretary of Agriculture himself. See Charles M. Hardin, *The Politics of Agriculture: Soil Conservation and the Struggle for Power in Rural America* (Glencoe, Ill., The Free Press, 1952), p. 106.

[6] The 1946 resolutions read in part: "A minimum of centralized control over agricultural programs from Washington is absolutely essential. Farmers in each State and county should develop and carry out programs to meet their particular needs and conditions.

"Duplication, overlapping, and unnecessary expense in governmental operations must be eliminated.

"We believe it incumbent upon the Secretary of Agriculture to consult with representatives of bona fide farm organizations in establishing agencies and agency responsibilities to carry out agricultural laws and programs. The foundation of our program is farmer participation in program planning and operation.

"We urge a program of conservation of soil, water, grazing and forest resources designed to secure a maximum of conservation with a minimum of expense.

"We urge decentralization of program planning and operation of conservation programs with authority and responsibilities placed in bona fide local, district, and State farmer committees.

"We urge that the conservation program be placed on a grant-in-aid basis to States, with each State determining what conservation practices are eligible for payment under existing law and that no practice be included unless approved by a State committee of farmers and representatives from land-grant colleges."

Quoted from summary of resolutions, Hearings on the Farm Program of the American Farm Bureau Federation, House Committee on Agriculture, 80th Cong., 1st sess., 1947, p. 40. These resolutions appear also in *Nation's Agriculture*, vol. 22 (January, 1947), p. 10.

[7] Farm Bureau spokesmen denied that they wished to *destroy* the S.C.S. They wished to continue "the technical help" of the S.C.S. by putting it in the Extension organization. In a further refinement of the argument, they stated that, in their plan, S.C.S. technicians would not be under the direction of the county agent but merely operating "through his office." See testimony of H. E. Slusher of the Missouri Farm Bureau, Hearings on the Farm Program of the American Farm Bureau Federation, House Committee on Agriculture, 80th Cong., 1st sess., 1947, p. 23. The committee, however, does seem to have understood the program of the Farm Bureau Federation as calling for the destruction of the S.C.S.

[8] Hearings on the Agriculture Department Appropriation Bill for 1946, House Committee on Appropriations, 79th Cong., 1st sess., 1945, p. 1053.

[9] *Ibid.*, pp. 1053, 1056.

[10] The resolution was read by O'Neal to the House Appropriations Subcommittee, in February, 1946, at Hearings on the Agriculture Department Appropriation Bill for 1947, House Committee on Appropriations, 79th Cong., 2d sess., 1946, pp. 1630–1632.

[11] *Ibid.* By "A.A.A. committees" at this time were meant Production and Marketing Administration committees, and by "F.S.A. clients" were meant Farmers' Home Administration clients.

[12] For a brief exposition of the activities carried on by the P.M.A., see issues of *United States Government Organization Manual* since 1946. See also Hardin, *op. cit.*, chap. ix.

[13] Cf. O'Neal testimony, Hearings on the Farm Program of the American Farm Bureau Federation, House Committee on Agriculture, 1947, p. 3. O'Neal held that the Extension Service should retain jurisdiction.

[14] See, for example, Resolutions, 1948 Convention, *Nation's Agriculture*, vol. 24 (February, 1949), pp. 18–20. The national federation has not been strong in this demand, but various state farm bureaus have been. The California organization is the leading example.

[15] See Hearings on the Farm Program of the American Farm Bureau Federation, House Committee on Agriculture, 1947, p. 3. The point has been made on nearly every occasion on which questions of administration have been considered by Farm Bureau spokesmen.

[16] See O'Neal's testimony in Hearings on the Long Range Agricultural Policy, House Committee on Agriculture, 80th Cong., 1st sess., 1947, Part I, p. 38. The statement made in text on the relative importance of duplication and extravagance is inference, though necessary inference, from O'Neal's testimony.

[17] The National Association of Soil Conservation Districts.

[18] See testimony of H. E. Slusher of the Missouri Farm Bureau: "Here is what happens. You set up your soil-conservation district and then you have another group of individuals out there who have a tendency to think that they should write the policies also of all agricultural programs for farm people."

Mr. Zimmerman: "What group is that?"

Mr. Slusher: "The soil-conservation districts—officers elected out there in the county. You would have some four or five that would immediately form a state organization and then the thinking is put back from Washington because individuals there would pretend to speak for the farmers." Hearings on the Farm Program of the American Farm Bureau Federation, House Committee on Agriculture, 1947, p. 22.

[19] O. M. Kile makes the explicit comparison from the point of view of the Farm Bureau in *The Farm Bureau through Three Decades* (Baltimore, Waverly Press, 1948), p. 336.

[20] Congressman Dirksen linked Bennett with "Brother" Tolley, C. B. Baldwin, and Rexford Tugwell. Almost all the letters of complaint came from Missouri. Hearings on the Agriculture Department Appropriation Bill for 1948, House Committee on Appropriations, 80th Cong., 1st sess., 1947, Part I, pp. 1009, 1059.

²¹ O'Neal testimony, *ibid.*, p. 1870.

²² The Farm Bureau Federation asked for a 20 per cent reduction in federal administrative expenditures. O'Neal told the committee that, if it would recommend this, "We will give our support to a similar reduction in the total expenditures for the Department of Agriculture, except appropriations for agricultural research and for Federal grants-in-aid to the States for the Extension services, the experiment stations, and the land grant colleges." *Ibid.*

²³ See, for example, Hearings on the Agriculture Department Appropriation Bill for 1949, House Committee on Appropriations, 80th Cong., 2d sess., 1948, Part II, p. 1088.

²⁴ Eventually several such bills were introduced. These and other agricultural bills concerned with administrative organization are analyzed in Black, *op. cit.*, pp. 50–63. Those carrying the title given here were the Jensen bill (H.R. 4417) and the Hope bill (H.R. 6054). See also Charles M. Hardin, "Current Proposals for the Organization of Conservation and Land-Use Programs in Agriculture, the United States," *Journal of Farm Economics*, vol. 30, no. 4 (November, 1948), pp. 619–644.

²⁵ Hearings on Long Range Agricultural Policy, House Committee on Agriculture, 80th Cong., 1st sess., 1948, pp. 1068–1069. The pattern of Extension domination of the Farm Bureau is restricted mainly to the Deep South and is not universal there.

²⁶ Black, *op. cit.*, p. 99.

²⁷ Association of Land Grant Colleges and Universities, *Proceedings*, 1944 Convention, pp. 233–276.

²⁸ *Ibid.*, 1945 Convention, pp. 60–61.

²⁹ See the statement by Noble Clark, *ibid.*, 1946 Convention, p. 200.

³⁰ The Committee on Post-War Agricultural Policy suggested this course of action: "Provide administrative protection and financial support for the county extension office so that extension workers may devote their full time to educational activities among all farmers and may, with discretion and judgment, engage in educational work on broad public issues without endangering their jobs." *Ibid.*, p. 74. Crocheron warned: "If county Extension agents are to find their greatest qualifications as greeters, or as community errand-boys, they will, in that event, then contrive to warrant only the wages and rewards that such an ability brings in the open market." *Ibid.*, p. 133.

³¹ *Ibid.*, p. 216.

³² *Ibid.*, 1947 Convention, pp. 174–175.

³³ *Ibid.*, 1949 Convention, p. 259. The 1947 statement on relationships between the colleges and the Department of Agriculture contained this remarkable statement: "It is a violation of the principle of our constitutional form of self-government for a Federal agency to by-pass a state agency having similar authority and responsibility to work directly with local groups and individuals." *Ibid.*, 1947 Convention.

³⁴ U. S. Department of Agriculture and Association of Land Grant Colleges and Universities, Report of Joint Committee on Extension Programs, Policies, and Goals, 1948.

³⁵ *Ibid.*, p. 1.

³⁶ *Ibid.*, p. 20. Dean H. P. Rusk of the University of Illinois took exception here: "I am not willing to accept the thesis of the majority of the committee that any formal agreement between the extension service and a general farm organization is *per se* undesirable. If any State extension service and a general farm organization forsakes the spirit and purpose of the Smith-Lever Act and the True-Howard agreement to play favorites and indulge in political give-and-take, it will be because of something more fundamental than the presence or absence of a formal agreement with some one of its farm organizations." *Ibid.*, p. 24.

³⁷ *Ibid.*, p. 15.

³⁸ U. S. Commission on Organization of the Executive Branch of the Government, *Agricultural Function and Organization in the United States* (Washington, D.C., 1949), Appendix M (Task Force Report). Its chairman was Dean H. P. Rusk; the other members were W. R. Rhea of the National Cotton Council, D. Howard Doane of Doane Agricultural Service, John M. Gaus of Harvard, Dean William H. Martin of the New Jersey

Agricultural Experiment Station, Frank W. Peek of the Farm Foundation of Chicago, Dean William H. Schoenfeld of Oregon State College, and Chester C. Davis.

[39] *Ibid.*, pp. 34–41. The old name of the service would be preserved, but the substance would be different.

[40] *Ibid.*, pp. 57–63.

[41] *Ibid.*, pp. 65–68.

[42] The commission's own report of recommendations on the Department of Agriculture differed at numerous points. However, on essential issues the recommendations were vague. The statement on field organization is particularly uncertain. When the commission suggests, "This would be a newly constituted Extension Service and not the present Coöperative Extension Service," a little skepticism seems justified. U. S. Commission on Organization of the Executive Branch of the Government, *The Department of Agriculture* (Washington, D.C., 1949), p. 11. The reorganization plan laid before Congress after the commission's report differed from the other two reports. This third plan was in turn rejected by the Senate.

[43] Unfortunately, the hearings were not published. The present account is drawn from the American Farm Bureau Federation, *Official News Letter*, May 20, June 5, July 17, and August 7, 1950; *National Union Farmer*, June, July, and August, 1950. The description of the bill is taken from *Digest of Public General Bills* (81st Cong., 2d sess.), Final Issue, Legislative Reference Service, Library of Congress (Washington, D.C., 1951), p. 151. The lone college whose representatives appeared against the bill was the University of Illinois.

[44] Congressman Hope is reported to have remarked that it was the bill's misfortune to have come up in an election year. *National Union Farmer*, August, 1950.

[45] The case was brought about by a new organization, Friends of Extension. *Ibid.*, December, 1950. It is notable, however, that in 1952 the Nebraska Farm Bureau voted to recommend separation of Extension from the Farm Bureau. In an assessment of this in *Nation's Agriculture*, vol. 28 (May, 1952), pp. 16, 17, Bernie Camp argued that separation would not hurt the Nebraska organization. He is undoubtedly correct.

[46] *Ibid.*, March, 1951. A Pennsylvania Farm Bureau has since then affiliated with the national federation.

NOTES TO CHAPTER 12

[1] This was hailed on the cover of the June, 1941, issue of *Nation's Agriculture*, vol. 16, with the single word "VICTORY" in letters three-quarters of an inch high. "Victory" at that moment in history was a word somewhat loaded with meaning.

[2] See O. M. Kile, *The Farm Bureau through Three Decades* (Baltimore, Waverly Press, 1948), pp. 310–323, for a description of the activities of O'Neal.

[3] The argument of the Farm Bureau was that the higher figure might be necessary to elicit additional production and that anyhow most prices would not rise to such a ceiling. The line of reasoning was painfully familiar to all concerned with price control in any field. What was novel here was the metaphysical nicety of 110 per cent of parity as an idea. For Farm Bureau testimony see the O'Neal statement, Hearings on H.R. 5990, Emergency Price Control Act, Senate Committee on Banking and Currency, 77th Cong., 1st sess., December, 1941, pp. 429–449.

[4] *Nation's Agriculture*, vol. 24 (March, 1949), p. 7.

[5] *Wallaces' Farmer* implied that the decision on this resolution was settled before the vote. Cf. issue of January 1, 1949, p. 23.

[6] *Nation's Agriculture*, vol. 24 (March, 1949), p. 7.

[7] *Ibid.*, September, 1949, p. 6.

[8] In 1948 and 1949 it was widely rumored that presidential candidate Dewey had offered Kline the prospective post of Secretary of Agriculture. *Time*, December 26, 1949, pp. 10, 11. These rumors were denied by Kline after the election. See American Farm Bureau Federation, *Official News Letter*, January 16, 1950, p. 4.

[9] *Wallaces' Farmer*, vol. 74 (August 6, 1949), p. 886.

[10] The Farm Bureau objections were listed by Kline thus: (1) It discards the idea of parity. (2) It repeals the philosophy of fair farm prices in the market. (3) It means government-administered prices and government control of production. (4) It introduces a cheap food philosophy. "It seeks to establish the principle that taxpayers should pay a considerable portion of the grocery bill of consumers." (5) It "puts a ceiling on opportunity in agriculture ... We view any unit limitation as a dangerous precedent—an opening wedge which eventually would result in Government supervised and stabilized agricultural poverty." (6) The cost would be staggering. (7) "The income of American farmers should not be made dependent upon annual appropriations from the Federal Treasury." Testimony of farm organizations, Hearings on the General Farm Program, House Committee on Agriculture, 81st Cong., 1st sess., April, 1949, Part III, pp. 440–442. There was disagreement on governmental supervision, as the president of the Georgia Farm Bureau testified in opposition to Farm Bureau policy on the Aiken bill. The Southern organization was willing to accept government restrictions in order to get high supports. *Ibid.*, p. 506.

[11] With "obvious reference to Farm Bureau officials," according to *Wallaces' Farmer*, Brannan said: "Leaders of some farm organizations apparently take the view that they, and only they, can speak for farmers. They seem to feel that farmers and the secretary of agriculture should be gagged and muzzled unless their voices are filtered through the purifying plants of a particular organization." *Wallaces' Farmer*, vol. 74 (December 17, 1949), p. 1441. For Farm Bureau reaction see *Time*, December 26, 1949, and *Nation's Agriculture*, vol. 25 (April, 1950), p. 22.

[12] The charge was leveled at instructions to the Production and Marketing Administration. See *Wallaces' Farmer*, vol. 74 (May 21, 1949), p. 632.

[13] Cf. testimony of Patton in Hearings on the General Farm Program ... , House Committee on Agriculture, 1949, pp. 360–361. Nearly every issue of the *National Union Farmer* since announcement of the Brannan Plan has contained some comment favorable to that plan.

[14] See testimony of A. N. Goss and John H. Davis, Hearings on the General Farm Program ... , pp. 595–602.

[15] This slogan appears on Farm Bureau membership signs issued for display on front gates.

[16] See the remarks of Secretary Brannan, quoted in note 11.

[17] As this is written, one of the basic problems of checking inflation is the difficulty presented by the definition of "parity."

NOTES TO CHAPTER 13

[1] In 1949 the Department of Commerce listed fifty-five national associations of farmers. See Jay Judkins, *National Associations of the United States*, U. S. Department of Commerce (1949), pp. 473–479.

[2] See Appendix, table 1, for membership data of American Farm Bureau Federation; Grange membership, given by letter from the National Grange office in Washington, D.C.; Farmers' Union membership, from *National Union Farmer*, January, 1951. It should be noted that the Farmers' Union issues membership cards to wives and to children sixteen years of age and older. The number of dues-paying family heads is less than 200,000.

[3] Hearings on Coöperative Extension Work, House Committee on Agriculture, 79th Cong., 1st sess., 1945, p. 3.

[4] Wesley McCune has emphasized the ties of this organization to the milk lobby under Charles Holman. *The Farm Bloc* (Garden City, N.Y., Doubleday, Doran and Co., 1943), pp. 91–104.

[5] Charles M. Hardin has developed the thesis that the committee system of the Production and Marketing Administration amounts in fact to a farm organization with great power. See Hardin, *The Politics of Agriculture: Soil Conservation and the Struggle for Power in Rural America* (Glencoe, Ill., The Free Press, 1952). So far as independent

tenure of power is the test of a farm organization (and it is the relevant test in the present context), this view seems somewhat to overvalue the independent strength of the P.M.A. system. The grounds for disagreement are given in note 2 to chap. 15.

⁶ Much on this point will be found in the following: Hearings on S. 1334, Permanent Farm Labor Program, Senate Committee on Agriculture and Forestry, 80th Cong., 1st sess., June, 1947; Hearings on H.R. 2102 and S. 724, Farm Labor Supply Program (temporary), Senate Committee on Agriculture and Forestry, 80th Cong., 1st sess., March, 1947. For a vivid account of the condition and treatment of farm migrants today see Report of the President's Commission on Migratory Labor, *Migratory Labor in American Agriculture* (Washington, D.C., 1951).

⁷ The American Institute of Public Opinion conducted two somewhat overlapping polls in 1944. This question was asked of a national cross section of farmers: "Do you happen to be a member of these farm organizations—the Farm Bureau, the Grange, the Farmers' Union?"

	Yes (percentage)	No (percentage)
August 1, 1944		
Farm Bureau	32	68
Grange	12	88
Farmers' Union	3	97
August 16, 1944		
Farm Bureau	22	78
Grange	17	83
Farmers' Union	13	87

⁸ This is borne out by a Cornell study of 3,000 farmers in New York State, in which it was discovered that "the organization-minded farmer is usually past thirty years of age, and an owner rather than a renter ... has a better education and a fairly large farm with a higher assessment value." Cited by DeWitt C. Wing, "Trends in National Farm Organizations," in U. S. Department of Agriculture, *Yearbook of Agriculture, 1940*, p. 942. It may be recalled that the strongest agricultural organizations in New York are the Farm Bureau and the Grange.

⁹ O'Neal rearranged the data from this *Fortune* poll to bring out a different point: "Who represents the farmer? Of all organized farmers—60 per cent are members of the Farm Bureau, the largest farm organization; 7 per cent are members of the Farmers' Union, the smallest farm organization; 42 per cent are members of the Grange and other farm organizations." Cooley Committee Hearings, 1943, p. 761. O'Neal added, "We have lots of Farm Security members."

¹⁰ Unsigned article, "Meet the Member," *Nation's Agriculture*, vol. 12 (December, 1936), pp. 1, 10. The following additional data were also given for every 100 Farm Bureau farms as against every 100 average farms.

	Farm Bureau	Average			Farm Bureau	Average
Chickens	26,240	8,693		Telephones	82	34
Beef cattle	1,557	478		Radios	80	21
Dairy cattle	1,349	376		Electricity	54	12.1
Horses, mules	510	239		Water systems	53	15.8
Hogs	3,341	624				
Sheep	2,728	729				

¹¹ See Gunnar Myrdal, *An American Dilemma* (New York, Harper and Bros., 1944), p. 1253, for such charges involving Negroes.

¹² There are now eleven states in the Northeast, but figures for the recently affiliated Maine Farm Bureau are not available. For further data see Appendix, tables 2 and 3.

¹³ See Appendix, table 3.

¹⁴ The Pennsylvania Farmers' Association and the Maine Farm Bureau Association have recently been organized and affiliated with the American Farm Bureau Federation.

The organization formerly bearing the name of "Farm Bureau" in Maine had never been affiliated, on the grounds that an organization formed for the purpose of coöperating with the county agents would be acting improperly by such affiliation. An earlier Pennsylvania organization had once affiliated with the national federation, but it withdrew.

[15] See Appendix, table 2.

[16] See the classic analysis by Robert Michels, *Political Parties* (Glencoe, Ill., The Free Press, 1949).

[17] This figure and the data that follow are drawn from a 1946 survey of the organization made by the national office of the federation. The results of the survey are reported in *Nation's Agriculture* in 1947. The present figure appears in an article by R. B. Corbett, "Know Your Farm Bureau," *ibid.*, vol. 22 (July–August, 1947), pp. 7, 8.

[18] In the Northeast there was only one full-time worker; in the South, the equivalent of 33 full-time workers; in the West, 46. California had the equivalent of 41 county workers. Corbett, *ibid.*, June, 1947, p. 7.

[19] Such papers were published by 444 of the county organizations in 1946. *Ibid.*, July–August, 1947, p. 8.

[20] *Ibid.*, April, 1947, p. 7. At this time only 50 cents went to the American Farm Bureau Federation.

[21] In the hearings on the Granger bill in 1950, M. L. Wilson, Extension Service head, is reported to have stated that he had received more than three hundred complaints since 1945. *National Union Farmer*, August, 1950. Testimony was also received that the use of the Extension Service was vital in organizing farm bureaus in Arkansas, Louisiana, and Mississippi. It was said that Minnesota county agents were required to maintain Farm Bureau membership or lose their jobs. Testimony on same bill, reported in *ibid.*, June, 1950.

[22] R. E. Short, in testifying on the Granger bill, cited the Gilbertson study to justify the statement that the violations of the True-Howard Agreement had "simmered down to about a dozen" and that these had been corrected since 1948. Quoted in Farm Bureau Federation, *Official News Letter*, May 22, 1950. It may be pointed out here that the strong resistance of the Farm Bureau to passage of the Granger bill is good evidence that the association between the Farm Bureau and the Extension Service remains useful to the former.

[23] Thus, in an article by an official of the Minnesota Farm Bureau, the remark was made: "The Minnesota Farm Bureau is not an office in St. Paul. Neither is it the College of Agriculture or the County Agent." "Farm Bureau in the Gopher State," *Nation's Agriculture*, vol. 13 (October, 1938), p. 1.

[24] The reasons for this statement are given in chap. 14.

[25] Thirty-five states reported no business activities in 1946. However, this does not cover the affiliated enterprises. Thus, the Illinois Farm Bureau, which owns no businesses, has sixteen affiliated companies. "Know Your Farm Bureau," *Nation's Agriculture*, July–August, 1947, p. 8.

[26] *Ibid.*, p. 7.

[27] These were selected from a list of activities of various federations in American Farm Bureau Federation, *Annual Report, 1937*.

[28] Illinois and California were the two largest employers among state federations. Others were Iowa, 43; Minnesota, 33; Ohio, 30; Michigan, 24. "Know Your Farm Bureau," *Nation's Agriculture*, June, 1947, p. 7.

[29] Northeast, 20; Middle West, 161; South, 40; West, 56. *Ibid.*

[30] *Ibid.*

[31] *Ibid.* By information given the Department of Commerce in 1949, the national staff then numbered between forty and fifty. Judkins, *op. cit.*, p. 473.

[32] *Ibid.*

[33] Harry L. Bryson, "This Farm Bureau of Ours," *Nation's Agriculture*, vol. 25 (June, 1950), pp. 4, 5.

[34] American Farm Bureau Federation, *Annual Report, 1937; Annual Report, 1939.*

³⁵ The 1946 survey revealed that among the state farm bureaus "a number report passing of 75% to 100% of the bills they sponsored." "Know Your Farm Bureau," *Nation's Agriculture,* July–August, 1947, pp. 7, 8.

³⁶ In the report for the second quarter of 1950, required by the Federal Regulation of Lobbying Act, $97,566.33 was the figure given for collections from state organizations. Income from investments was $12,984.01; newsletter subscriptions, $2,143.24; miscellaneous, $322.30; making a total of $113,015.88. The amount expended was $212,121.77 for the same period, all listed as spent for "public relations and advertising services." *Congressional Record,* August 22, 1950, p. 13253.

³⁷ One delegate is permitted for each federation having 500 members; two delegates for each federation having 7,501 or more; three delegates for each federation having 22,501 or more; four delegates for each federation having 37,501 or more; five delegates for each federation having 52,501 or more. Each of the four regions can have three directors plus one and not more than two additional for each 50,000 paid memberships. David Edgar Lindstrom, *American Farmers' and Rural Organization* (Champaign, Ill., The Garrard Press, 1948), p. 183. Data secured by Lindstrom from the American Farm Bureau Federation. See also Harry Bryson, "Field Director Outlines Farm Bureau Structure," American Farm Bureau Federation, *Official News Letter,* July 14, 1952.

³⁸ Cf. comments in *Wallaces' Farmer,* cited in note 26, chap. 6.

³⁹ In this connection, however, it should be observed that the organization has had six different national presidents, a greater number than many older organizations in the labor movement can boast.

⁴⁰ Conventions are reported rather sketchily, with emphasis on the text of resolutions and speeches. The most vivid official account is of the 1935 convention held in Chicago. Twenty thousand were present (including fifty-three voting delegates) to hear fifteen speeches by President Roosevelt, M. L. Wilson, president of the Association of Land Grant Colleges and Universities, General R. E. Wood, Chester Davis, Henry Wallace, and others. American Farm Bureau Federation, *They Pray! They Sing! They Fight!* (Chicago; pamphlet).

NOTES TO CHAPTER 14

¹ Dale Kramer, *The Truth about the Farm Bureau* (Minneapolis, Farmers' Book Store, 1938). In this pamphlet Kramer makes the charge, "Big business and Wall Street consciously set out twenty years ago to build 'company unions' among the farmers."

² M. S. Winder, executive secretary, and H. R. Kibler, director of information of the American Farm Bureau Federation, were removed by the board of directors when a scandal involving their activities reached the ears of Congress. The Farm Bureau was said to have offered to use its influence in "educational campaigns" on behalf of shipping companies and firms engaged in farm-home modernization and construction of farm-to-market roads. Cf. *Bureau Farmer,* vol. 9 (December, 1933), p. 6.

³ In the late 'twenties, when Senator George W. Norris was attempting to secure passage of legislation for development of Muscle Shoals, it was disclosed that one employee of the Farm Bureau federation was accepting money from the American Cyanamid Company in return for services given to help defeat the Norris proposals. See Alfred Lief, *Democracy's Norris* (New York, Stackpole Sons, 1939), p. 339.

⁴ One of the strongest statements of this view is by Russell Smith, legislative secretary of the Farmers' Union, "Big Business and the Farm Bloc," *Antioch Review,* vol. 4 (Summer, 1944), pp. 189–204. He cites testimony by Walter Reuther before the Senate Committee on Banking and Currency in December, 1943.

⁵ Although the present volume is a study of the national organization of the American Farm Bureau Federation, some mention should be made of the connection between the California Farm Bureau and the Associated Farmers. The La Follette Committee found that, while the Associated Farmers had been organized by the California Chamber of Commerce, Farm Bureau facilities were used in the original period of formation in 1934. "Key members of the California Farm Bureau Federation did collaborate in

laying the ground work for launching the Associated Farmers. The Farm Bureau, however, played a secondary role in the organizational activities. In fact the secretary of the California Farm Bureau Federation denied that the Associated Farmers had been 'sponsored' by his organization." Report of the Senate Committee on Education and Labor, 78th Cong., 2d sess., 1942, *Violations of Free Speech and Rights of Labor,* Part IV, "Employers' Associations and Collective Bargaining in California," p. 580. When the Associated Farmers were reorganized in 1935–1936, the Farm Bureau was a somewhat reluctant participant. The California Farm Bureau Federation board of directors, however, did decide to assist, and instructed the organization's new secretary to cooperate, against his judgment and desires. The principal notoriety of the Associated Farmers was gained after this reorganization. *Ibid.*, Part VIII, "The Associated Farmers of California, Inc.—Its Reorganization Policies and Significance, 1935–1939"; also Part IV, "Employers' Associations and Collective Bargaining in California," pp. 1148–1149. See also Clarke A. Chambers, *California Farm Organizations* (Berkeley and Los Angeles, University of California Press, 1952).

⁶ In a leaflet of the Farm Bureau Federation, *Voice of a Million Farmers* (1948), it was asserted that this law "as finally passed, embodied substantially the recommendations of the A.F.B.F."

⁷ One of O'Neal's wartime speeches was reported to include this statement: "He [the American worker] has so much money he doesn't know what to do with it. In the last war he bought two silk shirts and two quarts of whiskey. Now he has four silk shirts and a half case of whiskey." P. A. Waring and C. S. Golden, *Soil and Steel* (New York, Harper and Bros., 1947), p. 18.

⁸ This somewhat exceptional case involved licensing of processors. Cf. Hearings on Amendments to the Agricultural Adjustment Act, House Committee on Agriculture, 74th Cong., 1st sess., 1935, pp. 103, 156, 242, 291, 339, 363.

⁹ "Organization" is here taken to exclude what is sometimes called "informal organization." The reality of the latter is not denied; it is just not under discussion here.

¹⁰ James Patton has referred to the words of the act which permit private participation in the financial arrangements as the act's "historic legislative error." It would seem that an even more fundamental error lay in the selective quality of Extension teaching methods.

¹¹ Russell Lord, *The Wallaces of Iowa* (Boston, Houghton Mifflin Co., 1941), p. 454.

NOTES TO CHAPTER 15

¹ In practice, a secondary condition might be added: that no attempts were made to form superorganizations on top of the local organizations. This would become an important condition to the degree that the first condition were unrealized.

² Charles M. Hardin has suggested, in *The Politics of Agriculture ...* (Glencoe, Ill., The Free Press, 1952), pp. 127–155, and "Current Proposals for the Organization of Conservation and Land-Use Programs in Agriculture, the United States," *Journal of Farm Economics,* vol. 30, no. 4 (November, 1948), p. 632, that the committee system of the Production and Marketing Administration has many of the characteristics of a "farm organization." The department, by decentralization of P.M.A. administration, may be developing a constituency overlapping that of the Farm Bureau. To assume, however, that in a contest for the same constituency any P.M.A. "farm organization" could effectively compete with the Farm Bureau would seem unrealistic. The apparent strength of the P.M.A. "farm organization" is more probably the power held by the party administration.

The view that the P.M.A. "farm organization" is not, and is not likely to become, an independent holder of power is substantiated by the history of various attempts to form independent farm organizations from committeemen. The attempt to make the newsletter *Spade* into a committeemen's house organ as a preliminary to organization, the effort to form a national agricultural mobilization committee from these elements, and the drive to create an association of former committeemen, all failed.

[8] Charles M. Hardin places great stress on this distinction. He favors political decentralization, although in what form is not altogether clear. See "Reflections on Agricultural Policy Formation in the United States," *American Political Science Review*, vol. 42 (October, 1948), pp. 883 ff.

NOTES TO CHAPTER 16

[1] E. deS. Brunner and E. Hsin Pao Yang insist that it is a mistake to emphasize the association between the Extension Service and the Farm Bureau. Cf. *Rural America and the Extension Service* (New York Teachers College, Columbia University, 1949), p. 71. So far as emphasis is placed on the formal relationship implied in Farm Bureau contributions to salaries of agents, the point may be conceded. However, this is the least important aspect of the relationship. To lose sight of the relationship is to ignore an essential part of the structure of power, which in turn has colored the whole character of modern agricultural politics.

[2] Gladys Baker devotes considerable space to this in *The County Agent* (University of Chicago Press, 1939), chap. v, pp. 102 ff. It has been the focus of much criticism by the Farmers' Union and was the target of the Granger bill.

Index

Index

Adams, Henry, 5

Agrarianism, 7, 8; democracy and, 5, 6, 8, 9, 12, 17, 21, 181; effect of frontier on, 12, 13, 15, 36. *See also* Populism

Agricultural Adjustment: Acts, 71, 72, 129, 138; Administration, 72 ff., 80 ff., 114, 116, 123, 130–131

Agricultural Economics, Bureau of, 118, 121, 122, 128, 178

Agricultural education, 2, 20; experiment stations, 13, 22, 27, 28, 34; farmers' institutes, 22, 34; demonstration work, 24 ff., 29; businessmen interested in, 25, 26, 29, 30, 31, 32, 164. *See also* County agent; Extension Service; Land grant colleges

Agriculture, Department of. *See* Department of Agriculture

American Farm Bureau Federation, 2, 45 ff.; county agents as organizers, 47, 48, 49, 50, 153, 163, 164, 176; relation to Department of Agriculture, 47, 48, 53, 114, 118–133, 177; relation to colleges, 48, 49, 82, 164–165; objectives and program, 51, 58, 69, 79, 161 ff.; origins, 52, 56; lobbying, 52, 57–58, 179; membership, 56, 146 ff., 175; dues, 56, 153; power of, 57, 83, 125–126, 147, 173 ff., 179, 180; coöperatives, 59–62, 66; policy on farm surplus, 61, 62, 63, 64; regionalism, 61, 66–67, 76, 144; party system as rival to, 64, 143, 144, 174, 178, 180; sectionalism, 66, 76, 80; and Grange, 68, 69, 147; and Farmers' Union, 68, 69; and New Deal, 70, 71, 77, 123, 143; and A.A.A., 72–77, 114, 123, 130–131; relation to Extension Service, 73, 82, 83, 119, 120, 129–131, 133, 158, 163; commodityism, 76, 79, 80, 81, 143, 144, 179; attacks on F.S.A., 97 ff., 106, 112–113, 123, 178; and T.V.A., 123, 124; class basis of, 125, 148, 149, 150, 151, 164, 170, 171, 181; and Chamber of Commerce, 125, 160; attacks on S.C.S., 128–132; decentralization of, 129–130, 157, 159, 175, 177, 178; Granger bill, 137, 147, 176; Brannan Plan, 138, 141 ff.; organization of, 152 ff.; legislative projects, 155; conventions, 156; interpretations of, 158–160

American Federation of Labor, 38, 60

American Society of Equity, 41–42

Associated Farmers, 125

Association of American Agricultural Colleges, 22, 25, 33, 48, 134, 135, 137. *See also* Land grant colleges

Bailey bill, 82

Baldwin, C. B., 111, 112, 113

Bank of America, 145

Bankers: interest in agriculture, 30, 31; farmers' distrust of, 38

Bankhead Commodity Loan Act, 139

Bankhead-Flannagan Act, 133

Bankhead-Jones Act: of 1935, 82; of 1937, 88, 89, 91, 99, 111

Beech, Gould, 134

Brannan Plan, 138, 141 ff., 146

Bureau of Agricultural Economics, 118, 121, 122, 128, 178

Bureau of Reclamation, 91, 131, 135

Business: cycles, 4, 5, 37; interest in agriculture, 24 ff., 29, 30, 31, 32, 36, 47, 164. *See also* Capitalism

Byrd Committee, 102, 105, 123

Capitalism versus agrarianism, 1, 5, 6, 7, 8, 20, 37–38, 41, 113, 160, 180. *See also* Business

Carr, William G., 103, 104, 105, 109, 123

Catholic Rural Life Conference, 106

Chamber of Commerce: interest in agriculture, 32, 47; as auxiliary of A.F.B.F., 125, 160

Colleges. *See* Land grant colleges

Committee on Agricultural Development and Education, 30, 31

Committee on Post-War Agricultural Policy, 134 ff.

Commodity Credit Corporation, 79

Commodityism, 16, 76, 79, 80, 81, 143, 144, 179

Congressional committees. *See* Byrd Committee; Cooley Committee; President's Committee on Farm Tenancy

Cooley bill, 82

Cooley Committee, 107–110

Coolidge, Calvin, 64

Coöperatives, 27, 42, 58, 147; and Grange, 40; and A.F.B.F., 59–62, 66; and F.S.A., 91, 92, 93

no slavery entry

CPSIA information can be obtained
at www.ICGtesting.com
Printed in the USA
LVHW040013210423
744982LV00004B/333